MW00850184

THE
INTIMACY OF PAPER
IN EARLY AND
NINETEENTH-CENTURY
AMERICAN
LITERATURE

A Volume in the Series

STUDIES IN PRINT CULTURE AND THE HISTORY OF THE BOOK

Edited by

Greg Barnhisel
Robert A. Gross
Joan Shelley Rubin
Michael Winship

THE
INTIMACY OF PAPER
IN EARLY AND
NINETEENTH-CENTURY
AMERICAN
LITERATURE

Jonathan Senchyne

University of Massachusetts Press
AMHERST & BOSTON

Copyright © 2020 by University of Massachusetts Press
All rights reserved
Printed in the United States of America

ISBN 978-1-62534-474-8 (paper); 473-1 (hardcover)

Designed by Sally Nichols
Set in Alegreya
Printed and bound by Maple Press, Inc.

Cover design by Frank Gutbrod
Cover art: Detail of *Historic Ream
Wrapper* from Gilpin & Co. c. 1820.
Courtesy American Antiquarian Society.
Torn paper by Sarah Richter/Pixabay

Library of Congress Cataloging-in-Publication Data
A catalog record for this book is available from the Library of Congress

British Library Cataloguing-in-Publication Data
A catalog record for this book is available from the British Library

Portions of chapter 1 were published in a previous form as "Paper Nationalism: Material Textuality
and Communal Affiliation in Early America," *Book History* 19 (2016) 66–85. Portions of chapter 4 were
published in a previous form as "Bottles of Ink and Reams of Paper: *Clotel,* Racialization and the
Material Culture of Print," in *Early African American Print Culture,* ed. Lara Langer Cohen and Jordan
Alexander Stein (Philadelphia: University of Pennsylvania Press, 2012), 140–159.

CONTENTS

PREFACE AND ACKNOWLEDGMENTS

WHEN I WAS little my father took me on tours of the *Buffalo News* press-rooms whenever our family happened to be downtown. He worked as an electrician at "the *News*" for thirty-five years doing everything from maintaining and modernizing the presses to wiring the entire building for the internet revolution of the 1990s. At the time, the web offset presses were a massive and almost entirely mechanical system of rollers, plates, and belts that wove massive rolls of paper through the internal workings, soaring up into a high ceiling before cutting, folding, and loading finished newspapers onto pallets for distribution and delivery. I delighted in these trips because a child sometimes finds outsized joy in seeing what his parents do at work all day. Children are frequently asked what their parents do for a living, and I got to see close up. When I answered that my dad worked for the *Buffalo News*, a newspaper in print since 1873 and by the mid-1980s the city's only major daily, most people assumed I meant he was a reporter or a columnist, not an electrician. To me, "working at the newspaper" meant attending to the intricate machinery and other infrastructure necessary for the on-time delivery of a midsize metropolitan print run every single day before sunrise. To them: writing. Writing was important, I thought, but what was it without the whole system that my dad and his friends kept running? Later, I put it together that assumptions about what it is to work at "the *News*" were bound up with ideas about information, media, labor, and class. The material text, when noticed at all, was assumed to be a necessary but unremarkable carrier of the more important alphabetic text. Writing is privileged and romanticized, and it tends to render invisible all other information labor in service to it.

On reflection, these early moments of dissonance were influential to my decision to study the history of books and cultures of print. The questions in this field begin with the refusal to divorce the written word from scenes of its production and distribution. Jerome McGann, for example, reminds us that "because human beings are not angels, [symbolic exchanges] always involve material negotiations." And Thomas Tanselle's first axiom of bibliography is that "books are physical objects made by human beings."[1] Even at a young age, it was clear that not all methods and habits of reading are attuned to the layering of multiple kinds of human labor in each text. I was already in search for a way of reading that saw my father and his coworkers as part of an assembly of human beings behind the daily newspaper.

When my dad brought home the newspaper and handed it to me, I read in two ways. Articles about the then winning Buffalo Bills were favorites to read, but I also always looked for the registration marks (a circle with a cross through it) and the CMYK (cyan, magenta, yellow and key, or black) ink dots in the margin of the page. Perfect registration meant all four inks were layered on each page exactly as intended, mixing dots of color just right to produce crisp color images and text. More often than not, especially as the presses aged, the registration would be off. This made the images and advertisements look like off-kilter Roy Lichtenstein paintings. I had met the pressmen (at the time they were all men) who calibrated plates to work out registration problems. They made me newsprint hats when I visited to prevent ink from falling into my hair. I knew that the paper I held in my hand was a small remnant of the massive paper rolls I'd seen being moved around the warehouse. Each day's newspaper brought news of the city and the world, but it also brought to mind and hand the work of people and processes I knew. As a reader, I took pleasure in the newspaper by making sense of the writing and also sensing its making.

I also knew that any print object was the result of a series of contingencies that at any point could have gone wrong, been delayed, or otherwise been affected by the production of "the text." How many times did the phone ring at 11:00 p.m. because an intractable problem with the presses needed my dad's expert knowledge of the their electrical infrastructure? It couldn't be left until morning because the paper had to be ready for delivery before sunrise. Having witnessed the production of print from this side, it has been interesting to come into the process as an author. While this book was in the final stages of review, disruptions in the paper industry began to force others to see books and print from the production side. The *New York Times* reported that several bestselling books were unavailable to purchase during the last weeks of the

2018 holiday season because of extremely high demand for certain hit titles, such as First Lady Michelle Obama's memoir, combined with paper shortages and insufficient capacity at industrial printers. In the preceding years, the United States had initiated trade disputes with a number of nations, including Canada, where a significant amount of newsprint paper is produced. Mike Connelly, editor of the *Buffalo News*, wrote in May 2017 that the *News* was dangerously close to running out of paper and had almost been forced to skip publishing a Sunday paper. "A week ago," Connelly wrote, "three truckloads of newsprint failed to arrive at *The News'* downtown printing plant. We usually have 900 rolls of newsprint on hand. . . . As I write this, we have 56. It takes 20 rolls to print a typical weekday *News*. You do the math." The *News* didn't miss any days, but the publisher did reduce the number of pages per issue. Other small papers feared going under once Canadian manufacturers started passing the costs of U.S. tariff increases onto them, leading to 20–25 percent increases in the costs of printing. Even academic journal editors took notice of the downstream consequences of changes in the paper industry. Prefacing the October 2018 issue of *American Historical Review*, editor Alex Lichtenstein wrote, "If you are holding this journal in your hand as a printed object . . . you may have noticed a change in our paper stock from previous issues." He continued: "Severe disruptions in the paper market have made [the journal's regular paper] stock unavailable," which, he noted, will stand out in the middle of a single volume once the annual is bound together. As editor, Lichtenstein called the necessity to change paper stock "a potent reminder that publishing a journal is about much more than simply selecting the content the editor would like to see appear between two covers."[2]

The questions and anxieties from the rag paper period suddenly seem to be everywhere, and this book enters an interestingly unsettled market for books and their raw materials. The aim of *The Intimacy of Paper* is to understand how and why so many writers and readers from the late seventeenth through the nineteenth centuries found meaning quite literally *in* the materiality of texts, in paper as well as on it. The uncertainty in the voices of newspaper publishers, journal editors, booksellers, and literary agents over disruptions caused by an unpredictable paper market suggest that in our moment we have returned to questions about content, materiality, and meaning at the intersection of paper and ink.

☙

This book is in many ways about recognizing all of the people, processes, and materials that make a book. I'm grateful to have had the support of many people and institutions who made writing and publishing this book possible.

My teachers and mentors profoundly influenced my life through criticism, encouragement, and example. At Cornell University, Shirley Samuels was, and continues to be, a tireless mentor and example of how to be an engaged scholar and community builder. She taught me to see the layers of meaning in all things and to read the archives of American literature for their deeply suggestive proximities and meaningful, if fleeting, traces. I am grateful for her continued presence in my work and my life. Eric Cheyfitz also modeled how to work with early American literature and cultural theory while engaging meaningfully in the ongoing social and political movements in the United States. At Cornell, I also benefited from conversations with Ed Baptist, Richard Boyd, Richard Canfield, Grant Farred, Jason Frank, Cindy Hazan, Michael Jonik, Jane Juffer, Barbara Koslowski, Barry Maxwell, Masha Raskolnikov, Riché Richardson, Carin Ruff, Neil Saccamano, and Paul Sawyer. Visitors to the Cornell Society for the Humanities were also important and influential mentors, including Max Cavitch, Michael Cobb, Marcus Rediker, and Martha Schoolman. At Syracuse University (SU), I was first formed into a scholar of early and nineteenth-century America by Amy Schrager Lang. Gregg Lambert, Monika Siebert, and Adam Sitze filled out a team of skilled and patient teachers at SU who helped prepare me for doctoral work. At the State University of New York College at Geneseo, Christopher Dahl, the late Bill Edgar, Stacey Edgar, Tom Greenfield, and Ron Herzman were part of a deep bench of faculty committed to the public accessibility of a small liberal arts education. Geneseo alerted me to doors I could not have at first have imagined—and then helped open them.

The close-knit group of friends who launched and sustained the C19 Americanist Reading Group (better known simply as ARG) at Cornell between 2007 and 2012 were my sounding board while I conceived this book's questions. Conversations about the project with Alex W. Black, Jillian Spivey Caddell, Hilary Emmett, Sarah Ensor, Brigitte Fielder, Kamila Janiszewski, Toni Wall Jaudon, Melissa Gniadek, Daniel Radus, and Xine Yao were formative and continue to be sustaining. These folks make the ups of academic life possible and its downs bearable.

I also feel fortunate to be part of overlapping fields—American Studies, early and nineteenth-century American, early African American literature and print culture, book history—that are, on the whole, welcoming and collaborative. In particular, I have learned much in conversation with Sari Altschuler, Greg Barnhisel, Faith Barrett, Robin Bernstein, Jenni Brady, Michael Chaney, Sarah Chinn, Lara Cohen, Rachel Collins, Ryan Cordell, Pete Coviello, Pat Crain, Elizabeth Maddock Dillon, Marcy Dinius, Kathleen Donegan, Anna Mae Duane, Elizabeth Duquette, Michael Dwyer, Jonathan Elmer, Bert Emerson, Duncan Faherty, Stephanie Farrar, Molly Farrell, Jonathan Beecher Field, James Finley, P. Gabrielle Foreman, Travis Foster, Elizabeth Freeman, Ari Friedlander, Eric Gardner, Miles Grier, Kirsten Silva Gruesz, Daniel Hack, Danielle Haque, Sonia Hazard, Glenn Hendler, Nat Hurley, Leon Jackson, Honorée Fanonne Jeffers, Mary Kelley, Matthew Kirschenbaum, Lauren Klein, Greta LaFleur, Eric Lott, Dana Luciano, Mark Mattes, Meredith McGill, Koritha Mitchell, Amy Monaghan, Phil Nel, Meredith Neuman, Emily Pawley, Jason Payton, Donald Pease, Carla Peterson, Chris Phillips, Eliza Richards, Seth Rockman, Britt Rusert, Karen Sanchez-Eppler, David S. Shields, Cristobal Silva, Caleb Smith, Alexandra Socarides, Cheryl Spinner, Jordan Stein, Kyla Wazana Tompkins, and Nazera Wright. They have all heard, read, and responded to parts of this book and provided feedback that advanced the project.

Three somewhat ephemeral institutional affiliations were important to the development of this book. In 2005, I spent the summer at the School of Criticism and Theory studying with Hans Ulrich "Sepp" Gumbrecht. Sepp introduced me to questions about materiality and interpretation that later shaped this book, and he offered support and encouragement at a time when my scholarly prospects were more than a little nebulous. Between 2008 and 2012, I was a seminarian at the annual Futures of American Studies Institute at Dartmouth College, which transformed the way I thought about interpretation, argument, and scholarly community. Futures directors Donald Pease, Elizabeth Maddock Dillon, and Eric Lott annually create a generous space for collective thought that approaches a perfect balance of ardor and criticism. I have also learned a great deal about archival work, literary recovery, and feminist scholarship through membership in the Nineteenth-Century American Women Writers Study Group.

I reimagined and wrote this book at the University of Wisconsin (UW)–Madison. My colleagues in the Information School and the Center for the History of Print and Digital Culture helped me think about how literary history and book history enrich broad interdisciplinary conversations about information, archives, documents, and inscription. This project, and my life in Madison, has been sustained by conversations with colleagues from across the university, including Faisal Abdu'Allah, Monique Allewaert, Johanna Almiron, the late James Baughman, Susan David Bernstein, Joshua Calhoun, Russ Castronovo, Christy Clark-Pujara, Lisa Cooper, Jim Danky, Greg Downey, Stephanie Elsky, Kristin Eschenfelder, Danielle Evans, Brigitte Fielder, Martin Foys, Colin Gillis, Sara Guyer, Tracy Honn, Rob Howard, Eric Hoyt, Florence Hsia, Jenell Johnson, Steve Kantrowitz, Dennis Lloyd, B. Venkat Mani, Ann Smart Martin, Christa Olson, Christine Pawley, Jen Plants, Jennifer Ratner-Rosenhagen, Jordan Rosenblum, Reginold Royston, Alan Rubel, Dorothea Salo, Ellen Samuels, Catherine Arnott Smith, Molly Steenson, Mark Vareschi, Heather Wacha, Ethelene Whitmire, Rebekah Willett, Timothy Yu, and Jordan Zweck. Through their own scholarly development and ways of building the world they want to inhabit, my students—especially Courtney Becks, Oliver Baez Bendorf, Lauren Gottlieb-Miller, Carolina Hernandez, Harvey Long, and Sigrid Peterson—kept me invested in the work on even the most trying days. The Center for the Humanities at UW selected this manuscript for an intensive review seminar, an experience that helped focus the project and propel it toward final form. I am especially grateful to Lisa Gitelman and Meredith McGill who came all the way to Madison to participate, and to Sara Guyer for her leadership of the center. Support for this research was also provided by the University of Wisconsin–Madison Office of the Vice Chancellor for Research and Graduate Education with funding from the Wisconsin Alumni Research Foundation. I also thank my colleagues in the Information School and the College of Letters and Science, especially Director Kristin Eschenfelder, Associate Dean Sue Zaeske, and Associate Dean Greg Downey, all of whom helped make it possible for me to accept external residential research fellowships and to take parental leave.

This book would have been impossible to write without the staff and collections of several libraries and archives. First among these is the American Antiquarian Society (AAS). Gigi Barnhill, Ashley Cataldo, Ellen Dunlap, Paul Erickson, Tom Knoles, Jaclyn Penny, Elizabeth Pope, Caroline Sloat, and Nan Wolverton cultivated an ideal environment for research at AAS. My work at AAS was first supported by a Jay and Deborah Last Short-Term Fellowship and later by an AAS-National Endowment for the Humanities Long-Term Fellowship. Any views, findings, conclusions, or recommendations expressed in this book do not necessarily represent those of the National Endowment for the Humanities. Paul Erickson deserves special recognition for building a truly remarkable and dynamic networked community of scholars beneath, but extending far beyond, Worcester's "generous dome." Krystal Appiah, James N. Green, Nicole Joniec, Cornelia King, and Erika Piola aided my work at the Library Company of Philadelphia. Thomas Lannon's invitation to visit the New York Public Library's Manuscripts and Archives Division opened new archives for this project and others. Marianna Stell and Michael North in the Rare Books and Special Collections Division of the Library of Congress assisted my research on Bradstreet editions, as did the staff at the Rauner Special Collections Library at Dartmouth College. Within the University of Wisconsin Libraries, Anjali Bhasin, former director of the Information School Laboratory Library, Susan Barribeau, and Bronwen Masemann delivered excellent research support at home.

Time to complete the manuscript and finalize revisions was provided by the Pine Tree Foundation's Distinguished Visiting Fellowship in the Future of the Book in a Digital Age at the City University of New York (CUNY) Graduate Center. Matt Gold, Don Robotham, Kay Powell, Duncan Faherty, and Eric Lott gave me space, time to work, and encouragement that made it possible to finish writing this book while beginning to research another. Thank you to Szilvia Szmuk-Tanenbaum of the Pine Tree Foundation for supporting this position within the Graduate Center's Advanced Research Collaborative.

I was fortunate to deliver work in progress from this book at the invitation of scholars and groups whose feedback sharpened my thinking and writing. Audiences at Bard College Graduate Center, Bates College, Brown University, Clark University, Columbia University, CUNY Graduate Center, Dartmouth College, New York University, the University of Pennsylvania, and the University of Toronto asked questions that helped me to see these materials with fresh eyes and through different frameworks.

Brian Halley at the University of Massachusetts Press has been encouraging and patient; he is the ideal editor of both this book and the series in which it appears. Two anonymous readers for the University of Massachusetts Press provided a final round of important feedback that improved the work and its presentation. I am also grateful to the editors and peer reviewers of *Book History* and *Early African American Print Culture*, venues in which parts of chapters one and four appeared in preliminary form. Thank you to Johns Hopkins University Press and the University of Pennsylvania Press, respectively, for permission to include parts of those essays in this book where they now appear in revised and expanded form. When I was still in graduate school, the late Helen Tartar took an early interest in this project and gave me confidence to see it as a book worth writing. I'm grateful for the genuine interest she showed in developing the work of junior scholars.

Finally, I am grateful for my family's support of my education and career. I grew up among makers of texts and textiles. Watching them come into being in the hands of skilled craftspeople and technicians taught me to read the human stories of thought and work within things. My parents, Bill and Mary Ann Senchyne, are retired from careers well spent in the technologies of printing and sewing. Grandparents Bill and Marie Watson taught me to compose type and transform paper into print on the "venerable Vandercook" at Paradise Press. My brother, Dennis Watson, has long been teaching me how digital inscriptions are as material as print. My trilingual sister-in-law Shin-young Faith Watson is the family expert on languages and the materiality of their signs. Finally, Brigitte Fielder has been my unwavering partner in work and life and, more recently, my collaborator in the wonderful project of raising Ezra. Each day we pull new sheets from the stuff of life.

And if chance to thine eyes shall bring this verse,
With some sad sighs honour my absent Herse;
And kiss this paper for thy loves dear sake,
Who with salt tears this last Farewel did take.

—*Anne Bradstreet, "Before the Birth of One of Her Children"*

Printers do not print books. They print sheets of paper.

—*Peter Stallybrass, "'Little Jobs': Broadsides and the Printing Revolution"*

Paper, paper, paper. . . . I have always written, and even spoken, on paper: on the subject of paper, an actual paper, and with paper in mind. Support, subject, surface, mark, trace . . . inscription, fold. . . . The history of this "thing," this thing that can be felt, seen, and touched, and is thus contingent, paper, will have been a brief one.

—*Jacques Derrida,* Paper Machine

THE
INTIMACY of PAPER
in EARLY and
NINETEENTH-CENTURY
AMERICAN
LITERATURE

INTRODUCTION

D O YOU SEE this paper? The answer is likely "yes," but also "no." It is yes because the letters you read become legible against their papery substrate, and no because the technical and social codes of reading dictate that normally substrates should recede from view. John Bidwell, papermaking historian and curator of books at the Morgan Library, writes that paper is "the basic substance of which books are made, yet almost never impinges upon their communicative function." The less paper rises to a reader's attention, Bidwell contends, the more it succeeds as a technology of inscription. Paper "serves as a mute vehicle of text, rarely noticed except when it fails of its purpose, when defects inherent in its manufacture impede the transmission and preservation of printed information." Once it functions as a substrate carrying inscriptions, paper is meant to be self-effacing because it is supposedly secondary to meaning-making processes. This is so much the case that phenomenologists of reading, such as Georges Poulet, describe how paper "dissolves" during the reading experience, allowing a communion between the text and the reader's mind. "The book is no longer a material reality," Poulet writes, but rather "a series of words, of images, of ideas which in their turn begin to exist. And where is this new existence? Surely not in the paper object." Even among the early twentieth-century founding figures of the academic discipline of bibliography—those scholars who we might expect to take the greatest interest in the material facts of the book—we find that the flipside of attending to typography and composition is a tendency to overlook paper. In his 1927 Oxford *Introduction to Bibliography for Literary Students*, Ronald McKerrow writes that "knowledge of the processes by which paper is manufactured and of the substances of which it is composed has never . . . been regarded as necessary to the bibliographer."[1] Each of these

1

ways of reading and interpreting suggest that the hierarchy of inscription over substrate is both natural and necessary.

And yet, here you see and feel the paper even as you deprioritize these sensory signals in the process of reading text. Because I have made explicit mention of this book's paper, you might be giving it more attention than you normally would, rubbing it between your fingers, weighing it in your hands, examining its surface closely. If you became even more curious, perhaps you looked for a colophon that would provide additional information about this paper's origin: Is it recycled? What is its weight? Does it meet acidity standards for library preservation? If you work at the industrial printer where this book was produced, you likely touched and carried this paper object without stopping to read what I have written here. You may treat this paper similarly if you are the person or robot in an Amazon warehouse whose work was timed while boxing this book together with other books and household goods for delivery. Before it became the substrate for this particular printed book, this paper was cut from a massive industrial roll, which was manufactured in a facility that also likely makes rolls of newsprint, paper towels, and toilet paper. Do you wonder where the trees grew before they were cut, pulped, and made into paper, or what any recycled content did in a "past life"? If you are reading this on a digital device, you might now be asking related questions about glass, circuitry, software, and connective digital infrastructures (but that is a topic for a different book). Paying attention to the most mundane material elements of our reading surfaces brings focus to the processes of making and distributing language, art, and information through print.

Like the connections between this book's paper, printed text, and meaning, every book is the site of overlapping linguistic, bibliographical, and social codes. In these intertwined strands, Jerome McGann says, we encounter "the symbolic and signifying dimensions of the physical medium through which (or rather *as* which) the linguistic text is embodied" and how these, working together, are used by human beings. This insight is the primary contribution of book history to the humanistic disciplines, and its methods help us read the various layers of meaning and human history embedded within material texts. Bibliographers and book historians argue that such contribution is necessary because the hermeneutic tradition, at least since the mid-twentieth century, has established a "readerly view of the text . . . in which text is not something we *make* but something we *interpret*."[2] Book historians are not alone in pointing to all that is lost when the idealist interpretation of verbal texts takes precedence over the description and interpretation of material texts. Philosopher and literary theorist Hans Ulrich Gumbrecht argues that ever since the linguistic turn, the humanities have been organized around "the uncontested centrality of interpretation" and a commensurate "tendency . . . to abandon and even forget the possibility of a presence-based relationship to the world." "Presence," here, means the quality of cultural texts that are "tangible for human hands" and have an "immediate impact on human bodies."[3] Beyond your reading and interpretation of these words, this book is present to you and is in relation to your body. In another aesthetic register, when we listen to a live music performance we might interpret the formal qualities of the piece and contextualize it historically, but we also feel the presence of sound vibrating on our bodies and throughout the unique space we share with its performers and instruments.[4]

Paper might not at first seem to create sensory intensities that vibrate against our bodies as we dwell in its presence. *The Intimacy of Paper* shows, however, that ever since papermaking began in what would become the United States, readers, writers, printers, and papermakers have invested much in their relationship to paper. This book is about what paper makes present, how it creates meaning, and what difference this makes for literary criticism and book history. Specifically, I trace a phenomenology of reading that finds expression throughout the era of rag paper production in colonial America and the nineteenth-century United States, roughly between 1690 and 1867. During this period, paper was made from shredded and pulped linen, hempen, and cotton rags, many of which were collected from homes and recycled into paper. Studying paper and how writers and readers experienced it in this period changes the way we think about the interrelation of bibliographic and linguistic codes, of presence effects and meaning-making effects. Rag paper signifies from the rags embedded within it, as well as from the ink printed or written on it. Paper is the thin plane where presence and meaning, the ontic and the mimetic, the bibliographic and the linguistic cohere and become mutually constitutive.

Humanists, from book historians to philosophers, have tried to reconcile the seeming alienation of these ways of experiencing texts. We will see, however, that early and nineteenth-century American readers and writers did not experience intense alienation of the bibliographic code from the linguistic code. They were intimately and inextricably entwined. The intimate relationship of meaning and materiality is especially apparent when writers of this period discussed rag paper. Here they found the ideality and materiality of texts in lockstep.

In 1857, for example, Pastor M. Emory Wright toured a Holyoke, Massachusetts, paper mill and wrote about his experience in the heart of that region's biggest and most important industries. Rather than detailing paper machine technology, Wright instead expressed fascination with the relationship between rags and the written contents of books. "It is indeed a difficult matter for an inexperienced eye to discover any relationship between the tattered contents of the rag-bag in the kitchen closet and the beautiful leaves of a costly gift-book," said Wright. But once the eye is trained, we become able to see the connections "between the filthy bundles that weigh down the cart of the country tin-peddler and the fanciful packages that adorn the shelves and fill the drawers of the city stationer." "Strange as it may appear," he concluded, "the connection [between rags and books] is very intimate, and he who will attentively study the curious art of papermaking, will discover many odd companionships and dependencies, of which the world at large never dreamed."[5] Wright's narrative was published ten years before wood pulp would eclipse rag pulp as the primary ingredient of papermaking, and his paper mill narrative presupposes widespread knowledge about the industry among his readers. He cites the ubiquitous ragbag in the nineteenth-century kitchen, knowing that his readers had been saving irreparably torn or dirty household linens and selling them to rag peddlers their entire lives. To this day, elderly residents of western Massachusetts share childhood stories about rag collectors visiting the house to trade books and stationery for rags. Nineteenth-century memoirists also recalled trading their ragbags for books, paper, and cash. Rags had currency both as valuable items to save and trade and then as the substrate for paper money.[6]

Wright's paper mill tour narrative is just one example of literary writing about paper and papermaking in the nineteenth century. This book brings to the surface an archive of writing about paper from multiple genres and registers, including poetry, fiction, personal narratives, and advertisements. Across genre and period, writing about rag paper animates thought about readers' sensual relationships with material texts, revealing similarities in ways of writing and feeling. These works theorize sensemaking and dwell in the oscillation between attention to the presence of paper and attention to the meaning of letters and images written or printed on it. The haptic dimension of material texts becomes the site for political and aesthetic argument.

For example, women poets in the late seventeenth and the mid-nineteenth centuries turned to paper's origins in feminized labor with cloth as the basis of thought experiments about the connection between feminized domestic labor and women's writing. Historically and aesthetically, these poets belong to very different moments, but through the common thread of rag paper, a text technology shared in both periods, ways of sensing the material text are connected. Indeed, as we settle into the long digital present and renegotiate our relationship to paper, we are also questioning our sense of it, what it has meant to us, and how it positions us in a global supply chain of materials.

This book makes the claim that paying attention to rag paper and writing about it sheds new light on how early and nineteenth-century American readers and writers understood the materiality of texts. In everything from advertisements to popular poetry to magazine fiction, writers of the rag paper period theorized that narrative, memory, and meaning were inherent within paper's rag content as well as written on it. For readers and writers during this time, paper acted and was figured as a site of intimacy, where intriguing proximities and contacts became possible within the materiality of paper, books, and print. Reflecting on the relationship between cast-off rags and the paper within a book, Pastor Wright wanted his readers to share in the notion that "the connection is very intimate." He and other writers were drawn to the ways paper seemed to speak through the possibilities inherent within rags. Those who wrote what we might, adapting from Herman Melville, call "paper allegories," expressed in written form how paper mediated intimacy and what meaning was created in the contact between rags and readers.[7]

By engaging with early and nineteenth-century perceptions of the materiality of rag paper, I mean to address contemporary questions in the fields of book history, print culture, and bibliographical studies. Because paper is the meeting place of both written and material expression, I argue that paying closer attention to the layers of meaning-making on and within its surface calls us to rethink the definition of an important term in contemporary scholarship: "material texts." In the last decade, these three related fields have been arranged in coalition under the organizing principle that each is a way of approaching the "material text."[8] The earliest documented use of "material texts" in Americanist book history appears in Michelle Moylan and Lane Stiles's 1997 edited collection *Reading Books: Essays on Literature and the Material Text in America*, published by the University of Massachusetts Press in the same series in which this book appears. In *Reading Books*, Moylan and Stiles define the "material text" as the "collapse [of the] distinction" between "material form and textual content." For many readers and writers during the rag paper period, paper was always this sort of material text; it always presented the collapse of text into materiality and the eruption of materiality into text. *The Intimacy of Paper* shapes the understanding of "material textuality" as the literary or figurative dimension of a text's physical form. The study of this kind of material textuality is one type of Meredith McGill's proposed "book history style of literary criticism," identifiable by what she describes as a negotiation between "close reading of the text" and an "engagement with the material social economic forces that are invisible, occluded—even fetishized—at the level of the book-as-object."[9] What I take McGill's provocation to be here is that we need greater recognition that studying material texts does not mean that we read texts closely while also gesturing toward how they are packaged in particular material forms. Material textuality means that the material presence of something is itself figurative and demands close reading too.

We need to think further about the relationship between textuality and materiality that is implied when we say "material texts." There is a certain utility in organizing all types of scholarly attention to the physicality of books, print, and inscription under the umbrella of material text studies. But we would do well to think about the role of textuality here; what if these are not simply materials that carry inscription? *The Intimacy of Paper* offers rag paper as an object of study and reading in which both materiality and textuality are at work, where we see materiality *as* expression. Studying the tight relation of materiality and meaning is not a novel development in literary book history. Roger Chartier has written about how "readers . . . never confront abstract, idealized texts detached from any materiality. . . . They hold in their hands or perceive objects and forms whose structures and modalities govern their reading or hearing, and consequently the possible comprehension of the text read or heard." The very role of paper in making meaning is central to my thought on what constitutes material textuality. Coming at these questions from a slightly different angle, Bill Brown has offered "textual materialism" as "a mode of analytic objectification that focuses on the physical properties of an embodied text" that stages a "dialectical drama of opacity and transparency, physical support and cognitive transport."[10]

The Intimacy of Paper also contributes to the growing disciplinary formation of "critical bibliography" through its focus the ways material textuality has been used to make social and political claims about gender, labor, and race. When book history emerged in the U.S. academy in the early 1990s, some figured it as a positivist reaction against "theory" and the so-called culture war. They imagined that the study of books as objects returned the humanities to some desired solid ground. "Some people in literature are looking for ways to temper abstract theory with research," is how a *Chronicle of Higher Education* reporter put it at the time. This reactionary configuration offers a flattened-out version of the field, one that David Scott Kastan and Matthew P. Brown have characterized as "the new boredom" piling up dry-as-dust details in barricades against supposedly "sexy knowledge."[11] McGill and others have recently pointed out that the cultural turn in literary and historical research coincided with the drop off of scholarship in descriptive and analytic bibliography. The "recovery" of diverse writers and the expansion of the canon fed critical work on gender, sexuality, race, and class, which happened largely without detailed attention to bibliographical and book historical data.[12]

The recent project of developing a *critical* bibliography is a move to dissolve barriers between theoretically informed cultural studies and deep attention to the materiality of texts. Rag paper contains and represents narratives about gender, race, and labor, and the writers I study here try to bring these to the surface. *The Intimacy of Paper* studies how the materiality of paper directs attention back to the laborers who made it and to the layers of meaning inherent in rag paper. American women writers direct us to see that anything written or printed on paper takes residence on a surface that has been worked by women from the flax field to the linen rag to the sheet of paper. Anonymous ad copywriters and such canonical authors as Herman Melville theorized what forms of political and sensual community was made within paper after the gathering thousands of shreds of rags from communities near and far. Writers as dissimilar to each other as Benjamin Franklin and William Wells Brown both queried the ways that white skin and white paper appear alike within antiblack culture.

These are glosses of how the chapters of this book approach the embeddedness of culture within the materiality of paper. Just as *The Intimacy of Paper's* account of materiality textuality highlights the processes through which literature and materiality overlap, this book's alignment with critical bibliography insists on the disciplinary blending of cultural studies with bibliography and book history.

A Brief History of American Rag Papermaking

The history of papermaking is a subfield in its own right. It consists of histories of business, technology, printing and publishing, and arts and crafts.[13] To write this history would require several books, and each would have a different focus from this one. In fact, several comprehensive histories have been written by artists and scholars, including Dard Hunter, Cathleen Baker, and Nicholas Basbanes.[14] But to follow how American writers engaged with paper's material textuality during what I've called the "rag paper period," it will be useful to have a short history of the processes of rag papermaking and some of the more important changes that occurred during the period.

The first paper mill constructed in the colonies that would become the United States was built in Germantown, Pennsylvania, in 1690 by William Rittenhouse, a German-born immigrant to Pennsylvania by way of Holland. Rittenhouse learned papermaking in Germany and Holland, two continental centers of the trade since the twelfth century. There is one surviving report indicating that as early as 1674, "Paper hath been made in New England," but this is likely to have been an ill-equipped, small-scale operation, not a fully functioning mill.[15] Unlike in the New England colonies, the area surrounding Philadelphia supported the flax farming and linen weaving, along with German and Dutch immigrant communities skilled in these trades, necessary for papermaking to thrive at a large scale.[16] Several poetic pamphlets were issued in the late seventeenth century designed to advertise the successes of the Pennsylvania colony, and they tended to note the interdependence of nascent industries on one another. I will discuss the richest of these, Richard Frame's 1692 "A short Description of Pensilvania," at length in chapter 1, but another is worth quoting here. John Holme's 1696 poem, "A True Relation of the Flourishing State of Pensilvania," articulates the essential dependence of print on paper and, in turn, of paper on rags:

> Here dwelt a printer and I find
> That he can both print books and bind;
> He wants not paper, ink nor skill
> He's owner of a paper mill.
> The paper mill is here hard by
> And makes good paper frequently,
> . . . .

No doubt but he will lay up bags
If he can get good store of rags.
Kind friend, when thy old shift is rent
Let it to th' paper mill be sent.[17]

The reliance of one trade on another, the tireless search for rags for paper-making, and the transformation of material from seed to cloth to rag to paper are recurrent themes in nearly all writing about paper during this time.

Because the printer in this poem "is the owner of a paper mill" who "wants not paper," the poem also hints at the fact that paper was the most important upfront cost for a printer or publisher. Whether in the colonial, early national, or antebellum period, printers and publishers had most of their capital tied up in paper stock. This risk for each book or job was carried in paper that, unlike type, could not easily be reused, redirected, or recouped once a job was under way. Business historians of the book trade who have studied book costs of large nineteenth-century publishers have shown that paper represented most of the risk in the trade: Paper tied up substantial amounts of capital throughout the process of composing, printing, collating, and binding before a book finally hit the market, where publishers hoped it would sell.[18]

By the time papermaking was established in the American colonies, it had already spread from China through Japan and Korea to Africa and the Middle East before moving into continental Europe. The ancestor of paper as we know it was first made in China in 105 CE. Paper had become more common than papyrus and parchment in the Arab world by the end of the tenth century. Papermaking was established in Europe by Moors in the Iberian Peninsula in the twelfth century. In Spain, paper was called *pagamino de paño*, or cloth parchment, a neologism that acknowledged the essential ingredient of linen rags while maintaining a skeuomorphic connection to animal skin writing surfaces. Papermaking came to England relatively late, in the fifteenth century, owing to several factors, not least of which was the relative absence of flax farming and linen weaving and the prevalent use of wool, which is not conducive to making paper.[19] By the time papermaking was established in Pennsylvania in the late seventeenth century, it had already been developed by people in Asia, Africa, and the Middle East for centuries before being brought to the European colonial states that would move the technology to North America.

Broadly speaking, there were two "periods" of rag papermaking germane to this book's focus: the hand period and the machine period. Within these periods there were many innovations, closely held trade secrets, and experiments in materials and processes that deviated from or extended "norms." But within the scope of this book's literary critical study of material textuality, a general understanding of the main processes, materials, and laborers involved in each period suffices. Hand papermaking was the norm in colonial America and the early national United States from 1690 until 1817, when the first paper machine was built on the Brandywine River in the mid-Atlantic region. In Europe, the machine paper era began around 1800.

Hand papermaking involved three principal artisan laborers, usually men: the vatman, the coucher, and the layer. They were supported by teams of other laborers, often but not exclusively women and children, who sorted, shredded, and prepared rags and who also hung and managed paper while drying. Paper mills purchased rags from a variety of sources, including street ragpickers, household collectors, and importers. Once at the mill, rags were sorted by quality of weave, color and cleanliness, and strength. Depending on the quality of the mill or the paper desired, seams and stitches were removed, as were other inclusions, and dirt and dust was shaken out over a screen. Once sorted they were cut into small pieces by being passed over a fixed blade attached to the bins where the women and children worked. Until the early nineteenth century, these small squares of cut and separated rags would be left to ferment, or rett, for a time. This began the process of breaking down the cloth fibers, softening and opening them up to be recombined in the paper mould. Next came boiling in an open cauldron with the addition of alkaline solutions (which varied depending on the mill and the desired product) to further soften and open the rag fibers. Beating was then accomplished at first with a triphammer stamping machine that operated by cams on an axle, powered by a waterwheel. The stamping machines were very loud, which took a toll on workers and which made the rag room of paper mills difficult to be near. Beating, water, and chemical additives completed the process of breaking apart rag fibers and preparing their shape and surface area for recohesion as paper. The resulting pulp is called "stuff."

Once the stuff was prepared by sorting, cutting, retting, cooking, and beating, the slurry was dumped into vats. The vat is the basic workstation unit of the hand paper mill. A shop could be a one-, two-, or three-vat operation, and so on. After the vat was "charged," or filled with pulp and water, the vatman dipped a two-piece wire mould and deckle into the vat, drawing it toward himself creating a thin layer of pulp atop a wire mesh. Working quickly, the vatman needed to shake and even out the pulp on the surface of the mould as water began to dry out and the sheet began to settle. At this moment, rag fibers that were opened by beating and soaking begin to bond together again, making the surface of the sheet come together. The wire of the mould and deckle create the chains, lines, and watermarks you see within paper from this period when it's held to the light. The vatman then handed the mould off to the coucher, who pressed the wet sheet into a felt, transferring it from the wires to a stack of felt sheets. The vatman and the coucher did this continually. When a stack of wet sheets and felts reached a certain quantity, the layer placed the stack into a screw press and applied great pressure to remove more water from the sheets. Water was expressed several more times through pressing the accumulated pack. Sheets of paper were then hung to finish drying in the rafters of an upstairs room in the mill, usually with slats in the walls to regulate temperature, humidity, and airflow. The distinctive architecture of these buildings can be seen in engravings on nineteenth-century ream wrappers. After drying, and depending on the grade of paper and its purpose, the paper could be sized (to prepare the surface to accept ink without bleeding) by submersion in a gelatinous solution or buffed and beaten with stones and hammers. This three-person team and an eight-person support team working rags, pressing, and drying could make as many as fifteen hundred to two thousand sheets of good writing or printing paper per ten-hour day. The workflow of these three laborers is accurately and memorably depicted in the engraved illustrations accompanying Louis-Jacques Goussier description of papermaking in Diderot's *Encyclopédie* (1751–80). The best resources for studying the technical details of hand papermaking are the works of Timothy Barrett and Cathleen Baker, both of whom are paper scientists and papermakers who have reconstructed historical methods through practice in the present.[20]

The vat and mould structure of hand papermaking limited the amount of paper a mill could make. There were human limits: how fast humans could work, and how much they expected to be compensated for their skill and time. Near constant rag shortages were also a problem. The rag problem could not be solved by automation, but the speed and labor problem could be. After 1817, U.S. papermakers began replacing the hand mould with various kinds of paper machines. Eventually, these would replace the hand mould with a mesh belt. In terms of the paper itself, the replacement of the bounded rectangular mould with mesh belts meant that paper was now made in long rolls and then cut into sheets of different sizes, rather than made in discrete sheets limited by the size of the mould. The "endlessness" of the belt and emergent wet sheet captivated those who followed technology and even found its way to popular audiences. In 1830, one newspaper quipped that "the newspapers tell us that there is a paper mill in Delaware which can make a sheet of paper one hundred miles in length. This is a very decent sized sheet, undoubtedly, but there is a mill in Ulster Co. N.Y. which makes a sheet that has *no end*."[21] This comical editorial in the newspaper reveals both a fascination with the new technologies of papermaking and a projection of papermaking into the literary imaginary through humor and hyperbole. Eventually, people joked that papermaking machines worked such wonders of transformation that they could take a shirt in on one side and spit out a printed book on the other. One lecturer is reported to have marveled at a paper mill where "a person might throw in his shirt at one end and see it come out *Robinson Crusoe* at the other."[22]

In these water- or steam-driven machines, a wire belt passed through a charged vat, or "stock box," where it picked up a constant thin layer of stuff. The work of the coucher was replaced by several couch rolls that began drying the sheet and removing water with an "endless felt" belt that ran on a loop on the couch rolls. The sheet moved from the "wet end" of the machine to the "dry end," where it passed through several drying rolls before being rolled, cut into sheets, and hung to dry. The most widely adopted paper machine was the Fourdrinier, which became the standard machinery in mills up and down the eastern seaboard by the 1830s. Mechanization also changed how rags were converted into stuff. As early as 1756 the popular macerating engine called the "Hollander beater" largely replaced the water-driven triphammer beater in colonial America, greatly reducing the necessary time for beating rags from several days to several hours.[23] Like the eclipse of hand presses by machine presses for printing, the switch from hand to machine dramatically increased the speed and scale of papermaking, while lowering the cost. An 1818 newspaper account of this change mentioned that in one day's work "two men and one boy" could make "as much as the old machinery by twelve men and six boys."[24]

Increases in demand for paper and the capacity to manufacture meant that more rags than ever were needed. Experiments to add other materials to the stuff, from rope to vegetable matter, were always afoot at small scale. It wasn't until 1867 that a wood-based pulp replaced a rag-based pulp as the primary ingredient in the majority of American papermaking.[25] With the end of the rag period technologies of papermaking and ways of writing about one's relation to paper changed markedly.

How Rags Mediate Intimacy

The readings in *The Intimacy of Paper* explore how the rag content of paper mediates intimacy by transmitting material history and narrative, and by making bodies present to one another. Each chapter in this book takes up a different dimension of these possibilities and their representation in American written, visual, and material cultures. I want to present two examples at the outset that help ground our sense of how paper functions in these ways.

Like all things made by humans, and as scholars of material culture know well, paper bears visible signs that tell stories about its creation. Studying these signs, we can often recreate the processes, the decisions, the aesthetic priorities, and sometimes even the struggles of the artisans and laborers who design and make the things we use and encounter. Since creating a clean, smooth, and unmarked sheet was a priority of papermaking, traces of the various people involved in its creation can be hard to find. But when inspected closely, the seemingly two-dimensional surface of the page turns out to be three dimensional: there are visible fibers, bits of unshredded rag, bumps and depressions.

Though papermakers aimed for a clean sheet free of tell-tale marks, papermaking was often not very far from the cities and towns where printing and publishing took place, and also often not far from readers. Calls for rag collection were in the advertisements of almost every newspaper, a ragbag was a feature of most kitchens, and ragpickers walked the streets of cities and towns. Across differences of class and race, women and girls were instructed, or ordered, to save household rags and to prepare them for sale to paper mills. Children and adults who learned to read and write using *Webster's Elementary Spelling Book* or the *Columbian Orator* copied out and recited lessons about paper and papermaking by rote, as Pastor Wright noted, "There are probably few school-boys who are uninformed of the fact, so comprehensively declared in Webster's Elementary Spelling Book, that "Paper is made of linen and cotton rags."[26] Teamsters moved rags off ships coming to port from abroad. Paper mills were loud and could be heard amongst the din of mill industries whether in the center of a city or at the edge of a town. As we will see later in this book, during the rag paper period readers encountered the page both as something to read and as the product of an industry that they likely had some part in, however small.

The special collections library at the University of Illinois at Urbana-Champaign owns a copy of a seventeenth-century Italian book containing a remarkable sheet of paper. Holding this sheet of *Per la facciata del Duomo di Milano* to the light we find an impression of the vatman or coucher's hand (Fig. 1).[27] Seeing the hand of the worker within this sheet of paper confronts us with the presence of a human. The hand provokes us to realize that when touching this sheet, we are proximate to a particular person reaching through time from within this book's paper. Laying a hand over the seventeenth-century hand impression, you might share a kind of intimate contact through the materiality of the page. The hand raises questions that are very likely unanswerable: whose hand was this, what was the individual's life like, and so on. Lacking definitive answers, we might begin to imagine who this person was, crafting a story based in the intimate contact we make through this sheet of paper. The handprint in *Per la facciata del Duomo di Milano* is an unambiguous illustration of how paper mediates contact between humans. But as I will show in this book, people who encountered rag paper were attuned to its intimacies in ways that did not require something as visible as a handprint.

Every sheet of paper is an archive of human labor. This is true of the work of the paper mill, but it is also true of the rags that make up paper. We know hands touched each page as they came into being in the mill, but what about the cloth that became rags and the flax plants that became linen? These, too, are present within paper, and the literature of the rag paper period was also fascinated with how the histories of these objects and the people who encountered them were present within the sheet. The sense that a sheet of paper contained the history of all the people who encountered its material components was so strong that several "it narratives" exist in which a sheet or a quire of paper tells its story from flax seed to cloth to paper to print or manuscript and back to the earth again. The most well-known of these is probably the 1779 English magazine story "The Adventures of a Quire of Paper," but they were so common that schoolchildren could write them out from memory.[28]

One of them was James Knox, a school-age boy in Rochester, New York, who had an it-narrative about the material history of a sheet of paper ready at the tip of his tongue. He wrote it out for his classroom's manuscript newspaper,

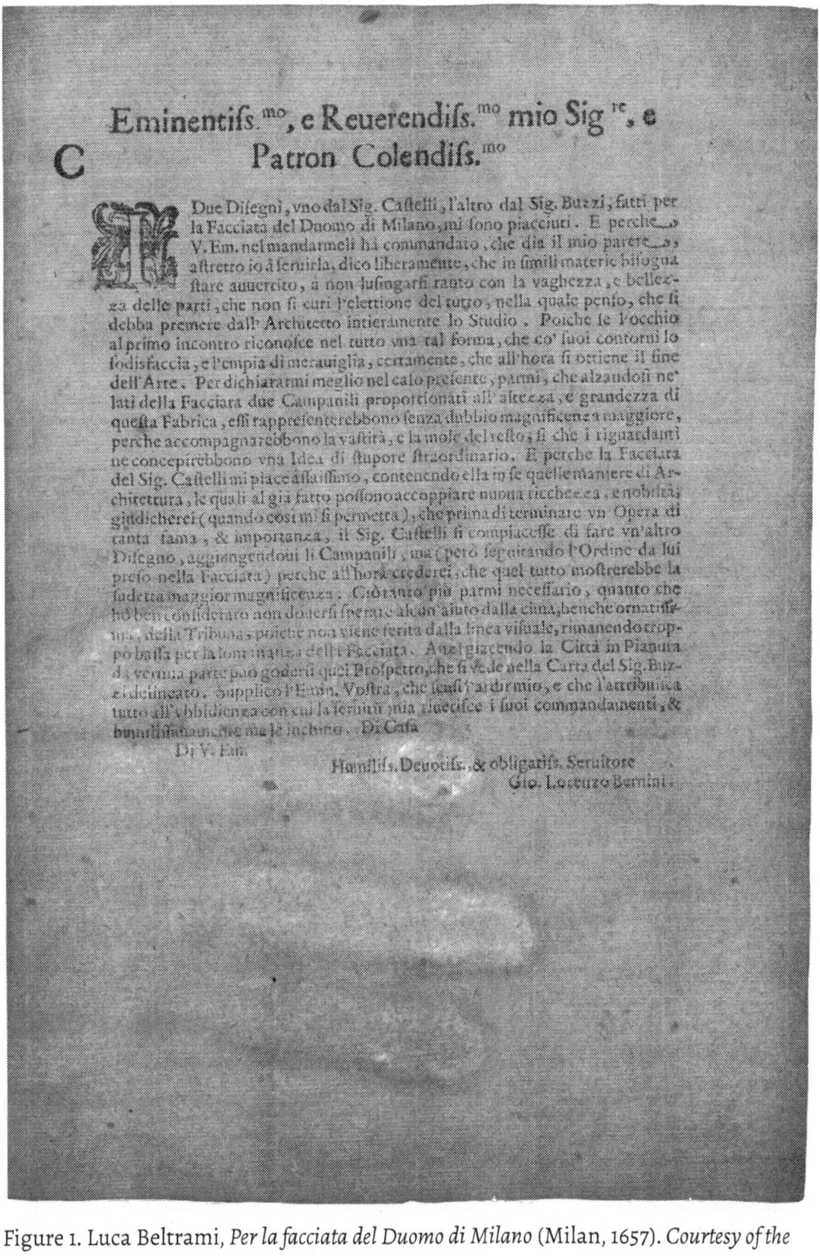

Eminentiss.^{mo}, e Reuerendiss.^{mo} mio Sig.^{re}, e Patron Colendiss.^{mo}

C

Due Difegni, vno dal Sig. Caftelli, l'altro dal Sig. Buzzi, fatti per la Facciata del Duomo di Milano, mi fono piaciuti. E perche V. Em. nel mandarmeli hà commandato, che dia il mio parere, aftretto io à feruirla, dico liberamente, che in fimili materie bifogna ftare auuertito, à non lufingarfi tanto con la vaghezza, e bellezza delle parti, che non fi curi l'elettione del tutto, nella quale penfo, che fi debba premere dall'Architetto intieramente lo Studio. Poiche fe l'occhio al primo incontro riconofce nel tutto vna tal forma, che co' fuoi contorni lo fodisfaccia, e l'empia di merauiglia, certamente, che all'hora fi ottiene il fine dell'Arte. Per dichiararmi meglio nel cafo prefente, parmi, che alzandofi ne' lati della Facciata due Campanili proportionati all'altezza, e grandezza di quefta Fabrica, effi rapprefenterebbono fenza dubbio magnificenza maggiore, perche accompagnarebbono la vaftità, e la mole del refto, fi che i riguardanti ne concepirebbono vna Idea di ftupore ftraordinario. E perche la Facciata del Sig. Caftelli mi piace affaiffimo, contenendo ella in fe quelle maniere di Architettura, le quali già fatto poffono accoppiare nuoua ricchezza, e nobiltà, giudicherei (quando cosi mi fi permetta), che prima di terminare vn Opera di tanta fama, & importanza, il Sig. Caftelli fi compiaceffe di fare vn'altro Difegno, aggiungendoui li Campanili, ma (però feguitando l'Ordine da lui prefo nella Facciata) perche all'hora crederei, che quel tutto moftrerebbe la fudetta maggior magnificenza. Ciò tanto più parmi neceffario, quanto che hò ben confiderato non doderfi fperare alcun aiuto dalla cima, benche ornatiffima, della Tribuna, poiche non viene ferita dalla linea vifuale, rimanendo troppo baffa per la lontananza delle Facciata. Auatgiacendo la Città in Pianura da veruna parte può goderfi quel Profpetto, che fi vede nella Carta del Sig. Buzzi delineato. Supplico l'Em. Voftra, che fcufi'l ardir mio, e che l'attribuifca tutto all'obbidienza con cui la feruitù mia riuecifce i fuoi commandamenti, & humiliffimamente me le inchino. Di Cafa

Di V. Em.

Humiliff. Deuotiff. & obligatiff. Seruitore
Gio. Lorenzo Bernini.

Figure 1. Luca Beltrami, *Per la facciata del Duomo di Milano* (Milan, 1657). *Courtesy of the University of Illinois Urbana-Champaign Libraries.*

Odds and Ends. A folio sheet formatted like a newspaper, students in this class composed articles and stories by hand and created a single copy of *Odds and Ends* each week. Upon completion, their teacher read it aloud. For the March 1, 1850, issue, young James Knox contributed a story entitled "The Flax Seed." I quote the entire story here for the sake of orienting us to how readers and writers like Knox understood the rag content of paper to "speak." Without much punctuation, and with a pace that communicates the boy's excitement, Knox writes from the perspective of a flax seed that becomes paper:

"The Flax Seed"

The first that I remember of myself I was laying in an old chest in a farmer's kitchen in the spring I was taken out and put in the ground I sprang up and was cut down again I went through a variety of performances till I was made into a piece of cloth I was then boxed up and sent to a dry goods store where I was taken out and placed on the shelf I had laid there for some time. When one day a little girl and her mother came into the store to buy some cloth. A great many articles were handed down but none suited them I was then taken down and placed before them they asked the price paid for me and and [*sic*] went off home I was then taken and placed upon the table I was worn around the house till I was all in rags I was then thrown in the rag bag. one day there came a man to the house and asked them if they any rags I was handed to him with the others and he gave them a few articles of tin-ware and went off I was then taken to the paper mills and made into a piece of paper I was then put into the printing press and made into a spelling book I was then placed into a book store I had lain there for some time when a little boy came into the store and asked them if they had any spelling books I was handed down he asked the price of me paid for me and went off the little boy did not like his book and I was left kicking around the floor one evening I was kicked out of the school I had lain there for some time when a large dog came along and shook me so that he shook the wits out of me and that is all I can remember.[29]

As a child, James knows that paper's origin is in flax seeds, which after growing into flax is woven into linen. Telling the story of this paper, James also tells the stories of the humans who encounter it along the way: a farmer, a little girl and her mother, a ragpicker, a schoolboy. James also associates all the places this seed, plant, linen, and rag have been with the paper. Within the paper are stories of the farm, the store, the home, the ragbag, the paper mill, the printer, the bookstore, and the classroom. James can imagine, and narrate in prose, the rag content of paper's ability to speak its material history and to make present all of the people it encountered along the way. James also resists the technodeterminist and archival fantasies that paper print and fix words and images in place and in perpetuity. The end of James's story contains a "dog ate my homework" joke, but it also delivers the realization that the elements of paper, once digested by the dog, will return to the earth from whence they came, perhaps as fertilizer for another flax seed. James's way of thinking about what he encountered when he touched the paper in his primer was not an uncommon one.

One of the qualities of rags and paper enabling the sense that it carries so many contacts and contexts within them is their absorptiveness. Rags and paper literally and figuratively absorb things around them and carry them forward. Other narratives about the raggy content of paper speak not only of the people who wove flax into linen but also about the tears absorbed into a pillowcase, or even about the conversations "overheard" by a piece of cloth. These tears and overheard conversations might later emerge out of the paper in the form of a tearjerking sentimental novel or, in the case of a novel called *The Tell-Tale Rag*, a tell-all exposé. *The Tell-Tale Rag*, for example, bills itself as a story in which "a cotton rag is made, as it were, a living oracle, giving its own history whilst serving as raiment on twelve different masters, relating each one of their secret besetting and popular sins, from the time it was planted in the cotton fields of South Carolina, until it became a portion of the body of a glorified saint."[30]

A sheet of paper constituted from thousands of pulped rags, the cellulose torn open and then rebonded through drying, contains within it what Carolyn Steedman calls the "irreducible traces of an actual history." Observing a rag rug in a nineteenth-century domestic space, she describes how it creates a floor covering out of interlocking pieces of waste rags. What interests Steedman is how "the rag rug is made from the torn fragments of other things, debris and leavings, the broken and torn things of industrial civilization." Looking at such a rug, Steedman wonders how the cultural historian could tell the story of the social relations literally knotted up within the thing itself: "The rug carried with it the irreducible traces of an actual history, and that history *cannot be made to go away*."[31] Such rugs, Steedman notes, were often sold by working families to paper mills for cash, and so these cloth-bound histories of domestic labor become subsumed into paper. And though, she notes, such it-narratives as *The Romance of a Rag* would try to speak on behalf of this material history within the generic constraints of the romance, a material history remains embedded within the rag rug and within the paper it goes on to make.

Material textuality combines the figural or storytelling dimension *with* the materially present object. We can look on the object itself as cultural historians and wonder "if these rags could talk . . . ," but we also encounter the object within a set of familiar generic expectations and narrative forms that supply us with no end of raggy expressions. The richest possibilities for reading "material textuality" present themselves when we are open to both the literal and the fanciful narratives that might accrue to a quire of paper. *The Intimacy of Paper* focuses on the relationship between literary writing about paper and paper itself, foregrounding how material metaphors, what N. Katherine Hayles calls "the traffic between words and physical artifacts," create different ways of sensing material texts.[32]

Rags and rag paper absorb and re-present what they carry within them. Beyond the realm of literary representation, people wondered about, and also feared, the possibly too intimate proximities that paper and rags put them in. In port and paper mill cities, people feared that rags and paper could spread disease. This was especially true of rags that were imported from abroad, and even more so if the country of origin stoked racist fears and prejudices. Rags were quarantined at port and rushed from port to remote paper mills without entering city centers lest they spread disease. A historian of early American quarantine, David S. Barnes, confirms that in the minds of early and nineteenth-century Americans, rags "represent[ed] the threat of direct or indirect contact with filthy human beings."[33]

The intimacies of rag paper could lead to imagination or contagion, or both. Either way, the rag content of paper made other people, places, times, and stories present within the page. Bill Brown has more recently commented that the lines between people and things become blurred. As a site of encounter between thing and person, as an archive of persons in things, rags and rag paper are sites of what Brown might call enmeshment: "Enmeshed as we are in the object world," he writes, "we can't at times differentiate ourselves from things, or because those things (however actively or passively) have somehow come to resemble us."[34] Others before me have taken up the way paper and books absorb and archive what happens around and over them. Stéphane Mallarmé wrote that "your act is always stuck to a piece of paper, / for mediation without traces becomes evanescent."[35] In "Unpacking My Library," Walter

Benjamin also links the scrap of paper and the trace of memory. Recalling the work of physically handling and reorganizing his book collection, he notices that "the floor [is] covered in torn paper." These scraps of paper and books bring him "not thoughts, but . . . memories," he says. In particular, touching these material objects makes present "the cities in which I found so many things."[36] Paper mediates presence and creates proximity; it absorbs traces of people, places, and actions, making them available for thinking and touching. *The Intimacy of Paper* excavates these traces stuck to pieces of paper. Through early and nineteenth-century American literature and culture, this book traces one path of these material memories through rag paper.

Paper Studies

"Many roads lead to paper," Christina Lupton writes, "both those of common sense, which aim to pin it down but end up vertiginously acknowledging the 'miracle' of papers that come and go as soon as we try to look at them too closely." In the book at hand I join a community of scholars in conversation about the different kinds of cultural and aesthetic work done by paper. In a December 2012 article in the *New York Times*, arts reporter Jennifer Schuessler described an "emerging body of work that might be called 'paperwork studies.'"[37] Schuessler's article focused a spotlight on several recent books studying the social, intellectual, and political structures that are made possible by the affordances of paper and paperwork. Under this umbrella, Lisa Gitelman, Ben Kafka, and others have loosed the archival and epistemological methodologies of book history and print culture studies from "the book" and "print," focusing rather on *documents* and the technologies of paper that make them possible. In *Paper Knowledge: Toward a Media History of Documents*, Gitelman argues that book history and print culture have dominated the history of communication but are "insufficient" rubrics for the task. "One aim" of Gitelman's work, she writes, "is to discourage [the] use" of the terms "book history" and "print culture," dislodging them long enough to see around the edges, to let other sorts of media objects come into focus. Taking up paper and the document as the organizing principle opens up different questions about the materiality of texts. "Surface" and "inscription" become more important terms for analysis than are "book" or "print." The way paper cuts across, or under, as it were, the division between manuscript and print dissolves the hold of that division on the mind. Gitelman calls attention, for example, to the massive archive of job printing, including blanks and forms. Forms and blanks have no authors or readerships in the traditional, literary sense, yet they made up the bulk of a printer's daily work and they play a crucial role in the establishment and management of governmental and corporate infrastructures. Ben Kafka takes up this very question in his book, *The Demon of Writing: Powers and Failures of Paperwork*. He studies how paperwork, documentation, and bureaucracy create and frustrate forms of power. Kafka argues that the bureaucratic regime created by the French Revolution gave rise to the notion that government could be called to account and that this accounting was based in new possibilities of paperwork, record keeping, and record storage.[38] Both Gitelman and Kafka are influenced by Bruno Latour's actor-network theory, particularly the suggestion that objects act on and organize the behavior of humans around them. Paper *works* on the humans around it, affording some possibilities while foreclosing others. *The Intimacy of Paper* is similarly interested in the ways that rag paper prompts those around it, calling readers to look into its fibers or to think about whose hands they encounter when touching the sheet.

In addition to Gitelman's and Kafka's work, this book's conversational constellation includes the work of several scholars who study the links between paper and the literary content it carries. For example, the sheet of paper emerges as the crucial analytic scale in Alexandra Socarides's *Dickinson Unbound: Paper, Process, Poetics*. Socarides offers a wholesale reevaluation of Emily Dickinson's fascicles, the poet's hand-stitched, book-like gatherings of poems in manuscripts. Socarides observes that critics tended to analyze Dickinson's fascicles as if they were booklets, making claims about the relationships between and among poems in the fascicles as if they were purposefully arranged in order in booklets. So accustomed are we to "thinking in books" that we forget, as another scholar, Augusta Rohrbach, has written, to "think . . . outside the book."[39] We become unprepared to see other possible units of meaning and formats for carrying them. By doing the fundamental bibliographical work of collating the sheets in the fascicles, Socarides found that Dickinson composed not with booklets in mind but in sheets of paper. Socarides's close readings of the poems, informed by bibliographical data, show that the unit of coherence and relation among poems in Dickinson's fascicles is actually the sheet of paper. Dickinson's "poetics . . . is guided by paper," finds Socarides.[40] The single sheet of paper puts poems in relation to one another in the fascicles, an important and revealing fact that remained invisible as long as we go with the assumption that Dickinson intended the fascicles to resemble books, not sheets. Socarides reveals the extent to which paper literally shaped Dickinson's work and how self-conscious Dickinson was about the material influences on her writing. "There isn't room enough; not *half* enough to hold what I was going to say. Won't you tell the man who makes sheets of paper, that I hav'nt the *slightest respect* for him!" Dickinson wrote in a letter from her home in Amherst, halfway between the major paper mill capitols of Springfield and Pittsfield, Massachusetts. Socarides's work shows that "paper shapes what [Dickinson] has to say" and issues a call to scholars using methods born in book history and bibliography to remember that, while we usually focus on print and script, paper is a platform and studying what it makes possible is both necessary and revealing.[41]

No one has taken further the insight that paper is a technological platform than Bonnie Mak, whose book, *How the Page Matters*, studies "the page" as a long-lasting architecture of information. The page has organized information for readers in loose sheets of papyrus, paper, or vellum, bound in codex form, reproduced in Xeroxes and microfilms, and in digital environments where selecting "new" in the menu of word processing software produces what looks like a digitally remediated fresh sheet of paper. Across textual media and technological periods, "the page" endures as an interface and organizing structure. As scholars increasingly study the remediation of texts across formats—Gitelman, for example, studies the link between print, microfilm, and digital versions of texts—"the page" turns out to be a more useful frame for tracking content across platforms than "the book." Like Socarides, Mak argues that book history and print culture "demarcate[d] the printed book as a locus for the investigation of reading and writing" and "fractured the broader history of the codex and communication technology" by overshadowing other components like the page. "Mattering," Mak writes, means significance, and signification in the textual sense, "but also to claim a certain physical space, to have a particular presence, to be uniquely embodied." This interweaving of matter and signification, the interrelation of meaning, presence, space, and embodiment, is at the heart of *The Intimacy of Paper*'s approach to material textuality. "The matter and mattering of the page are entangled in complicated ways as they reconfigure each other," Mak writes.[42]

Closely related to Mak's analysis of the layering of embodiment and meaning within the page, Sarah Kay's *Animal Skins and the Reading Self* asks questions about the relationship between animal skin writing substrates like vellum or parchment and the genre of the "bestiary" inscribed upon them. Here, visual and textual representations of animals are borne on skins of goat and calf; pores, hair, and holes from wounds to the animal and to the text carry visual and verbal representations of the very same fleshly animals. What is the relation of the skin writing surface to "skin" represented in text and image? "By focusing on the page itself, as much as what is written, drawn, or painted on it," Kay "sketch[es] a speculative phenomenology" of the page. How does the substrate of skin intervene in reading by making its presence known to the reader, "how would it feel to become absorbed in the contents of a page that can be perceived as an extension of the reader's own skin?" "Guided and preempted by the texts themselves," how do such texts reconfigure the stable categories of book as object and reader as subject, she asks.[43]

The Intimacy of Paper is similarly invested in the real and imaginary boundary crossings between the reader who collects rags in her kitchen and the rag paper pages over which she runs her fingers. What emerges between embodied reader and embodied text? Here I argue for an approach to material textuality that asks readers to dwell in the structures where meaning and matter are entangled. The Intimacy of Paper joins a growing body of scholarship that looks to paper, the page, and the substrate to think about the generative feedback loops between textuality and materiality.

Material Turns and Theories of Material Presence

As a field, book historians have been moving toward the framework of "material texts" at the same time that other humanist interpretive frameworks have taken their own "material turns." To what extent does the study of material texts intersect with these? Bibliography, book history, and print culture studies' attention to the details of material objects was once held out as a rejection of "theory" after the linguistic turn, a refusal to permit "the text" to float free of any particular manifestation in the world. Similarly, new materialism and "thing theory" offer possible models for staging the relationship between thought and things. With so many thinkers attempting to articulate how materiality shapes thought and experience, what models matter, so to speak, for those of us focused on material texts?

The "new materialism," for example, proposes to think outside the dualism of the subject/object paradigm in order to regard the agency of things, and further to do so without appealing to personification or the value human subjects assign to objects. This mode of thinking seeks to reveal the networks, assemblages, and relations that form without human input or that are perhaps even indifferent to humans altogether.[44] The idea of assemblages that emerge from this body of theory may be particularly useful for the study of material texts. We are used to talking about books and print as conglomerations of different kinds of human labor and craft assembled into book form. But the notion of the assemblage that comes to use from new materialism prompts us to think about other, nonhuman actors in these negotiations of material textuality. Sonia Hazard has argued that the move away from anthropocentrism allows humanists, in particular, to see the interrelation of humans and objects as complex assemblages. "Humans and things are fundamentally co-constitutive, whether cooperatively or agonistically so," she writes." "Assemblages," Hazard continues, "challenge the commonplace idea that agency—the capacity to make effects in the world—is the unique province of deliberate actors like humans . . . in assemblages, things are not inert."[45] When human blood soaks into a rag, and then is made into paper, what sort of assemblage of human, vegetable, and textual matter is it? How do we account for the presence of the animals whose bones and hooves supply gelatin for the sizing that prepares paper to accept ink? The vocabularies of new materialism permit us to talk about the tense molecular bonds always moving between fibers in a sheet of paper and the DNA dwelling within rags as part of the encounter between human readers and the sheet of paper.

The way Bill Brown describes "things" as different from "objects" can be another useful framework, one that resonates with this book's interest in paper's becoming visible and meaningful in the rag paper period. Things, Brown says, are excessive objects that "exceed their mere materialization as objects or their mere utilization as objects—their force as a sensuous presence or as a metaphysical presence, the magic by which objects become values, fetishes, idols, and totems." Things are objects that suddenly "seem to assert their presence and power." Fibers in rag paper assert their presence, visible within the surface of the page. Rag and fiber within the page assert their thingliness in the way Roland Barthes says that the punctum in a photograph "rises from the scene, shouts out of it like an arrow, and pierces." It is the "accident which pricks me." I am particularly drawn to Barthes's use of "accident" here, because an accident does not only mean contingency or circumstance but also signifies that which is "present but not necessarily so," the material embodiment of something seemingly absent.[46] For both Brown and

Barthes, things harbor the ability to exceed their supposed inertia, to gain the attention of the viewer, and "infuse the world with significance."[47] Rag paper calls out from its surface to be engaged in its presence and its sensuousness.

In this book, I am especially interested in bringing the study of material texts into conversation with a body of scholarship on "the materialities of communication" not often engaged by American scholars, even in the current wave of material turns. The way *The Intimacy of Paper* thinks about the relationship between presence and meaning in material texts is informed by Hans Ulrich Gumbrecht's work on "presence effects" and the "presence dimension" of aesthetic and cultural objects. In a series of books, including *Materialities of Communication* (1994), *The Powers of Philology: Dynamics of Textual Criticism* (2003), and *The Production of Presence: What Meaning Cannot Convey* (2004), Gumbrecht embarks on a project to articulate an approach to aesthetic experience that is not completely subsumed by the metaphysical, including the subject/object dichotomy of the Cartesian worldview and hermeneutics/interpretation. Gumbrecht laments how various approaches to the "attribution of meaning," which he credits as the dominant paradigm of the humanities, dull our capacity to perceive and describe the effects that objects have on our bodies: "If we attribute a meaning to a thing that is present, that is, if we form an idea of what this thing may be in relation to us, we seem to attenuate, inevitably, the impact this thing can have on our bodies and our senses."[48] Throughout his work, Gumbrecht aims to restore the haptic to our critical toolkit by dwelling in the oscillation between the "presence effects" and the "meaning effects" of cultural artifacts. As a book historian working today, I am particularly interested in how easily presence and meaning map onto materiality and textuality, respectively. Throughout this book, I am keen to dwell in the oscillation between materiality and textuality, between presence effects and meaning effects. This oscillation is at the heart of what material textuality, a configuration that links these terms and creates generative tension, offers as a paradigm for our field.

In Gumbrecht's framing, the search for meaning, symbolism, context, and interpretation has become so dominant to critical practice, and it sets in so immediately, that it forestalls recognition of sensation and its intensities on the body. In the Cartesian worldview, the work of the mind is separate from the body and objects. In the hermeneutic tradition, meaning is latent in objects and must be drawn out. The work of the scholar is to find the meaning "behind" something, to look "through" its surface to reveal the spirit that lies within the body. To think around and outside this paradigm, Gumbrecht and a number of other German philosophers and critics, including Friedrich Kittler, turned their attention to, as they framed it, the "materialities of communication." We should recall here that in one of the earliest uses of the concept of "material textuality," Peter Stallybrass and Margreta de Grazia say that material texts are objects that "demand to be looked *at*, not seen *through*."[49] The call to meet the text *at* itself rather than to immediately look into or through it unites both early articulations of de Grazia and Stallybrass's material texts studies and Gumbrecht and Kittler's "materialities of communication." "Not taking into account . . . the materiality of characters on wax, papyrus, or parchment was seen as the historical condition for the dominance of 'meaning' and 'spirit' in Western culture," Gumbrecht writes. Gumbrecht, Kittler, and others in their working group of media theorists organized their work around a "main fascination" with the "question of how different media—different materialities—of communication would affect the meaning that [material texts] carried."[50]

The main thrust of Kittler's work, probably the most influential so far to emerge from this group, is that human thought does not happen outside the affordances of available inscription systems. Therefore, in this model, the work of the scholar is to understand the media conditions of possibility for certain expressions of literature, rather than to interpret individual expressions. In any historical period, Kittler would say, the technological capacities of media determine the shape of what can be written. Technologies of inscription are prior to meaning-making.[51] Kittler's work has influenced media studies far more than book history, though these fields do share some conceptual and disciplinary overlap. Kittler's work is also foundational to prominent Americanist scholars of material texts, such as Lisa Gitelman.[52]

One of the features of Gumbrecht's thought that makes it more attractive to me than Kittler's is that he leaves more room for oscillation between meaning and materiality, especially in literature. "Poetry is," he writes, "the most powerful example of the simultaneity of presence effects and meaning effects—for even the most overpowering institutional dominance of the hermeneutic dimension could never fully repress the presence effects of rhyme and alliteration, of verse and stanza." Here we have an outline for literary criticism, moving back and forth between how some material condition, the way rhyme sounds or moves the mouth, and the meaning made by what is said in the way it is said. "We no longer believed that a meaning complex could be kept separated from its mediality, that is, from the difference of appearing on a printed page, on a computer screen, or in a voicemail message," Gumbrecht writes. But, he admits some room for ambiguity in the relation between meaning and mediality: "We didn't quite know how to deal with this interface of meaning and materiality."[53] Kittler's work centers around historical epochs and their media systems; another of his widely influential books is titled *Gramophone, Film, Typewriter*, and in his reading, each of these new media technologies inaugurates a distinct era of discursive possibility. Where Kittler turns to media, Gumbrecht turns to philology, a field closely related to bibliography and book history. And this is why I think his focus on the presence effects of media are as, if not more, important for book historians to engage as Kittler's. Philology is the discovery, editing, and presentation of historical texts, a field of study in which one must literally get close to the problematic interface of meaning and materiality at the surface of text. Dealing with the fragmentary text, for example, the philologist works with the artefact to articulate its relation to a whole. "Philological practices generate desires for presence, desires for a physical and space-mediated relationship to the things of the world (including texts)," Gumbrecht writes.[54] To get around the dominance of interpretation, Kittler makes interpretation secondary to technological systems; Gumbrecht urges physical tangibility and closeness of the body to aesthetic objects and events.

To situate this argument in practice for a moment, let us think about the intensity of feeling that arises in you when you are presented, in the archival or special collections reading room, with an object you have called from the vault. I do not think I am alone in having and valuing an intense bodily reaction to the manuscripts, books, and other objects I study—especially those that come to me across great stretches of time. Who has not been moved in some way by being present with an object in an archive? A person we care about very deeply for one reason or another moved their hands over this paper in the creation of this manuscript, and it is possible to lay our hand there too. My eyes are struck by the bite of very black type on astonishingly white rag paper; my fingers move over the bumpy echo of eighteenth-century type pressed through to the recto of a sheet. I wonder about the enslaved African American man who I know printed this sheet and place my hands where his were. Encountering the first edition of a book I've read in modern reprint a hundred times before arranges my body to the text anew. When these material texts are brought forth in space we experience their presence effects. But, typically, when we begin to produce scholarship about them, we narrow our focus to meaning effects. Almost immediately we get set on the "real work" of reading, interpreting, and contextualizing. It would be almost embarrassing to acknowledge the intensities we feel during these moments of physical encounter.

And yet, firsthand archival research remains crucially important to the field. Fellowships at archives like the American Antiquarian Society, the Library Company of Philadelphia, the Newberry Library, and the Huntington Library, among others, are important catalysts for research, teaching, and career development. As teachers, we take our students to special collections to see, touch, and smell material texts. In these moments we cultivate a certain enchantment with material texts, but do we have a vocabulary to offer students to give shape to their embodied encounters? We rightly insist on the value of being present with the material texts that we study, even as digital surrogates make reproduced texts more readily available for us to read on digital screens nearly anywhere. In these moments, material texts vibrate on our skin in the same way that low bass notes register in our bodies, shaking us; how would we even begin to talk about this? We have not abandoned the presence dimension of material texts, but we lack the vocabulary necessary to acknowledge and interpret it. One wager of this book is that readers and writers of the rag paper period did not lack the words or concepts that acknowledged and described how paper's presence dimension worked on their bodies and created meaning in their time. Let their example be instructive to us as we try in the digital age to communicate the value of being present firsthand with other people among art, books, and sound.

In *The Intimacy of Paper*, I work through Gumbrecht's challenge to "think a layer in cultural objects and in our relation to them that is not the layer of meaning" and then to view the presence layer and the meaning layer at work together in specific written expressions.[55] The language of layering is useful for thinking about paper. Paper itself is a three-dimensional structure of pulverized rag fibers constantly pushing and pulling off one another, coated with a layer of sizing, and sometimes imprinted with a layer of ink. Some layers we want to read representationally because they contain words or images to be interpreted. But the presence layer can be something else entirely. When I speak of finding the presence of women workers in the rags that their hands touched, I am speaking of this "presence layer." In the real world that you and I inhabit, when we go into archives and special collections and handle rag paper, we are literally presented with traces of thousands of people, plants, garments, and labors. Across time and space, our bodies and minds are put in some form of relation to theirs, just as the bodies and minds of early and nineteenth-century American readers were. Working in multidisciplinary teams, humanists and scientists today engage in advanced imaging and chemical testing to attempt to scientifically represent the complex world inside of paper. They may eventually be able to tell us with certainty where this or that flax came from or what whose DNA survives within the raggy contents of a sheet of paper. Before there was multispectral imaging of paper, however, there was literature, and the writing that I take up in this book is deeply engaged in animating the world inside of paper. Readers in early and nineteenth-century America did not need to be reminded that paper was made of rags or that the encounter with paper was an oscillation between the presence of its materiality and the meaning conveyed by what is written on it. But much could be done through literature to animate the presence dimension of paper, of the real and imagined relations embedded within the sheets. Presence effects and meaning effects are simultaneous in the model Gumbrecht offers and emerge in relation to each other, a process that literary writing about paper enacts to different political, aesthetic, or cultural ends.

The purpose of introducing Gumbrecht's framework of oscillation between presence and meaning effects is not to argue that it ought to become the chosen model for describing and interpreting material texts. I am uninterested in strict adherence to any particular "theory" and prefer rather to adopt aspects of bodies of thought when they illuminate something about a particular problem, genre, or interpretive tradition. Gumbrecht acknowledges a key feature of aesthetic objects: they have immediate effects on both the body and the mind. More important, the mind and body work together to understand the object in its multidimensionality. This carries great utility for our still-developing understanding of what the framework of material textuality brings to book history, print culture, and bibliography. What is admitted to perceptibility and interpretation by the specific linkage of textuality and materiality of a text's presence dimension and its meaning dimension?

Throughout *The Intimacy of Paper* I am also interested in challenging and displacing one of the more dominant theories, or set of questions, that has organized Americanist book history and print culture studies since at least the early 1990s: the notion of the print public sphere, specifically as inherited from Jürgen Habermas. I am certainly not the first to criticize the utility of the Habermasian model of the public sphere because of its reliance on the

Kantian notion of disembodied and disinterested use of reason in print or its fantasies of political affiliation through self-reflexive shared reading. The first two chapters of this book are concerned with how communities of readers and, crucially, makers understood themselves as embodied participants in the creation of a material world of paper letters, rather than as subjects in a free-floating sphere of ideas and thinkers in dematerialized print. The Habermasian model of the print public sphere limits participation in textual production, aesthetic expression, and communal/political affiliation to those who read and write, usually in English, French, or German, and who have privileged access to printing presses. But if we pull back to the book as a material object, we find a more diverse range of actors, many of whom are women and laborers. Early and nineteenth-century American print often conveyed the printed words of elites, but these words are carried by paper made of the rags worked by women's hands, collected by ragpickers, and made into paper by artisans and factory laborers. Traces of these people are available in the presence dimension of rag paper, and they allow us to conceive of books and print on paper as archives of a drastically different kind of community to be read and sensed within the raggy contents of the sheet.

In this book, I explore these questions in four chapters and a concluding reflection on rag papermaking in the contemporary book arts. The book moves roughly chronologically through the rag paper period in early America and the nineteenth-century United States, beginning in the late seventeenth century and lasting until the late 1860s at the end of the Civil War and the beginning of Reconstruction. Chapters 1 and 2 are concerned largely with literary representations of handmade rag paper, and they challenge the print public sphere model to account for diverse communities of makers whose presence inheres in rag paper. Chapters 3 and 4 take up technologies of papermaking and inscription from the machine paper era and trace larger-scale "socialities" within the endless sheets of white paper rolling off of paper machines.

Chapter 1, "Paper Publics and Material Textual Affiliations in American Print Culture," focuses on paper as the grounding possibility for communal affiliation, not only through acts of reading but also within the material substrate of texts. I assemble an archive of writing about papermaking during the revolution and early republic, noting how these calls for rags and reflections on the industry describe the material survival of the nation in terms of its ability to make paper from the new nation's rags. The way these calls for rags represent the materiality of early American periodicals necessitates a reevaluation of how we have long understood, following Jürgen Habermas and Benedict Anderson, the relation between reading and the formation of the public sphere. Paper becomes the material substrate of both the literary public sphere and and the body politic. In the eighteenth century, the early republic was figured as a commoning of rags in paper that had to emerge before a community of readers became possible. These concerns about paper and the maintenance of nations and publics resurface during the Civil War, when conditions of material lack, especially in the Confederate States, occasion a crisis in printing a paper and maintaining a public. Paper publics ground communal affiliations by making people present to one another in the contents of paper. Encountering these paper publics is still possible when rag paper is ready to our hands.

Chapter 2, "The Gender of Rag Paper in Anne Bradstreet and Lydia Sigourney," follows the trade in rags and their movement from the feminized domestic sphere and into the masculinized public sphere as its material substrate. Anne Bradstreet and Lydia Sigourney, American women poets who lived several hundred years apart, both turn to the rag content of paper to mount a feminist argument about their gendered exclusion from the literary print public sphere. In their poetry, they both draw a direct link from domestic work with rags and cloth to artistic and writerly work on paper, noting how the latter is dependent on the former. By insisting on these material intimacies, they reframe the possibilities of female authorship by making visible the women's work embedded within all paper.

Herman Melville would later develop these themes for different purposes in "The Paradise of Bachelors and the Tartarus of Maids," an 1855 story about the masculine and feminine spheres represented by writing and papermaking. Chapter 3, "The Ineffable Socialities of Rags in Henry David Thoreau and Herman Melville," examines how Thoreau and Melville, two male writers living in the capital of mid-nineteenth-century papermaking in western and central Massachusetts, understood the presence dimension of rags. Thoreau takes Sigourney's assertion about the intimate embedding of meaning within rags to its logical conclusions, believing that he can read narratives within rags better than he can after narratives have been printed on rag paper. Melville focuses much more strongly on how relationships are embedded within rags and paper, which are, for him, a site of highly intimate, even erotic interpersonal communion. Both Melville and Thoreau react to the midcentury scalar changes in machine papermaking. For Melville, what he calls in one instance the "socialities" within paper become "ineffable" because instead of collecting rags from a bounded community, they are gathered from around the globe and mixed into an unending "riband" of paper emerging from a Fourdrinier machine.

Chapter 4, "The Whiteness of the Page: Racial Legibility and Authenticity," examines the racial logics behind the production of whiteness in white paper as the invisible substrate against which other marks become visible. The blank sheet of white paper, real or imaginary, was called to signal various social formations, especially the gendered construction and "preservation" of white femininity. Here we see the specific production of a medium and mediation across human and paper bodies. Just as paper's materiality is intertwined with embodied relations to gender, sexuality, and nation, so is it intertwined with social processes of racialization. As technologies for producing, protecting, and discerning racial whiteness consolidate during the nineteenth century, so do technologies for producing whiteness in paper. Black/white legibility emerges in a form analogous to the legibility of black ink on a white page, a structure that is further supported by the history of constructing white womanhood through reference to unmarked sheets of white paper. These processes are read through the techniques of relief engraving racialized figures to be printed on white paper. In particular, the engraved image of William Wells Brown's title character in the novel *Clotel* ought to appear as white as the paper on which she is printed, but her face is represented with black ink in order to render legible the legal logics of race on the surface of the page, acting within its logics of print legibility.

Finally, I close *The Intimacy of Paper* with a scene taken from contemporary rag papermaking practiced by the Combat Paper, Peace Paper, and Panty Pulping projects. These paper artists work with veterans to pulp their military uniforms and with survivors of intimate partner violence to pulp their undergarments, transforming these rags and the material memories embedded within them into paper. Participants and project leaders describe the overlap of materiality and meaning within rag paper in language that re-creates the early and nineteenth-century American sensibility of rag paper's material text. Their papermaking draws on ways of sensing paper and making meaning out of materiality that keep seventeenth- through nineteenth-century ways of knowing material texts alive in the present.

Collected in the papers of Isaiah Thomas—early American printer, founder of the American Antiquarian Society (AAS) in Worcester, Massachusetts, and author of the earliest monograph in what today we would call "the history of the book in America"—is a folio gathering of three blank sheets of paper. The AAS is one of the most complete archives of early and nineteenth-century American books and print, so these blank sheets stand out somewhat for their very blankness. Isaiah Thomas was a printer, but this folio is an artifact of his business as a papermaker. This folio contains the first sheets of writing paper made in his paper mill. An accompanying note reads: "1794. First writing paper Made in Worcester. Mill erected by I. Thomas 1st sheet molded [sic] in latter part of July 1794—this paper finished Aug. 1 1794."⁵⁶ Holding these sheets up to the light reveals the distinctive chain and wire marks of hand-moulded paper. It also reveals the watermark, "IT," and "Thomas" for Isaiah Thomas.⁵⁷

In this introduction, I have proposed that these blank sheets should be experienced and also read, even though there is no alphabetic writing inscribed on them. They contain rags collected from homes in the Blackstone River valley and Boston.⁵⁸ Those rags carry traces of bodies and stories of lives. "Rags are as beauties, which concealed lie, / But when in paper, how it charms the eye; / Pray save your rags, new beauties discover," read a late eighteenth-century Boston newspaper.⁵⁹ This poetic advertisement asks readers to participate in the process of making concealed rags visible and of recognizing the "charming" effect they have on the senses. Such are the modes of reading paper that this book tries to bring to the study of material texts.

Isaiah Thomas built a paper mill on the Blackstone River in Worcester in 1793 because his printing operations required more paper than existing mills could supply. When writing the *History of Printing in America*, Thomas progressed only a few pages into the "introduction of the art" of printing in the colonies and the United States before shifting from printing to paper, papermaking, and paper mills.⁶⁰ Paper and paper mills come before discussions of type foundries, printing presses, and the histories of printers working in each colony and state. As the twentieth-century typographer Eric Gill said, "Paper is to the printer as stone is to the sculptor." On February 7, 1776, before he built his own mill, Thomas wrote in his pro-Revolutionary newspaper, the *Massachusetts Spy*: "We are sorry we cannot oblige our customers with more than a half's sheet this week owing to the want of paper. The present scarcity throughout this country will certainly continue unless a paper-mill is established in this neighborhood."⁶¹ Chapter 1 dwells in this very problem at the nexus of paper, neighborhood, and public.

CHAPTER 1

PAPER PUBLICS AND MATERIAL TEXTUAL AFFILIATIONS IN AMERICAN PRINT CULTURE

I N MARCH 1857, on the verge of the United States Civil War and mere days after the Dred Scott decision, Pastor Wright wished that for just one day the disjointed social order of humanity would be like a paper mill. Wright visited the Parsons Paper Mill in Holyoke, Massachusetts, and was fascinated with the size of the machine and its minute calibrations. The whole of the machine coordinated its many parts, producing a single unbroken roll of paper out of the shreds of diverse rags. "In the movements of this wonderful machine," he writes, "with its almost infinitude of parts, the least degree of success requires well-nigh a hair-breadth accuracy in the adjustment of every feature." Talking to millworkers and observing the machine, Wright's admiration of the paper-making process heightens as his imagination grants the paper machine the character of a nation. "In reply to some remark of mine . . ." he continues, "the operator philosophically observed: 'We can't do anything unless all parts of the machine draw together.'" Although "the machine occupies . . . eleven hundred square feet" and the riband of paper travels "one hundred feet" through it, the machine runs with a "completeness and perfect correspondence of all the parts, that, aside from occasional breakages, which are inevitable, and the adjustments which the different varieties of paper always require, no extraordinary interruption may occur for weeks, or even months." The ability to draw together, to correspond, and to mend inevitable disruptions seemed to him an impossible wish for the United States, which President Abraham Lincoln would the next summer compare to a house divided. "A thousand pities," Wright concludes, "that the multitudinous wheels, and cranks, and pinions of human society, which so often so ruinously break, or hideously creak, could not, for at least one diurnal revolution, as smoothly and harmoniously move as the complicated machinery of the paper mill."[1]

Wright was not alone in his admiration of what others called the "beautiful machinery" of papermaking. In 1835, the anonymous author of a tract for use in schools called all those "who love to contemplate the results of human ingenuity, as manifested in complicated machinery," to observe the paper mills outside Boston. "The rags, by the operation of some simple, yet well devised combination of wheels, are reduced very rapidly to a sort of paste . . . then spread out, by the movement of other machinery, unassisted by hands, into a thin broad sheet, which goes onward . . . till it finally makes its appearance . . . in the form of a beautiful ribbon of white, dry paper, fit for immediate use." The message that paper mills "must be regarded as one of the most extraordinary productions of the age" was a popular one. This author's admiration of papermaking's coexistent simplicity and complexity was widely reprinted in newspapers from New England to Ohio within a few months.[2]

The author of "Beautiful Machinery" is not as explicit as Wright about the link between the "complicated machinery" of papermaking and republican democracy, but as Laura Rigal has shown, "metaphors of manufacturing" were frequently used to characterize the "collective forging, framing, or fabricating of a thing called the United States." The complicated machinery of both American manufacture and American federalism were imagined to distribute and balance power within a complex system. The manufactory and the nation were thought to produce a product that is vast in scale, diverse, and yet unified. "Millions of yards [of paper] might be easily manufactured," out of thousands of shredded rags, but emerge from the mill "in one unbroken piece."[3]

Paper, as long as it was made from cloth rags, and its production offered writers of everything from advertising copy to poetry and fiction a set of material metaphors through which to figure the nation.[4] Because a sheet of paper was made from the particles of thousands of rags that were shredded, pulped, and reconstituted into a single sheet, and because those rags were often collected from the homes of those living near the mills, the sheet of paper came to be seen as a concrete manifestation of the body politic. Put simply, one could say of both the nation and the sheet of paper: *e pluribus unum*, that is, out of many, one. Wright recognizes this not only in the machine but also within the sheet of paper itself.

Figure 2. Ream wrapper for the Eliphalet Thorp Mill in Athol, Massachusetts. *Courtesy of the American Antiquarian Society.*

Wright observed: "The floors [of the mill rag room] are piled and littered with rags, of all imaginable sorts, sizes, and colors, mingled in such hopeless confusion as apparently to defy the most patient efforts to classify them. An unpractised [*sic*] eye would surely not select those torn and filthy fragments as representatives of even a nominal value. But a few hours shall witness the truly marvelous transformation of that unsightly mass of 'shreds and patches' into an article of such beauty and utility that the admiration of the nicest critic may be successfully challenged."[5] The diversity of rags, shreds, patches—all plural nouns—are incorporated into a singular noun, *the* "article." This trope is repeated elsewhere too. Papermakers emblazoned the wrappers that held reams of paper together with the "e pluribus unum" motto. The printed engraving on a ream wrapper for Eliphalet Thorp's paper mill in Athol, Massachusetts, juxtaposes the national motto with "one ream" (Fig. 2). The presence of this motto indicates not only that nation building was linked with commodity production in the early republic but also that papermaking offered a metaphor, grounded in familiar material practices, for turning the many into the one. Just as the eagle represents the union of federated states, the ream wrapper makes "one ream" out of hundreds of sheets of paper, each of which is, in turn, the product of many rags. Holding a ream of rag paper emblazoned with federalist symbols was an object lesson in affiliation and its scales.

৩ৎৎ৴

The question of the relationship between texts, publics, and nation has occupied Americanist criticism and literary history for some time. Since Michael Warner's *Letters of the Republic*, Americanists have, in Sandra Gustafson's words, "integrated Habermas's concept of the bourgeois public sphere with history of the book methodology" in ways that strongly influenced the shape of the field. Warner linked questions of print technology, public-making circulation, and early republican nationalism. Around the same time, Benedict Anderson's *Imagined Communities* offered a model of national communal affiliation that engaged both print circulation and imagination or narrative, further solidifying critical connections between the study of nationalisms, literatures, and print cultures. Warner influentially demonstrated how in the late seventeenth and eighteenth centuries it became "possible to imagine oneself, in the act of reading [the impersonal printed object], becoming part of an arena of the national people that cannot be realized except through such mediated imaginings." Reading practices and the circulation of print contributed to the development of a print public sphere in which "an individual reads in a manner that implicitly relates him- or herself to the indefinite others of a print public."[6] Numerous scholarly projects responded in ways that questioned the strong tie between print and public by positing the importance of other media, such as voice and performance (Chris Looby's *Voicing America*, Sandra Gustafson's *Eloquence Is Power*), or that identified the gendered and raced subjects and bodies structurally denied access to Habermasian disinterestedness (Elizabeth Maddock Dillon's *Gender of Freedom*, Joanna Brooks's *American Lazarus*, Anna Brickhouse's *Transamerican Literary Relations and the Nineteenth-Century Public Sphere*). But even within these critiques, questions of who is represented in print, to and through whom print circulates, and how these issues shape our understanding of nations, publics, and communal affiliations represent the dominant thread of scholarship on early and nineteenth-century American print cultures. Because these models focus the circulation and consumption of printed texts, Americanist book history and print culture scholarship has been delayed in paying attention to how the production of the material text was itself both a mediated imagining and materially grounded relation of self to others in the colony and nation. Along the way we have, by and large, taken the material existence of texts for granted even though writing of the period focuses on the difficulties and uncertainties of sustaining the production of printed materials and, through them, communities.[7]

This chapter is concerned with the ways rag paper drew people together into recognizably political, even national, affiliation before it circulated and was read as a printed text, or even as a precondition of a printed text's circulation. The assemblage of what I call "paper publics" is readily visible in historical moments of crisis when paper's continued production and its availability was highly uncertain. During the lead-up to the Revolutionary War and later during the Civil War, the viability of nations and local communities is, interestingly, figured in whether or not a newspaper can be maintained. This chapter will look closely at papermaking during these moments of crisis, as well as how it was discussed, to understand how early and nineteenth-century Americans understood paper as a material enactment of political affiliation. Paper modeled and materialized forms of "drawing together" in common and as a community. What does this tell us about the theories of print and publics that have structured our work?

Following feminist critiques of the Habermasian public sphere model, centering paper and its materiality in our accounts of print and nation brings into a view a wider range of subjects, bodies, and relations. For example, on November 14, 1777, the *North Carolina Gazette* issued a promise to young female readers: "The young ladies are assured, that by sending to the paper mill an old handkerchief, no longer fit to cover their snowy breasts, there is a possibility of its returning to them again in the more pleasing form of a *billet doux* from their lovers."[8] Borrowed from the *Spectator*, such a call for rags imagines an intimate circuit between the white female body, the paper mill, and the circulation of a material text. This is not an anonymous public sphere of letters where reason floats free of bodies. Paper is not the accidental and negligible substrate bearing important words through an impersonal public sphere. Rather, because the paper in question has been made from cloth taken from intimate contact with a woman's body, both the content written on it and its circulatory routes are intimate.

This call for rags constructs a sensual encounter with paper, and not only because of its sexualized imagery. It suggests that paper engaged the senses of those who wrote on it, read from it, exchanged it, and sent rags from their bodies and homes to make it. This sensual engagement with the material text meant that traces of women, children, laborers, and unknown others inhered in encounters with paper. Gillian Silverman has argued that books "positioned" nineteenth-century readers "in intimate even bodily relation to imagined others." "Readers," Silverman continues, "have a voluptuous relation to books, and in handling these texts they initiate a fantasy of touching and being touched by those people affiliated with a book's narrative world, particularly the author or a fellow reader."⁹ What Silverman calls the "fantasy of communion" arose not only through reading but also through the making of the material texts. The imagined community of early national America did indeed construct itself through reading, but that was with the knowledge that many hands collected rags from diverse corners the community before mingling them together at the mill: an act of commoning more literal than imagined.

Imagining Community in Paper Publics

Joseph Addison's *Spectator* for May 1, 1712, imagines the commons of material textual community within the paper of its own pages. In this entry, "Mr. Spectator" concerns himself with papermaking. Posing the question of how the *Spectator* organizes its public, Mr. Spectator argues that the paper on which his magazine is printed has a unifying power beyond, or at least before, what is printed on it. This account of how eighteenth-century texts give rise to publics is different from what we are used to. In Jürgen Habermas's account of the rise of the print public sphere in the late eighteenth century, shared reading of such periodicals as the *Spectator* and public debate in spaces like the coffeehouse created the conditions through which private subjects understand themselves as having a public life and as being assembled in a public forum. In this account, because print abstracted words and ideas from the bodies of speakers and writers, and because it circulated, was read, and debated in shared time and space, the printed page modeled the disinterested use of reason in a recognizable public of shared readers.

And so the May 1, 1712, issue stands out as an interesting exception to the typical Habermasian account. This particular account of how the *Spectator* performs public-making work privileges paper more than the reading of what is printed on it. Here, Addison fashions the *Spectator* as the connective tissue of the English public through both the "Material and the Formal . . . Benefits which accrue to the Publick" but places considerably more emphasis on the material. Included in the "formal" benefits of the *Spectator* are what Addison describes as "those Advantages which my Readers receive, as their Minds are either improv'd or delighted by these my daily Labours."¹⁰ These "formal benefits" hew to the typical Habermasian model of the rise of a public sphere. Yet Addison's purpose here is to put these formal benefits of the publication on equal footing with the material. He spends the rest of this column expounding on what the materiality of the *Spectator* does to bring together its public.

"By the Word Material" Addison says he means "those Benefits which arise to the Publick from these my Speculations, as they consume a considerable quantity of our Paper Manufacture, employ our Artisans in Printing, and find Business for great Numbers of Indigent Persons." The *Spectator*'s need for paper, and the production of it, draws together everyone from the "Prince" to "Indigent Persons." Reading and discussing content is an important aspect of the *Spectator*'s service to the public, but it cannot happen, Mr. Spectator argues, without the production of paper, a process that "takes into it several mean Materials which could be put to no other use, and affords Work for several Hands in the collecting of them. . . . The whole Nation is in a great measure supply'd with a Manufacture, for which formerly she was obliged to her Neighbours."[11] Papermaking links the nation through hands along a supply chain; here we find the ragpicker, the merchant, the industrialist, and the landlord. Further, domestic manufacture of the product protects "the whole nation" from dependence on foreign sources and markets, an issue that had been the subject of proposed government regulation in England as early as a 1585 request to ban the export of rags to other countries.[12]

What links England together in this narrative is not a national character, race, or culture: it is having had physical contact with rags or rag paper somewhere in the process of producing and consuming the *Spectator*. Congratulating himself, Mr. Spectator writes, "In short, when I trace in my Mind a Bundle of Rags to a Quire of Spectators, I find so many Hands employ'd in every Step they take thro their whole Progress, that while I am writing a Spectator, I fancy my self providing Bread for a Multitude." We find in this account that circulations of rags and paper create material links between people and across the social body. "It is pleasant enough to consider the Changes that a Linnen Fragment undergoes, by passing thro' the several Hands above mentioned." Dutch linens come into England as cloth and leave as letters in the post: "The finest pieces of Holland, when worn to Tatters, assume a new Whiteness more beautiful than their first, and often return in the shape of Letters to their Native Country."[13] Later, in chapter 4, we will explore how the production of "a new Whiteness . . . beautiful" links ideas about bodies politic and racialized bodies. But for now, as with the example of the fair lady's handkerchief taken from her "snowy breast," we also find here that what is written on paper is dictated by the origins of the rags inside it. Depicted in the "return . . . to their Native Country" is a textual network oriented around hands that make more than hands that write, where the content of letters is dictated more by the raggy contents of paper than by the holder of the pen.

Explaining how paper manufacture links the public together, Mr. Spectator provides an alternative, materially oriented account of how the *Spectator* organizes publics beyond the political reading and conversation of the coffee-house. Rags, along with their collection and use in papermaking, link strangers to one another in the very materiality of the text, which occurs before reading of script or print. Such a paper-centric account of the *Spectator* links the chiffonier picking rags in the dung hill with the royal family: "In a word, a Piece of Cloth, after having officiated for some Years as a Towel or a Napkin, may by this means be raised from a Dung-hill, and become the most valuable Piece of Furniture in a Prince's Cabinet."[14] When thinking about the circuits and networks through which print moves, we have tended to focus on writers, editors, printers, and readers. These are privileged positions not always readily available to women, the poor, and nonwhites. The orientation toward rags and paper over print, an orientation made visible here in the *Spectator*, reveals a wider range of actors around the material text: female domestic laborers working with cloth, indigent ragpickers, papermakers. These people are memorialized within paper through their trace encounters and labors with rags, then made visible by writers who imagine the assembly of people within the paper public that subtends the print public.

Paper Nationalism

In the American colonies and early republic, worry about the availability of rags, and thus the availability of paper, became a site to express concern over the very viability of communities in what would become the United States. One Providence, Rhode Island, newspaper connected the availability of rags and paper to the success of the army during the Revolutionary War: "As paper is now much wanted for the army, and other necessary purposes (which cannot be manufactured without rags) it is hoped every friend of America will encourage the saving and collecting them."[15]

A popular legend about Benjamin Franklin's attic warehouse illustrates the worry. Before the Battle of Monmouth in 1778, soldiers searched Philadelphia for paper that could be used to make cartridges and wadding for rifles. Twenty-five hundred copies of the Reverend Gilbert Tennent's *Late Association for Defence Farther Encouraged: Or, Defensive War Defended, with True Christianity* are said to have been held for nonpayment in the "garret" attic of Benjamin Franklin's print shop. These were then torn up and used for cartridges and wadding at Monmouth. When this story is retold, emphasis is placed on the relation of the content of the printed matter, defensive war, and its use in the world not as something to be read but as weaponry. An early twentieth-century history of papermaking retells the story under the heading "A sermon effectively delivered," playing, of course, on the "delivery" of the sermon at the end of a rifle. "These [pamphlets] were used for musket cartridges and 'wadding,'" begins the retelling before going further in connecting the author and the scene of war. "The battle . . . raged about old Tenant [*sic*] church, where fought representatives from every one of the thirteen colonies, mingling their patriotic blood upon the historic field, the sermon proved one of the most effective ever delivered. The Rev. Mr. Tenant, when he penned his discourse, probably had no idea that it would ever be delivered in so forceful a manner, just outside the doors of his church."[16] Paper, here, is more important as wadding than as a public-sphere medium for ideas and debates about defense. Whether in search of paper for rifle wadding or for printing newspapers and government documents, eighteenth-century American writers linked the viability of the emergent state to the availability of paper.

To use a term of Jacques Derrida's, a very real sense exists in which the state is a "paper machine." Derrida argues that paper "hold[s] a sacred power. It has the force of law, it gives accreditation, it incorporates, it even embodies the soul of the law, its letter and its spirit." Paper is "indissociable from the Ministry of Justice . . . from the rituals of legalization and legitimation, from the archive of charters and constitutions for what we call, in the double sense of the word, *acts*."[17] In more concrete terms, Matthew S. Hull and Ben Kafka have both studied modern bureaucracies by paying attention to systems of paperwork, documenting how procedures of documentation, handling, and storage give rise to (and sometimes frustrate) modern governmentalities.[18] And at the level of the individual, we need look no further than "undocumented persons," or those who are *sans-papiers*, to understand how paper literally and figuratively constitutes the state and its imaginary. For it is still through "the legitimating authority of paper" that we are (or are not) accredited as citizens, workers, visitors, and bearers of rights. "Here I am," Derrida writes, "this is my body, see this signature on this paper—it's me, it's mine, it's me so-and-so, I sign before you, I present myself here; this paper that remains represents me."[19]

In the context of the twenty-first-century United States, Kate Vieira has shown that "documentation" and "having papers" surpasses literacy as a marker of legitimacy and a tool for liberation. In this case, the primary suture of a state and its people, a public and its members, is made through paper rather than through language. Studying immigrant communities and their relation to the United States and its culture, Vieira finds that what she calls "sociomaterial considerations," who has papers and who doesn't, takes precedence over sociolinguistic ones, such as who speaks and reads. While it is widely assumed that "English literacy can unlock the door to the American Dream," the ability to "leverage" language "profitably" depends heavily on "ideologically loaded literacy artifacts, specifically immigration papers." Literacy, citizenship, and papers are irrevocably entwined.[20]

Similarly, where we have studied the effects of print in the construction of collectivities, nations, and publics, we have largely taken the sociomaterial dimensions of texts for granted, even though their writers and readers emphatically did not. The link between the materiality of paper documents and the ability to conduct the business of the state was frequently expressed in protest of the Stamp Act, for example. In 1765, Benjamin Franklin Mecom, nephew of Benjamin Franklin, printed *A New Collection of Verses Applied to the First of November, A.D. 1765, &c. Including a Prediction that the S——p-A-t shall not take Place in North-America, Together with A poetical Dream Concerning Stamped Papers*, a thinly veiled protest against the Stamp Act. In the "poetical dream," the speaker happens upon a group of anthropomorphized papers complaining about the adverse effects the Stamp Act will have on their role in mediating the colonies. "One Night," recalls the dreamer:

> [A]s I lay slumbering in my Bed,
> Dark Images crouded [*sic*] into my Head.
> I thought, as through the Town I walk'd alone,
> I, at a Distance heard a grievous Moan.
> Attention rous'd; I then approach'd more near,
> And found a Croud of PAPERS gather'd there.
> To each of them, as to the Prophet's Ass,
> A Tounge was giv'n to tell his wretched Case.
> . . . .
> They spoke by Turns: In this they all agree,
> To plead the Cause of *English Liberty*:

> And deprecate the Woe, which each one thought
> Would, by the St—p-A-t, soon on them be brought.[21]

One by one, anthropomorphized papers spoke about how, by taxing official documents and other papers, the Stamp Act will be injurious to the health of the colonies and to the "English Liberty" of colonists. In order of appearance, the personified papers are the "Bond," the "Papers of the Court: Summons and Writ," "Probate Papers," "Diploma," "License Paper," "[News]Paper," and the "Almanack." The papers include those that perform acts of the state, such as the bond that is "so much Use / To Men of all Professions, rich and Poor, / Whose Property I daily do secure," or the summons and writ that "call'd the Debtor to discharge his Debt" and that "many Rogues at Justice' [*sic*] Bar have set." They also include papers that constitute the print public sphere, such as the almanac that "try'd . . . to please / Both Rich and Poor, and Men of all Degrees" by talking about "the Stars and future Scenes." The newspaper claims a position of prominence among all the papers, crying out:

> Who, of ye all, has shewn a readier Mind,
> At once to please and profit all Mankind?
> I travel far and near; the World I range
> And carry with me all that's *new* and strange.
> Advices of Importance I convey;
> As well as merry Tales, to please the Gay.
> Must I be burden'd with this cruel St—p,
> Which will my Speed and Progress greatly cramp?[22]

The Stamp Act, according to the speaking papers, threatens not only the production of persons documented in deeds and diplomas but also the association of "Men of all Degrees" within reading publics.

Any discussion of the "speed and progress" of the periodical press with respect to the health of a polity should make us recall *Imagined Communities*, in which Benedict Anderson theorizes the importance of print periodicals in generating a large, impersonal population's realization of its own national consciousness. The newspaper produces a ritual of reading with unknown others in both simultaneity and anonymity; it emplots national consciousness. Anderson writes: "The obsolescence of the newspaper on the morrow of its printing . . . creates this extraordinary mass ceremony: the almost precisely simultaneous consumption ('imagining') of the newspaper-as-fiction. We know that particular morning and evening editions will overwhelmingly be consumed between this hour and that. . . . The newspaper reader, observing exact replicas of his own paper being consumed by his subway, barbershop, or residential neighbors, is continually reassured that the imagined world is visibly rooted in everyday life. . . . creating that remarkable confidence of community in anonymity which is the hallmark of modern nations."[23] Thus in the *Poetical Dream*, the speaking newspaper emphasizes that the Stamp Act will impede the paper's function in time and space. The newspaper's "far and near" reach and the temporality of its serial publication, its "speed and progress," will be "greatly cramp[ed]." The same goes for the almanac which is published annually but "if deny'd [reprieve from the Stamp Act] I fear / I cannot live to see another Year."[24] The speaking papers of the *Poetical Dream* unsettle the notion of a stable material world of print from which print culture or print nationalism might arise.

Anderson's foundational narrative relies on the promise of serial time, the notion that today's newspaper will be obsolete tomorrow when it is replaced by tomorrow's edition. However, the rituals of community in anonymity come under threat as the *Poetical Dream*'s speaker hears "The wretched Papers [sic] dying Groans."[25] The *Poetical Dream* requires us to think about what happens when the ritual consumption of the newspaper comes under threat. Even though Anderson is willing to treat the newspaper as a commodity, paper appears in its fetish character within his imagination of community. That is, the newspaper appears to readers for consumption without consideration of how it was produced. As offered, Anderson's theory of print nationalism depends on readers' belief—Anderson calls it their "remarkable confidence"—in the future consumption of newspapers without offering an account of the material conditions that would allow this. Despite what we know about Robert Darnton's well-known "communication circuit" that visualizes the ecosystem of printers, suppliers, shippers, and booksellers adjacent to the reader and the printed text, Anderson's account asks us to accept that the newspaper will simply be there.[26]

This is not how colonial Americans experienced the newspaper. Rags were always in short supply, threatening to choke the progress of papermaking, which meant that pleas for rags were present in the everyday lives of readers. These pleas yoked the fate of printed material to the fate of the colonies and then the nation, recruiting readers to do a patriotic duty by collecting rags for the production of paper. It makes sense that newspaper printers would express the most concern over the scarcity of paper, given that newspaper publication first drove demand for a ready supply of paper in the colonies. During the seventeenth century, before the earliest mills began operation, few books and pamphlets were published in the colonies. During the first decades of the eighteenth century, periodical publication took off in such urban areas as Boston and Philadelphia. While books and pamphlets could be printed in London and imported to the colonies, the periodical press was, owing to the spatial and temporal necessities of newspapers, far more local in its production.[27] Necessary for the periodic issue of print were paper mills, which proved to be a fairly lucrative industry. William Bradford, William Rittenhouse, and Benjamin Franklin all secured contracts to provide paper to periodical publishers and to colonial government offices. The scale of the burgeoning colonial paper industry and the declining need for imported English paper were both drivers behind the taxation of paper under the Stamp Act.

As the colonies approached the Revolutionary War and independence, paper became a literal and figurative ground for negotiating nationhood. This was apparent in the many calls for rags that were issued in the print periodicals of the day. But it was also apparent in domestically made paper itself. Sheets of paper made in Massachusetts during the late eighteenth century bear the watermark, "Save Rags."[28] The demand called out to readers from within the sheet itself, bringing to mind an interrelated set of political and material conditions in the colonies and early republic. After declaring independence, American colonists were no longer able to import paper from England. Dutch papermakers welcomed the trade with Americans, and one took advantage of the ability to embed messages within the page itself to show solidarity. Adriann Rogge made paper bearing a watermark image of the "Stars and Stripes" flag flying from the mast of a ship.[29] Paper was an important material and symbolic front for eighteenth-century Americans at the moment of revolution.

Echoing these themes, Eugenie Andruss Leonard argued in a 1950 essay that paper should be understood "as a critical commodity" necessary to support the patriot cause "during the American Revolution." She traced how shortages of mills, rags, and skilled labor posed material problems for the Continental Congress, to the point where the body closely regulated trade in paper and rags and even kept men out of the military who had papermaking experience. In the late summer of 1776, one man was ordered to leave military service so he could resurface worn paper moulds, which the Continental

Congress then claimed for their own property as critical wartime infrastructure. Individual colonies also passed measures to support papermakers, including Massachusetts, where incarcerated papermakers were released from prison so they could resume the trade and maintain the supply of paper. New Hampshire and Connecticut gave loans and raised lotteries for the establishment of mills. And, of course, encouragement of rag saving came from public and private quarters.[30] As Leonard documents, in both everyday life and legislative chambers, securing the materials and means to produce paper was seen as a way of securing the independent United States.

While many of the actions to promote the paper trade were taken by legislative bodies, calls for rags were present in the everyday experiences of readers. In broadsides and newspaper ads, calls for rags linked the material processes of papermaking and the ideological processes of political life. A broadside advertisement printed and distributed in January 1777 provides one example of how these matters of trade, production, and demand were not only linked but also put before readers, connecting statehood with the very paper in their hands, as well as the rags on their backs: "Among the necessary articles wherewith America has usually been supplied from abroad, PAPER was a very considerable and important one; we could not subsist, in a state of society without it. And very large sums were annually paid and lent out of America for the purchase of it; but since our disunion with Great Britain, our supplies of paper from thence have totally ceased, and almost from every other part of the World; so that the United States of America, are reduced to the necessity of suffering the great inconveniences, through want of that necessary article; or of becoming manufacturers of it themselves."[31] The author suggests that paper is necessary to maintain the cohesiveness of society. Such a claim may seem hyperbolic, but it is hardly exceptional in writing about paper and papermaking during this moment. A column in the *Connecticut Courant* from September 1777 makes a similar case. "Consider their [the paper mill owners'] distress on account of the scarcity of RAGS. The business of Paper-Making and Printing is at an end if Rags are not to be had. . . . The News Paper must inevitably stop, or be reduced to a half sheet—The Schools will be essentially affected, and all writing business cease."[32] The making of paper itself becomes a primary concern for building and conducting the nation. The state of society is maintained on paper through documents, newspapers, and literate activity in the public sphere, but early American newspapers reiterate that the fate of their uncertain existence lies in the hands of readers who are called to contribute to the process of producing paper. This is hardly representative of Anderson's "remarkable confidence of community in anonymity . . . the hallmark of modern nations" but rather a deep worry about the existence of paper and the precariousness of the communal or national frame of mind made possible by print. These calls for rags suggest that if the United States is to become a separate entity from Great Britain, then communities must become "manufacturers of it themselves," both through papermaking and the ceremonies of reading off of paper that give rise to national consciousness.

As early as the 1690s, paper had already figured in the symbolic logic of the colonies' independence from England. The first large-scale paper mill in North American was established in Germantown outside Philadelphia in 1690, and it figures prominently in Richard Frame's 1692 poetic survey of Pennsylvania, "A Short Description of Pennsilvania, Or, a Relation What things are known, enjoyed, and like to be discovered in the said Province Presented as a Token of Good Will to the People of England." Frame describes the riches of Pennsylvania with an eye to attracting investment from fellow Englishmen across the Atlantic:

> TO all our Friends that do desire to know.
> What Country 'tis we live in, this will show.
> Attend to hear the Story I shall tell,
> No doubt but you will like this Country well
> . . . .
> Here are more things than I can well express,
> Strange to be seen in such a Wilderness.
> By Day we work, at Night we rest in Peace,
> So that each Day our Substance doth increase:
> O blessed be his Name, who doth provide
> For you, and us, and all the World beside.

The many apparent riches of Pennsylvania include livestock, vegetation, metals, and strong building materials. At the conclusion of the poem Frame, offers a long stanza noting a certain synergy between the work of German and Dutch inhabitants, whose expertise in producing linen and paper merge to produce a symbiotic relation through papermaking.

> The German-Town of which I spoke before,
> Which is, at last, in length one Mile and More,

Where lives High-German People, and Low-Dutch,
Whose Trade in weaving Linnin Cloth is much,
There grows the Flax, as also you may know,
That from the same they do divide the Tow;
Their Trade fits well within this Habitation,
We find Convenience for their Occupation.
One Trade brings in imployment for another.
So that we may suppose each Trade a Brother;
From Linnin Rags good Paper doth derive,
The first trade keeps the second Trade alive:
Without the first the second cannot be,
Therefore since these two can so well agree,
Convenience doth approve to place them nigh,
One in the German-Town, 'tother hard by.
A Paper Mill near German-Town doth stand,
So that the Flax, which first springs from the Land,
First Flax, then Yarn, and then they must begin,
To weave the same, which they took pains to spin.
Also, when on our backs it is well worn,
Some of the same remains Ragged and Torn;
Then of those Rags our Paper it is made,
Which in process of time doth waste and fade:
So what comes from the Earth, appeareth plain,
The same in Time returns to Earth again.
So much for what I have truly Compos'd,
Which is but a part of what may be disclosed,
Concluding of this, and what is behind,
I may tell you more of my Mind;
But in the mean time be content with this same,
Which at present is all from your Friend
RICHARD FRAME.[33]

The fraternal manufactures of linen and paper produce a perpetual harmony.
Flax grows from the ground, is woven into linen, which is worn out and eventually sent to the paper mill. Paper, too, wears out and returns to the ground
where it will become flax. The circularity of this process is mirrored in the
poem's rhyming couplets; paired "brothers" form codependent units as the

poem progresses. Frame himself is drawn into this pairing process as the poem anticipates his name and positions him as its final rhyme. The rhyming couplets establish a system of pairings like linen and flax, and these pairings do not leave room for interruption from outside. Thus the rhyme scheme is uninterrupted from beginning to end, just as the cycle of dirt to flax to linen to paper to dirt continues apace: "So what comes from the Earth, appeareth plain, / The same in Time returns to Earth again." In Frame's description, papermaking does not require the importation of rags from abroad. Unlike the 1777 New Haven writer who notes that paper "has usually been supplied from abroad," Frame imagines a polity that is perfectly capable of producing its own paper self-sufficiently. Political independence may not have been one of Frame's express goals in 1692, but he nonetheless produces an account of a place where material abundance permits "the first trade" in rags to "[keep] the second Trade" in paper "alive" without outside influence. During the Revolutionary moment, this line of thinking about the material and political economy of rags, paper, and print emerged as a strong expression of independence.

Richard Frame's poem offers a fraternity of end rhymes to create a perfect order of productive abundance in late seventeenth-century Pennsylvania. We are given a vision of Germantown where paper will never be out of supply because flax, linen, rags, and dirt are in harmony with papermaking. The archive of calls for rags in eighteenth-century newspapers suggests that rags were not as abundantly available from the homes and workers surrounding paper mills as Frame imagined. While Frame's writing offered end rhymes that mimic cycles of production leading to the harmonious production of linen and paper, then later eighteenth-century calls for rags warned of something more like caesura. Eighteenth-century newspaper readers were reminded that newspapers and printing would cease unless they collected the rags off their backs, and did so patriotically:

> The Subscribers therefore, to prevent these inconveniences, and as far as they are able to promote the public good, confidently with their own private advantage, have . . . lately erected and finished a PAPER MILL, at New Haven. . . . But as the success of this undertaking absolutely depends upon their receiving sufficient supplies of COTTON and LINEN RAGS, without which, the manufacture of paper cannot by any means be carried on, hereby earnestly solicit and hope to obtain assistance and encouragement from all persons of both sexes, more especially from the good women, who are friends to the freedom and interest of America, and this place in particular, in collecting supplies of this essential requisite to paper-making; which might easily be done, by a

constant care and attention to save the cotton and linen rags. . . . The great difficulty of obtaining supplies of rags to support a paper manufacture, arises, not from their real scarcity or insufficient quantity; but from their inconsiderable value, which affords no immediate inducement equivalent to the trouble of saving them;—the inducement therefore must arise from the love of our country, and the benefit that individuals will receive, in a full enjoyment of freedom and property in common with the whole community in general. . . . We are the public's humble servants, THE PROPRIETORS OF THE MILL, Who will give Two Pence per pound for clean cotton and linen rags.[34]

According to these advertisements, it is not reading newspapers and participating in public debate that generate the public sphere or a print-nationalist structure of feeling but rather people entering into the material circuit of linen and paper. National feeling—"love of country" and a sense of the "public good"—here pertain to "collecting supplies of this essential requisite to paper-making." Nationalism is not produced merely by the arrival of the newspaper in serial time but from the specter of the newspaper's absence. In these cases, national consciousness arises out of awareness of the strangers whose rags are mixed into paper in contact with your own, not the notion of strangers who read the same text elsewhere.

Women and the Material Public Sphere

As the appeal to "the good women" and "ladies" in calls for rags suggests, this form of being in "common with the whole community in general" is not limited to men. The promotional literature issued by papermakers linked rag collection to "republican motherhood," an ideology of white womanhood and white women's role in reproducing the young nation, in order to mobilize white women's para-industrial labor. Papermaker calls for rags attempt to harmonize the interests of nation, commerce, and citizenry in acts of women's work and domestic order. While John Locke's 1690 *Essay concerning Human Understanding* makes an early link between the raising of children and the nature of paper ("white Paper receives any characters"), papermakers linked women's work as rag collectors to the republican imperative to raise and educate patriotic, capable children, nurtured into proper forms of citizenship.[35] An 1808 advertisement from a paper mill in Fort Edward, New York, is but one example of the way giving rags was associated with the work of republican motherhood in which "the Republican Mother integrated political values into her domestic life": "It is not thought that this appeal to our countrywomen will prove unavailing when they reflect that without their assistance they cannot be supplied with the useful article of paper. . . . For clean cotton and linen rags of every colour and description, matrons can be furnished with bibles . . . [and] mothers with grammars, spelling books, and primers for their children." If, in Linda Kerber's account of republican womanhood, "righteous mothers were asked to raise the virtuous male citizens on whom the Republic depended," then ensuring the supply of paper by collecting rags was an activity understood to directly connect domestic and political life.[36] This demonstrates how manufacturers framed women's domestic labor as an essential prerequisite for the fulfillment of the ideal role of educators and moral influencers. Without rags, there was no paper, and without paper, no books, bibles, or primers.

Such arguments were common in calls for rags. Near the turn of the eighteenth to the nineteenth century, a Portland, Maine, newspaper called for "the attention of the LADIES, [and other] inhabitants of the District . . . ," to "invite all persons, whether rich or poor, old or young, male or female, but more especially of the sex last mentioned, to be very attentive to the *Saving of Rags*." The owners of the new paper mill declared: "It must afford pleasure and satisfaction to patriotic minds to reflect that while in the pursuit of any private business . . . they are at the same time promoting that of the public. . . . They will receive a generous price for the Rags they may have and be intitled [sic] to the thanks of all their fellow citizens: For there is not a man, woman or child who *reads* or *writes*, nor one who uses PAPER for the various purposes to which is constantly applied, but would be benefitted by the manufacture of that useful article, Therefore, *Save your Rags*." This call for rags deploys the rhetoric of republican motherhood by explicitly "politicizing private behavior," framing the domestic space of the home and the domestic space of the nation as parallel spheres of women's influence without granting women full citizenship in the nation.[37] Thus we see the paper mill owners making the case that saving rags harmonizes the private interests of domestic economy with the public interest of domestic manufacture: "It must afford pleasure and satisfaction to patriotic minds to reflect that while in the pursuit of any private business . . . they are at the same time promoting that of the public."

This call also hints at an appeal to the republican mother to educate and prepare male children for citizenship, through the figure of the literate child and his or her need for material: "For there is not a man, woman or child who *reads* or *writes*, nor one who uses PAPER for the various purposes to which is constantly applied, but would be benefitted by the manufacture of that useful article." Saving rags for the paper mill is patriotic not merely because it conserves resources during uncertain political times—like in the midst of war—but also because of the special nature of its products (bibles, newspapers, primers) and their use for raising citizens. Extending the work of the paper mill into the home was seen as a necessary precondition for other responsibilities of republican women, such as instruction in reading.

It was not uncommon for women to be hailed in poetry and prose by newspapers and papermakers. Periodicals frequently reprinted simple verses meant to both encourage and reward women to collect rags and supply them to mills. After the Revolution, others appealed more to the romantic interests of "the ladies" than to their republican virtues. "Save your rags!" implored the Hawley mill of Fort Edward, New York. "This exclamation is particularly addressed to the ladies, both young and old and middle aged. . . . Without their assistance they cannot be supplied with the useful article of paper. If the necessary stock is denied the paper mills, young maids must languish in vain for tender epistles from their respective swains."[38] Whether promising the erotic charge of a lover's note, encouraging virtuous republicanism, or simply begging the pardon of a needy industry, women were at the center of these appeals. "Sweet ladies pray be not offended," an upstate New York mill owner wrote in 1807, "Nor mind the jest of sneering wags: / No harm, believe us, is intended, / When humbly we request your rags."[39] Through these material textual routes, women were highlighted as crucially important figures in the production of the text and of the nation alike. We will return to the gendered labor of rag collection in chapter 2, where we will see how women poets figure the world of print as a world made up of remnants of women's domestic labor with cloth.

"Want of paper": Crises of Confederate Paper

What would happen if, as late eighteenth-century papermakers and newspaper publishers feared, there actually were not enough rags and paper to produce the newspaper? While rags were frequently scarce throughout the eighteenth and nineteenth centuries, there was an acute crisis in the paper industry during the Civil War's economic depression and wartime disruptions. In 1864, publisher and economist Henry Charles Carey wrote a series of public letters to Speaker of the House Schuyler Colfax on what he dubbed "the paper question." Carey urged Colfax to enact international protections and domestic encouragements for small paper manufacturers, who, Carey thought, were needed if paper supply was going to meet demand at a reasonable price. "The day is close at hand," he warned, "when we shall have to provide literary food for sixty millions of people."[40]

The idea of paper mills providing "literary food" for the nation resonates with Oliver Wendell Holmes Sr.'s 1861 essay, written for the *Atlantic Monthly*, on the effects of wartime mass mediacy on the Union homefront. In "Bread and the Newspaper," he recalls: "[A] most eminent scholar told us in all simplicity that he had fallen into such a state that he would read the same telegraphic dispatches over and over again in different papers, as if they were new, until he felt as if he were an idiot. Who did not do just the same thing, and does not often do it still, now that the first flush of the fever is over? Another person always goes through the side streets on his way for the noon *extra*,—he is so afraid somebody will meet him and *tell* the news he wishes to *read*, first on the bulletin-board, and then in the great capitals and leaded type of the newspaper." Experiencing the Union at war in regular intervals and in print is a hallmark of both this scene and of Benedict Anderson's theory of the national imagined community under print capitalism. Local gatherings around the bulletin board and a national sense of connectedness mark Holmes's descriptions of the appetite for news. The community of readers is described as a body, "a network of iron nerves which flash sensation and volition backward and forward to and from towns and provinces as if they were organs and limbs of a single living body." The "perpetual intercommunication" of battlefields and the home front, continues Holmes, "keeps us always alive with excitement. It is not a breathless courier who comes back with the report from an army we have lost sight of for a month, nor a single bulletin which tells us all we are to know for a week of some great engagement, but almost hourly paragraphs, laden with truth or falsehood as the case may be, making us restless always for the last fact or rumor they are telling. And so of the movements of our armies. Tonight the stout lumbermen of Maine are encamped under their own fragrant pines. In a score or two of hours they are among the tobacco-fields and the slave-pens of Virginia."[41] The typography of ink on paper and its appearance at quick intervals links Maine to Virginia in "perpetual intercommunication," as if linked by nerves and organs.

Indeed, access to the newspaper becomes like access to food, and together they form a sort of bottom line for life in wartime. Holmes repeats over and

over, "We must have something to eat, and the papers to read": "Only *bread
and the newspaper* we must have, whatever else we do without." In fact, if the
production of print became too costly to sustain, then, and only then, would
it be okay to surrender the cause of the Union according to Holmes: "The time
may come when even the cheap public print shall be a burden our means cannot support, and we can only listen in the square that was once the marketplace to the voices of those who proclaim defeat or victory. Then there will
be only our daily food left. When we have nothing to read and nothing to eat,
it will be a favorable moment to offer a compromise. At present we have all
that nature absolutely demands,—we can live on bread and the newspaper."[42]
Both Holmes and Carey figure paper and newspapers as the daily bread of
communities, and when Holmes speaks of living on newspapers, it is almost
hard to discern at moments whether or not he is talking about literally eating
paper. Like their eighteenth-century wartime counterparts, these writers
ponder the specter of paper starvation. Carey's letters on the "paper question"
are an expression of a paper industry in which wood pulp papermaking had
not transformed the supply of raw material and in which the Civil War had
disrupted the supply and affordability of necessary rags within the Union
States. Further, destruction of the Confederate States' infrastructure deci-
mated the South's already minimally developed paper industry.

The 1863 diptych cartoon "The Paper Panic" from Frank Leslie's comic
newspaper, *Budget of Fun*, links the high cost of rags that so worried Carey to
the sense of material lack he warned of with the word "hunger" (Fig. 3a). In one
panel, a husband asks his wife, "Where are my shirts?," to which she responds,
"You see, my dear, the premium upon linen rags was so high that—a—I was
tempted to sell them to the junk man." The next panel of the comic shows one
rural newspaper editor meeting another who is rifling through the contents
of a barrel. Says one rural newspaper editor to the other, "What's this Smith,
turned rag-picker, eh?" Smith answers, "Yes, 'pon my soul, I'll have to gather
the materials and get the paper made before I can print my next issue." These
linked panels pick up two important threads of my argument in this chapter.
First, the panel on the right insists that before printing, the necessary work of
rag collecting and papermaking must be done. It is significant that this comic
depicts the editor of a paper out looking in barrels for rags. The comic refuses
to obscure the work of ragpicking behind the more visible scenes of writing
and printing. Second, the panel on the left plays on the ways that women
manage work with cloth in the household, making clear that women are

THE PAPER PANIC.

SCARCITY OF PAPER IN THE RURAL DISTRICTS.

Figure 3a and 3b. "The Paper Panic" and "Scarcity of Paper in the Rural Districts" from *Frank Leslie's Budget of Fun*, ca. 1863. *Courtesy of the American Antiquarian Society.*

key agents in the papermaking process. There is humor in pretending that a man's shirts are worth more to the household once they've been sold as rags to the mill, but it is also an expression of the material routes that run between the home and the print public sphere, with women in the middle. The link between the domestic space of the home and the publics of writing and print is made in another Frank Leslie cartoon: "Scarcity of Paper in the Rural Districts" (Fig. 3b). This cartoon depicts rural townspeople writing on old shutters and directly onto clothing—completely and comically cutting out the paper mill. The panel on the left reads, "The boss sent me to yez. . . . He's got no paper for a letter, so he's wrote on this shutter what he wants, and you place the answer on the other side." In this depiction of lacking paper, those who would correspond with each other have resorted to taking apart the house to find a substrate for writing, not mere cartoonish fancy when Confederate printers later used the undecorated side of wallpaper to print newspapers, as we will see shortly. The caption to the right panel imagines a need for paper so urgent that writers skip over the papermill, choosing to write directly on their underclothes instead: "All the paper being used up, the Potterville people have to write their correspondences upon their under-clothing. The above picture shows the expressman in the act of mailing said letters." Earlier calls for rags promised that handkerchiefs sent to the mill would return to the donor as paper correspondence. This cartoon literalizes fantasies about intimate apparel within paper, imagining underclothes as the writing surface.

What was humorous for cartoonists in Union papers was actually happening on the ground in the Confederate States. On April 15, 1863, the *Southern Literary Companion* suddenly issued a half-sheet instead of a full-sheet newspaper. Under the heading "Want of Paper," the editors announced that "the destruction of the Bath Paper Mills by fire on the 2nd . . . near Augusta Ga., and the impossibility of the other paper mills furnishing a supply equal to the demand of the publishers, have rendered it necessary for us to print the *Companion*, for the present, upon a half sheet. . . . Money will not now buy paper. The material (rags) of which it is made, is the only thing with which we can purchase it." In another column, readers learn about a rise in subscription rates due to the rising cost of paper: "The cost of paper on which the News is now issued is fully ten times as great as the price of paper on which we formerly printed, and much more than our former subscription price." New subscriptions were discouraged since "all the paper mills of the Confederacy are now monopolized to their fullest capacity by press engagements," with existing levels of production still exceeding supply. For this particular issue, the editors explain, "we have been fortunate enough . . . to procure a temporary supply at a great cost, and we this morning present the News on English paper brought through the blockade from Nassau to Charleston."[43]

From the North, the *New York Times* proclaimed that "for the moment, Paper, not Cotton, is King." This writer seemed happy to report that "the skies seem big with disaster" for Confederate counterparts, whose supply of paper "each day [becomes] beautifully less." "Paper is indispensable to the Confederate

Government if the rebellion is to continue," the *Times* notes. "It is essential for the manufacture of Confederate State Bonds; it is necessary to expand the system of shinplasters in the different States, so that it may meet the requirements of a currency; and it is wanted especially for the proclamations of the rebel leaders, to say nothing of the smaller quantities required for correspondence and the printing of rebellious newspapers."[44] By naming paper king over cotton, the *Times* put the a nation's material economy of writing and communication ahead of its market economy in commodities. As in the comics, cotton is figured as more valuable to the state within rag paper than it is on the market. The state depends on its paper infrastructure for its very being.

Confederate newspaper publishers openly worried about the fate of their paperless national body. "Scarcity of paper throughout the Confederacy," began one writer for the *Savannah Republican*, meant that "newspapers would stop, and all correspondence be suspended.—The necessary blanks for the army could not be furnished, its accounts could not be kept, or its efficiency maintained. The Post Office Department would expire with the absence of paper with which to carry on correspondence, and we should be reduced to the expedients of savage nations who only communicate at a distance by means of special couriers, and pieces of bark." In this expression of anti-Indian colonial racism, paper serves as the dividing line between so-called civil and savage, a meme about paper and legal documentation that extends into the present. Also these comments show that anxieties about the lack of paper for written communication not just the stuff of jokes. With wallpaper newspapers in circulation, jokes about writing letters on shutters seems less far-fetched. Under General William T. Sherman's explicit orders, Union forces burned paper mills all over Georgia, a move that speaks to an awareness of paper's importance in the maintenance of governments and publics. The Marietta Paper Mill was under the supervision of Confederate general William Phillips, supplying paper for Confederate stationery and gun wadding, when the 17th Indiana Infantry Regiment marched on and burned it.[45]

Further south, printers resorted to printing newspapers on wallpaper, making real the idea of taking apart the house and writing on the shutters. On April 8, 1863, the editors of the *Pictorial Democrat* in Alexandria, Louisiana, finally ran out of paper. Finding that they couldn't smuggle any through the coastal blockades or from the dwindling number of Confederate paper mills, they printed the newspaper on the blank side of rolls of unused wallpaper. The *Pictorial Democrat* was only one of several newspapers to issue a "wallpaper newspaper." The *Pictorial Democrat*'s editors lament: "We are forced, contrary to our expectations, to come down to the pictures, (or wallpaper), and issue this scant specimen of a newspaper. We have done all in our power to avert this evil, but all our plans and arrangement . . . have been frustrated. . . . As this is the first time under our control the Democrat has flukered, we hope our many patrons will look over it and be content with our pictorial, containing the latest compendium of news." One week later, the situation had not improved. The editors lamented that they have nothing to show by way of improvement: "Here we are again, dear patrons, roaming and scrambling among the pictures! The fates, for the while, seem to be against us . . . no paper yet! Well, it's no use offering excuses, and our patrons must bear it with becoming grace and dignity. Let it be understood that, we will make no charge against them for our illustrated as we merely issue it to keep them posted in the latest . . . items, and to give circulation to the advertisements of our patrons."[46] Wallpaper newspapers introduce another material textual path between private and public spheres, between domestic space and national space. The material for the newspaper is paper meant for the walls of the home; the periodical that ties the community together in print is itself an artifact of the home. A similar dynamic is working when readers' attention is drawn to the necessity of collecting rags at home, but the connection between home and print is even more apparent when wallpaper and newspaper are merged. Such connections result from a particularly scarce market for printing paper and rags but are also an extreme example of a circuit that is always running between the intimate cast-off cloth rags of a home. Wallpaper newspapers are an object lesson on the always-present linkage of the private domestic sphere and the public sphere within texts printed on paper.

Wallpaper newspapers are literalized expressions of the fears of the eighteenth-century newspaper editors and paper mill owners that I discussed earlier in this chapter. What if there is no paper? What if there is no "literary food" to nourish public demand for news and common reading? The editor of the *Pictorial Democrat* remains dedicated to circulating "the latest [news]" about the war and also fulfilling obligations to advertisers but admits that the "fates seem against us." The material lack and precariousness of the Confederate States as a nation are apparent in the wallpaper newspapers—the desperate attempt to maintain a reading public through the circulation of a paper object, going so far as to figuratively take apart the home to go to print.

The *Vicksburg (MS) Daily Citizen* of July 2, 1863, *and* July 4, 1863, is probably the most famous wallpaper newspaper. It bears two datelines because of the circumstances of its printing. Most of the lead type for this issue was set by Confederates anticipating Grant's imminent capture of city. "The great Ulysses . . . has expressed his intention of dining in Vicksburg on Saturday next, and celebrating the 4th of July with a grand dinner and so forth. . . . Ulysses must get into the city before he dines in it. The way to cook rabbit is 'first catch the rabbit.'" These original compositors and pressmen fled the office before they went to print, leaving the type standing in a galley tray. After taking the city on July 4, Union soldiers found the standing type and amended the text. They then printed the issue on wallpaper. Immediately following the passage concerning Grant's proximity, the Union soldiers composed in lead and printed the following:

> NOTE.
> July 4th, 1863.
>
> Two days bring about great changes, The banner of the Union floats over Vicksburg, Gen. Grant has "caught the rabbit;" he has dined in Vicksburg, and he did bring his dinner with him. The "Citizen" lives to see it. For the last time, it appears on "wall-paper." . . . This is the last wall-paper edition, and, excepting this note, from the types as we found them. It will be valuable hereafter as a curiosity.[47]

Who is the "Citizen" who "lives to see it?" On July 2, 1863, the newspaper addresses itself to the Confederate citizens of Vicksburg. When the original compositor refers to the "the Yanks outside *our* city [emphasis added]," the *Daily Citizen* is indeed using what little wallpaper was left at hand to emplot Confederate Vicksburg in time and space with a public identifiable by an "our." But less than an inch down the page of printed wallpaper, the Union response reframes what it means to be a citizen of this paper's public: "The banner of the Union floats over Vicksburg." Who constitutes the public hailed and assembled by this paper? Printed on wallpaper intended to cover the walls of homes in town, the newspaper's original intent was to circulate beneath a Confederate banner on July 2 as the *Daily Citizen*, a title that recalls the daily circulation and shared reading among people that gives rise to imagined community. But, ultimately, the newspaper issues on a later day than its masthead indicates and is addressed to a citizenry that no longer exists. Wallpaper newspapers are the physical embodiments of the dread with which newspaper printers and papermakers spoke of paperless futures. No rags and no paper, they warned, would mean no daily citizenry.

After the war, "Confederate paper" was more a curiosity than the substrate of an actual print public. Two books, one published in 1866 and the other in 1867, claim to be the last ones published on "Confederate paper." Within two years of the close of the Civil War, the circulation of "Confederate paper" made it possible to "touch" the Confederacy again. Rags gathered from Confederate homes, pulped and drawn together as paper in the space of Confederate mills, allowed a very material sense of the Confederacy to continue to circulate even after its dissolution.

Both books were written by Fanny Murdaugh Downing and published by two different Raleigh, North Carolina, printers. The first of these, *Nameless: A Novel*, was published in 1866. The copy held by the American Antiquarian Society (AAS) is inscribed, in bold late nineteenth-century script, "The last book which was printed on 'Confederate' paper."[48] Published a year later, Downing's long poem *Pluto: being the sad story and lamentable fate of the fair Minthe*, has no indication either in print or manuscript annotation that it is made with so-called Confederate paper. The metadata in its record at the AAS reads: "Said to be the last book printed on Confederate paper. Last page blank." What does it mean in 1867, or in the present, to put a blank sheet of Confederate paper before one's eyes and into one's hands? Knowing it to be "Confederate paper" makes a haptic experience of a particular political community possible across time and space. These books call attention to their paper substrates and designate them the physical remnants of a political formation. Their sheets evidence material traces of the Confederacy within them, which are carried forward for future readers to touch.

Paper Futurity

"I think," the contemporary novelist Jonathan Franzen told a reporter, "for serious readers, a sense of permanence has always been part of the experience. Everything else in your life is fluid, but here is this text that doesn't change. Will there still be readers 50 years from now who feel that way? Who have that hunger for something permanent and unalterable? . . . I do fear that it's going to be very hard to make the world work if there's no permanence like that. That kind of radical contingency is not compatible with a system of justice or responsible self-government. The technology I like is the American paperback edition of *Freedom*. . . . And what's more, it will work great 10 years from now."[49] Franzen's claim is odd, but it makes a certain kind of sense within the long history of worrying about the relationship between a political or communal body and the textual substrates that record, circulate, and preserve it. Like the eighteenth-century colonists who fretted over what the Stamp Act taxes would do to their ability to conduct government, Franzen ties what he thinks is the impermanence of and atemporality of e-books to the very form of democratic "self-government."[50] His twenty-first-century anxiety over the materiality of texts is part of a long historical concern over the material supports for both texts and nations. A writer for *Harper's New Monthly Magazine* in 1887 makes a similar argument: "Without paper, the modern world would be literally impossible," because it stitches together both the "social and commercial machinery without which we could not and would not be what we are."[51] Paper is seen here as a privileged site where social and material life meet and are secured, archived, for the future.

In his 1740 poem "The Paper-Mill," Joseph Dumbleton speculates how social and material relations are embedded within paper. The poem both praises and advertises a Virginia paper mill owned by William Parks, Virginia's first printer, and opens by connecting thought and community within the materiality of paper.

> Tho' sage Philosophers have said,
> *Of nothing, can nothing be made;*
> Yet much thy Mill, O *Parks* brings forth
> From what we reckon nothing *worth.*
> Hail kind *Machine!*—The Muse shall praise
> thy Labours, that receive her Lays.
>
> . . . .
>
> The Substances of what we think,
> Tho' born in *Thoughts*, must live in *Ink.*

Dumbleton's "The Paper-Mill" takes its epigraph from Ovid: "My heart makes me tell of forms that have been changed into new shapes." The theme of metamorphosis begins the poet's thinking about the transformation of rags into paper, the bearer of words. The speaker observes that though physical things may transform from one form to another, nothing can be made from nothing. Immaterial thoughts must take shape in ink and paper material texts. Having established that thoughts must take physical form in the world, Dumbleton explains what people must do to provide the materials necessary for thoughts to take form in ink: they must make paper out of rags collected in their community:

> Ye Brave, whose Deeds shall vie with Time,
> Whilst Mill can turn, or Poet rhime
> Your tatters hoard for future Quires;
> So Need demands, So *Parks* desires.
> (And long that gen'rous Patriot live
> Who for soft Rags, hard Cash will give!)
> The Shirt, Cravat, the Cap, again,
> Shall meet your Hands, with Mails from Spain;
> The Surplice, which when whole or new
> With Pride the Sexton's wife could view,
> Tho' worn by Time and gone to rack,
> It quits its Rev'rend Master's Back;
> The same again the Priest may see
> Bound up in Sacred Liturgy.

The poem is not only an advertisement for the willingness of Parks mill to buy rags but also a reflection on the constitution of the social body. The stanza defines the brave and the patriotic as those who contribute rags to the paper mill, ensuring that colonial Virginia is able to correspond with Spain. The circuit of rags and paper operates on a local scale too. The Sexton's vestment is worn, turned to paper, and returns to the church as the priest's sacred book; a young lady's handkerchief makes its way back to her as a lover's note. By producing paper, patriots ensure that the communicative circuits within this community will endure. These relationships are figured by imagining that the metamorphosis of shirt to book exchanges materials meaningfully. The Sexton's shirt returns to the Priest as holy book and the young lady's handkerchief makes its way back to her as a lover's note:

> Ye Fair, renown'd in Cupid's Field
> Who fain would tell what Hearts you've killed
> Each shift decay'd, lay by with care;
> Or Apron rubb'd to bits at—Pray'r,
> One Shift ten Sonnets may contain,
> to Gild your Charms, and make you Vain,
> One Cap, a Billet-Doux may shape,

> As full of Whim, as when a Cap,
> And modest 'Kercheifs Sacred Held
> May sing the Breasts they once conceal.[52]

In this poem, paper ties the past to the future. Because a quire of paper supposedly contains the tattered remnants of a sexton's shirt, it will be made into a holy book and return to the church on the property he cared for. A woman's tattered apron and shift contain sonnets that can be unlocked by a paper mill, before returning to her. Paper functions as an object that carries the past into the future. It is not merely that memories are recorded *on* paper, ensuring a continuity of knowledge, but also that relationships are maintained and even occasioned by the exchange of materials *within* paper. The poem pronounces that because we are in paper, because our bodies are recorded within the raggy material textual substrate, the future will contain us.

In 1777, the *Connecticut Courant* worried that "if Rags are not to be had . . . The News Paper must inevitably stop."[53] On its centennial celebration in 1864, that very same newspaper looked back across its century of publication and noted its essential role in both publishing the news of the late colonies and early republic ensuring that there would be a proper supply of rags for paper. "During the war of Independence, our publishers erected a paper mill in Hartford, and made the paper on which they printed." Nearing the end of the Civil War, in the midst of the "paper crisis" of 1864, the *Courant's* publishers celebrated that "numerous appeals and entreaties are to be found in our files to the good people of Connecticut to save every scrap of rags or other material that could be converted into paper, and bring it to the Courant office for the use of the mill." Significantly, the *Courant* here claims the role of printer of the news as well as maker of paper. "The good people of Connecticut" are assembled not only as readers but also within the very pages of the *Courant*. Both the printed text and the material text are available to posterity, to the archive, and thus both the ideas and the physical presence of Connecticut rags survive for reading and the creation of historical knowledge. "Historians," the newspaper boasts, "like Bancroft, Trumbull, Stuart, Hollister, and other writers and politicians have freely quoted and cited from the files of the Courant." Without the assemblage of "the good people of Connecticut's" rags made into paper at the *Courant's* mill, we would lack archive historical records from which the likes of George Bancroft can weave historical narrative. Communal affiliations survive *within* paper as much as their records are printed *on* paper. Thus, in 1864, before the resolution of the Civil War, the *Courant*'s editors recall the long-ago assembly of the "good people" through the rags they sent to the mill and made into paper. The editors wish that "we be permitted in these days when the perpetuity of the great Republic is at stake, to offer our private prayer: 'THE COURANT: est perpetua.'"[54] If the *Courant* remains, then so must the republic—the people, through their rags, remain too. Here "remains" signifies both endurance over time and the remnants of bodies preserved and memorialized.

Presence and the Material Public Sphere

Narratives about paper and community explored in this chapter rely on fantasies of intimacy mediated within the fibers of paper. A lover's note makes its way to a woman because its paper is made from her old underclothes. The sexton's shirt, tattered from labor in the graveyard, is transformed into paper for a Bible inside the church. Rags collected from Confederate towns and transformed into paper at nearby mills make "Confederate paper" specifically and later offer a way to physically encounter the remnants of a defeated political body. I have argued that these intimacies—real and imagined—assemble publics and create common feeling differently than do print circulation and reading. For one, as countless printers and papermakers have exclaimed, before there is print, there must be paper. But more important, to make paper, communities were called to mingle their cast-off cloth. In times of crisis, readers were even bombarded with messages that urged them to bring rags to local mills to be transformed into paper, or else, they were told, their communities would cease to exist. The assemblage of rags in paper mirrors the assemblage of people within paper. I name these fantasies of intimacy to highlight how much work literary writing and figurative language are recruited to perform in the service of technology and statecraft. Poetry about papermaking allows the literal and the fantastical to coexist. Papermaking truly recycles cloth rags into paper, but it is very unlikely that a woman would reencounter her own handkerchief in a sheet of paper. The space of the unlikely but not unimaginable is the terrain of the literary.

From Richard Frame's seventeenth-century poetic exploration of the colonies' first paper mill through nineteenth-century newspaper calls for the gathering of rags from communities, writing about paper has consistently highlighted how communities of communication are persistently and some-times frustratingly *material*. As Dumbleton had it, "The Substances of what we think / Tho' born in *Thoughts*, must live in *Ink*." The "materialities of communication," Hans Ulrich Gumbrecht writes, "are all those phenomena and conditions that contribute to the production of meaning, without being meaning themselves."[55] Earlier, I criticized the tendencies of public sphere theories popularized by Habermas, Anderson, and Warner because of their collective tendency to take the materiality of print for granted and to focus on reading and interpretation of what has been printed. But when the *Spectator* imagines its public through the collective work of papermaking, or when newspapers broadcast the precarity of the material processes necessary to produce print, readers are being called to account for the presence of print. These accounts use language, including literary language, to reassert the presence of print. A present thing is tangible to the hand, and Gumbrecht theorizes that things of the world and cultural objects can at times "produce presence" or intensify their impact on human bodies.[56] In these moments when the presence of a thing is intensified, when its impact on the body is heightened, then we are left to sense it, rather than interpret it. Sensing paper and its raggy content, for example, asks us to momentarily suspend the desire to read and interpret, to look behind the words and into the page. When scarce paper and rags place a limit on the desire to print, read, and interpret, paper asserts its presence negatively, or as we will see in subsequent chapters, it can assert its presence positively, as when a shred of unpulped linen sticks out within a page. In this chapter and throughout this book, I am also tracing how writing about the materiality of print seeks to heighten readerly sensitivity to paper's presence.

I have been arguing that paper represented a kind of community in materiality, an affiliation of people related through their cast-off rags remade in paper. These affiliations are often imagined in writing about paper and papermaking, hinting at the possibilities within paper's rag content. By asserting the presence dimension of rag paper, writers from the seventeenth though nineteenth centuries urged others to consider that what increasingly became identifiable as a public sphere of letters, of reading, writing, and debate, emerged out of, and in some cases on top of, a material sphere that needed to be encountered and considered—felt, even. Emergent in the oscillation between throwing one's own ragged linen into a ragbag and reading appeals to women to save rags is the awareness of rags and women's work within the paper one reads. The public sphere of authors and readers is inseparable from the materials and the labors that support it: meaning making words and presence making paper are simultaneously available in the encounter with print. We will further investigate these oscillations and their use in feminist arguments about print, writing, and material labors in the next chapter.

I close the chapter with a final example where the intimate relations within paper are forcefully made present in quite concrete ways by text—an example that offers a real, rather than speculative or fantastical, account of the presence of people and a community represented within sheets of paper. This is not to discount the imaginative work of eighteenth- and nineteenth-century writers and papermakers read throughout this chapter. Imagined communities are no less real for having been imagined into being. However, in the colophon of *Old Ream Wrappers: An Essay on Early Ream Wrappers of Antiquarian Interest*, we are given the names of people whose clothes are in the paper it is printed on, realizing the fantasies of intimacy that so many have imagined in paper.

Old Ream Wrappers is a 1968 artist book by paper historian Henk Voorn exploring Dutch ream wrappers and the history of papermaking. Henry Morris, of the Bird and Bull Press, made all the paper for this edition, save one sheet in each copy of the book. In the colophon, Morris explains that he has bound into each copy of the book one sheet of paper from a seventeenth-century book: "To return to the business at hand, the one sheet of paper in this book which I did not make is a sheet of old Dutch paper supplied from a large blank book." Morris calls attention to this seventeenth-century paper and its main visible inclusions, orienting us to a way of reading the materiality of paper. He writes, "It is full of all sort of lumps, wool, wood, stones, plaster." Opposite this sheet, Morris has included another blank sheet. Of this one, he says: "The other colored sheet is something else again. This sheet is made from the collected shirts, underwear and handkerchiefs contributed by the following people, who are all active in the field of books, printing, or papermaking: James Anderson, Joseph Blumenthal, Herman Cohen, Jack and Remy Green, Leonard Schlosser, Norman Strouse and Henk Voorn. The pulp made from these collected rags was used by members of the audience at a talk I gave at Gallery 303 in New York City, on September 18, 1968."[57] Here we have a sheet of paper that can be explicit and detailed about its internal material textual affiliations. Holding it, we know we touch the underwear and handkerchiefs of James, Joseph, Herman, Jack, Remy, Leonard, Norman, and Henk. When I first encountered this book, I mentioned the remarkable colophon to a curator in the rare books room at my university as she passed behind me. "Oh," she said, "I knew Henk," and touched the page. Voorn died in 2008, but today it is still possible to lay hands on this sheet of paper and to touch a remnant of him that we know is present. It is also possible within this sheet to touch—to sense—this community of book artists. This sheet of paper contains traces of identifiable people in "the field of books" who came together in sharing rags to make pulp for this paper, and so there they remain within.

I have argued in this chapter that the materiality of rag paper contains a form of sociability within itself and that this form of affiliation within material texts complicates theories of the print public sphere, calling our attention to communities of makers and material traces as well as communities of readers and writers. I focus in the next chapter on how women writers constructed and deployed a feminist theory of the print public sphere by following the movement of rags from the home into paper. I explore the arguments made by poets, including Anne Bradstreet and Lydia H. Sigourney, who trace a form of feminist labor at the material level of the rag that links domestic work to literary production.

CHAPTER 2

THE GENDER OF RAG PAPER IN ANNE BRADSTREET AND LYDIA SIGOURNEY

ALTHOUGH HE WAS famous for being a printer, several of his biographers point out that Benjamin Franklin became the largest wholesale dealer of paper in the thirteen colonies and derived a great share of his income from these interests. He invested in mills throughout the colonies and sold 166,000 pounds of rags between 1739 and 1747. It was a lucrative business for the founding father and the secular patron saint of printers.[1] Paper also played a role in Franklin's ever-present self-fashioning as a credible and, most important, creditable character. In his *Autobiography*, Franklin memorably describes how he turned the calamity of dumping a day's worth of set type into an opportunity to appear busy by sorting and resetting everything in front of his shop window late into the night. Less frequently remembered are his conspicuous trips through the streets of Philadelphia with a wheelbarrow full of paper. "In order to secure my Credit and Character as a Tradesman, I took care not only to be in *Reality* Industrious and frugal, but to avoid all *Appearances* of the Contrary," he writes. "I sometimes brought home the Paper I purchas'd at the Stores, thro' the Streets on a Wheelbarrow." It brought in more business to be seen carrying paper about town, to visually associate himself with the materials of his trade. Eager to work with the man who moved so much paper, "the Merchants who imported Stationery solicited [his] Custom," and "others propos'd supplying [him] with Books." "I went on swimmingly," in gaining credit and new business, Franklin says, by flaunting an association with the materials of his trades, whether in type or reams of paper.[2]

But behind Franklin were women working to make his paper-laden persona possible. Franklin may have gone through the streets with barrows full of paper, but the rags in that paper had already been used, sorted, and shredded, likely by many women's hands. One of those women was his wife, Deborah Franklin. He writes in the *Autobiography* that "it was lucky for me that I had [a wife] as much dispos'd to Industry and Frugality as myself," because "She assisted me cheerfully in Business, folding and stitching Pamphlets, tending Shop, purchasing old Linen Rags for the Paper-makers, etc. etc."[3] Though fame and money would accrue to him for his printing and his writing, it was the work of Deborah Franklin and women like her, collecting and sorting rags, that provided the material supports for Franklin. Excavating the history of Franklin's sister Jane Franklin Mecom, Jill Lepore argues that Jane's life spent caring for her and Benjamin's parents, maintaining the family soap business, and keeping the family records in her memory was a quarry of domestic labor that her brother mined for his own success. While Benjamin Franklin sold paper, print, and his own writing, "Jane's life," Lepore writes, "was cluttered with a different sort of rags: rags for washing, rags for diapering, rags for catching blood."[4] Beneath every printed word is a shred of washrag or diaper, and behind every Benjamin there is a Jane.

In the preceding chapter, I argued that animations of the real and imagined intimacies within in the materiality of paper offer us real and imagined traces of the many people who worked with rags. This chapter explores how writers highlight and animate the presence of rags within paper to make feminist claims about print and the print public sphere. Anne Bradstreet and Lydia Sigourney, women poets from different centuries who both rebuffed claims that they should not make themselves available in print, argued in their poetry that because print required women's domestic labor with rags for its material existence, women were always already present in print and therefore belonged as writers too. For these women writers, the rag content of paper served as the crucial material link uniting private and public spheres. Bradstreet and Sigourney traced the material intimacies between feminized domestic labor and masculinized print publicity. Reflecting on his tour of a paper mill, Pastor Wright noted that "strange as it may appear, the connection" between the kitchen ragbag and the printed book "is very intimate."[5] Bradstreet and Sigourney laid claim to this strange intimacy to contend that print was dependent on women's work with textiles. While some sought to enforce a strict and gendered separation of private and public spheres, Bradstreet,

Sigourney, and others looked to the transformation of household linen into paper as a material continuity that collapsed the separation of spheres.

From the late seventeenth- through the late nineteenth-century, women and girls were frequently offered lessons about maintaining the household economy of rags, as well as the value of rags for papermaking. In one of the most prominent domestic advice manuals of the nineteenth century, *The American Frugal Housewife*, Lydia Maria Child writes that the "ragbag" was an essential fixture in the home for the housewife to maintain: "Rags should never be thrown away because they are dirty," Child writes, "mop rags, lamp rags should be washed. . . . Linen rags should be carefully saved; for they are extremely useful in sickness." An essential part of this work was also managing the life cycle of cloth, from clothing to rag to much-used rag, without waste: "After old coats, pantaloons, &c. have been cut up for boys, and are no longer capable of being converted into garments, cut them into strips and employ . . . in sewing and braiding them for doormats."[6] Other advice pieces suggested that the ragbag could become a fashionable and functional decoration in the parlor: "The ladies in several of the large towns" of Connecticut and Massachusetts "display an elegant work bag, as part of the furniture of their parlors, in which every rag that is used in the paper mill, is carefully preserved."[7] The fingers of the paper mill stretched into the management, and even the decoration, of domestic spaces organized and overseen by women.

And, as we saw in chapter 1, once household rags were no longer useful for domestic tasks, women were instructed to sell them to ragpickers or directly to paper mills. In the 1780s, bookbinder and stationer Benjamin January made this connection between the home and the paper mill, writing "it is well worthy the attention of every one to save all the RAGS which may be made in their families, as by this they will have the pleasing reflection of having given their mite towards promoting a very useful and important manufactory."[8] Calls for rags from papermakers also appealed to the sense that housewives were obligated to stretch the most value out of every scrap of material in the home. "SAVE YOUR OLD PAPERS AND RAGS," emphasize the editors of the Pennsylvania *Delaware County Republican* in an 1862 note directed to "housekeepers": "Those who practice domestic economy will . . . see the necessity of saving . . . during the present scarcity of stock for making paper," they wrote, adding that "all families and individuals will benefit themselves and the public by saving everything adapted to the manufacture of paper, and promptly putting it into the market."[9] As we observed in chapter 1, to read a newspaper in the eighteenth and nineteenth centuries was to be constantly confronted with calls for rags. Like these, they tended to appeal directly to women and connected household economy to virtuousness and citizenship.

Domestic conduct manuals and newspaper advertisements were joined by poetry, which circulated in newspapers and on handbills and ream wrappers. Such printed pieces literally made women's domestic labor rhyme with the interests of the paper and printing industries:

> Sweet ladies, pray not be offended,
> Nor mind the jest of sneering wags
>   No harm, believe us is intended,
> When humbly we request your rags.
>
> The scraps which you reject, unfit
> To clothe the tenant of a hovel,
>   May shine in sentiment and wit,
> And help to make a charming novel.
>
> The cap, exalted thoughts will raise,
> The ruffle in description will flourish;
>   Whilst on the glowing work we gaze,
> The thought will love excite and nourish.
>
> Each beau in study will engage,
> His fancy doubtless will be warmer,
>   When writing on the milk white page,
> Which once, adorned his charmer.
>
> Tho foreigners may sneer and vapor,
> We no longer fore'd their books to buy
>   Our gentle belles will furnish paper.
> Our sighing beau will wit supply.[10]

This poem makes visible how women were understood to be "behind" writing and printing on paper; for every novel there are women discarding rags deemed unfit for the resident of a "hovel." Writing here is done by "beaus" on paper furnished by "belles." A hat cast from the home returns, in a way, to the head in the form of exalted thoughts, the discarded ruffle becomes a literary flourish. In the eighteenth- and nineteenth-century imagination, it was possible to imagine a direct connection between the rag in the page and the writing on it. This connection also meant that women's work—domestic work with cloth—was figured as a form of prerequisite labor in the background of all writing and printing on paper.

Such poems as the one above promise love letters in exchange for rags, while the bulk of domestic advice literature offered frugality and the moral superiority of avoiding waste as a reward. Other writers, however, especially women, wondered whether their role in securing the material conditions for paper and print should secure women something more. If all writing and printing on paper depended to such a great extent on women's domestic work, shouldn't that guarantee women's access to reading and writing? This is, in short, the argument that two women poets, Anne Bradstreet and Lydia H. Sigourney, made.

As women poets thinking about the routes rags take from home to paper mill to print shop, Bradstreet and Sigourney are our best theorists of gender and the materiality of the public sphere. Because they are poets, both of them think through the relation of figure and ground, of the seen and not seen, of metaphor and its vehicle. Bradstreet and Sigourney are thus able to oscillate between the making of literary meaning through language and the making of presence within the paper it is printed on. In "The Author to Her Book," the poem we turn to next, Bradstreet makes apparent that the diapering and dressing of a child with cloth is prelude to the making of a book from rags.

Anne Bradstreet's "Raggs"

If, as the story goes, Anne Bradstreet had no knowledge of the 1650 London publication of her poetry in printed book form as *The Tenth Muse, Lately Sprung Up in America*, then the often-imagined moment of her first introduction to the book would have been filled with great surprise. Elizabeth Wade White imagines that "when the little book of her own poems . . . was put into her hands," it was "the most dramatic moment of Anne Bradstreet's not uneventful life."[11] Literary historians have exhibited a certain fascination with the potential meanings and purposes of the publication of *The Tenth Muse*, the first published book of poems by an "American woman." Did her family need to demonstrate that its women were properly pious in the wake of the public preaching and subsequent divorce of younger sister Sarah Dudley Keayne?[12] Was the moment of publication an occasion for fear of being either publicly chastised for her writing, as Anne Yale Hopkins was, or publicly tried, shamed, and exiled like Anne Hutchinson? Was publishing her work an act of betrayal or even appropriative violence carried out by men who felt they had license to do with her intellectual property what they pleased?

Whatever else happened or did not happen in that moment of discovery, we can be certain that Bradstreet was presented with a book printed on paper. Though we cannot recover with certainty what that dramatic moment meant to its poet, Bradstreet later wrote "The Author to Her Book," a poem that provides a version of her reaction to, and reflection on, the event. In this poem, she exhibits a great deal of technical knowledge of the book's material text, including about how its paper was made. Her knowledge of papermaking is an essential part of her construction of the poem's central metaphor of the book as child. In the poem's first eight lines, she writes:

> Thou ill-form'd offspring of my feeble brain,
> Who after birth did'st by my side remain,
> Til snatcht from thence by friends, less wise than true
> Who thee abroad, expos'd to publick view,
> Made thee in raggs, halting to th' press to trudge
> Where errors were not lessened (all may judg).
> At thy return my blushing was not small,
> My rambling brat (in print) should mother call.[13]

Bradstreet's critics have tended not to consider how her technical knowledge of the object set before her may have contributed to her reaction to the book. As a result, interpretations of the poem have preserved a surprised and ignorant Bradstreet. To the contrary, she knew how books were made and understood her role in bookmaking in more than one dimension. In fact, despite the book's careful defense against the possible improprieties of being a published woman, "The Author to Her Book" signals that Bradstreet saw rag paper as a site of women's presence in all print and writing on paper.

Use of the book-as-brainchild trope was not unique to Bradstreet's "The Author to Her Book"; early modern writers, women especially, had already developed the metaphor. What is original to Bradstreet is how she turns to the technical language of papermaking in the fifth line. Here she unites the metaphor's tenor and its vehicle (book and child respectively) together in the same object: "raggs."[14] In citing paper's rag content, Bradstreet argues that this book object combines the child, parenting, and authorship. Rags and children introduce the language of the domestic into the poem and signal the literal continuity of domestic work and print publicity. The very rags that clothe the child and wipe its face become the rags that constitute the paper underlying writing and print.

Observing the material continuity that links domestic labor to print authorship collapses the distance between the public and the private. John Winthrop had already articulated a separate spheres ideology in colonial New England when he sought to keep separate "household affairs . . . as belong to women" from "things as are proper for men, whose minds are stronger." These words of Winthrop's come from his discussion of Anne Hopkins in his journal, where he notes that Hopkins had "fallen into a sad infirmary . . . by occasion of her giving herself wholly to reading and writing" and had "written many books."[15] For Bradstreet, rags unsettle the opposition between the needle and the pen, private women's work and men's public life, and biological reproduction and artistic production.

According to John Bidwell, paper "almost never impinges on [the] communicative function" of books. It ought to serve "as a mute vehicle of text, rarely noticed except when it fails its purpose, when defects inherent in its manufacture impede the transmission and preservation of printed information." Bidwell's description of the encounter with paper is indicative of common practice but incongruous with Bradstreet's description of paper and her figurative use of it in her poetry. In "The Author to Her Book," Bradstreet consistently points to the defected, malformed, and blemished nature of the ragged object of her address. She draws the reader's attention to the textures of the plane of communication, to highlight not the manifest failures of paper but the significant material of its constitution. Reading Bradstreet's "raggs" in all their suggestiveness is essential for understanding how, in one of her most frequently read and taught poems, the poet confronts the gendered distinction between the work of needles and pens and of all the constrictions apparently warranted by that division.[16] But while much has been said about how the poem engages questions of motherhood and authorship, little has been made of how these are theorized within the object of the rag paper book.

"The Author to Her Book" has assumed a central importance in writing about Bradstreet because the poem offers a window into the poet's thoughts about, and reactions to, the social regime of gender and writing in Massachusetts Bay Colony. Bradstreet juxtaposes artistic production and biological reproduction in a construction of metaphorical equivalence between book and child. Because she also references the specific circumstances under which *The Tenth Muse* was printed, the poem has special significance as an expression of Bradstreet's negotiation of her position as both a pious Puritan woman and a published woman in public. Feminist critics, in particular, have been interested in Bradstreet's figuration of the literary text as a child. In discussing the poem in her book on self-representation in lyric poetry of the colonial period, Ivy Schweitzer succinctly outlines the general debate over the meaning of the trope. The "double-edged metaphor of motherhood" allows Bradstreet either to "subversively [reconnect] what patriarchal culture severs: woman's body and her brain," or on the other hand, it "put[s her] back into the place that, according to Governor Winthrop, God had set her," that of the "satisfied child-bearer."[17]

Those who assume that Bradstreet in some way resigns herself to the role of motherhood tend to read "The Author to Her Book" as a pivot between the elegies, quaternions, and histories of *The Tenth Muse* and her later poems about domestic life in Massachusetts. Representative of this line of argument is Timothy Sweet, who views Bradstreet's work following "The Author to Her Book" as having been "written within a discourse of domesticity . . . display[ing] an acceptance of the 'woman's place.'" Sweet praises Bradstreet's early work for "demonstrat[ing] that subjectivity could . . . be detached from the gender assigned to the poet" but laments that her later adoption of the position of mother-author constrained her to the writing of "domestic poems" that " merely reproduced the ideology of social discourse which reifies gender."[18] In a similar fashion, one critic has contended that Bradstreet's poetry can be easily divided by period and quality according to her gendered voices: "the public voice is imitative, the private voice original." According to this view, the difference in voice between Bradstreet in *The Tenth Muse* and Bradstreet as motherly domestic lyricist evidences that she "never fully resolved for herself the conflict between what she considered to be her principal vocations as housewife and mother and her role as a poet."[19]

More recent critics, however, have sought to disassociate Bradstreet's use of motherhood from an act of simple capitulation to social norms or as evidence of her settling into easier, more topically appropriate forms. These scholars historicize the childbirth metaphor and argue that Bradstreet's use of motherhood keeps her within the realm of acceptable Puritan discourse while granting her the leverage to explore subversive aspects of the connection between creative production and human reproduction. Jean Marie Lutes, for example, "assumes that physical experience is itself discursive" and thus that Bradstreet's exploration of childbirth and authorship does not signify acceptance of an externally defined role but rather represents her "active engagement with doctrines designed to *create* authentic versions of female physicality."[20] According to this view, motherhood, the female body, and creation are not assumed to be stable categories within which Bradstreet presents herself but are investigated as contingencies of her social world, a symbolic order that she opens for exploration. While Puritan men used their linked religious and political influence to define and interpret which female bodies and bodily uses were proper, Bradstreet used her writing to renegotiate the terms of the dominant ideologies of "theology and gynecology." Instead of reading Bradstreet's metaphorical motherhood as a return to a traditional role, Lutes argues that the poet "uses medical and spiritual principles of generation to connect her physical reproduction to poetic reproduction, acknowledging the potential risks while also declaring the power of her own imagination." In this way, the child of Bradstreet's "The Author to Her Book" is "a metaphor for power and constructing a female body that could legitimately produce not only children but ideas as well."[21]

In similar fashion, Bethany Reid historicizes the poem's child metaphor. She finds in the child's illegitimacy and deformity the establishment of allegiance between Bradstreet and Anne Hutchinson, disrupting readings that make Bradstreet and Hutchinson representative Puritan women only to set them in contrast. Citing the history of Hutchinson's miscarriages and the use of them as confirmation, and a physical manifestation, of her heresies, Reid argues that through the image of an "ill-form'd offspring," Bradstreet "enters a female discourse that extend[s] well beyond womanly fears of childbirth to embrace charges of illegitimacy not unlike those leveled at Anne Hutchinson." "Discrete and playful" where Hutchinson was "direct and defiant," Bradstreet places herself in proximity to Hutchinson to question the contours of the power structure that determined the legitimacy of a woman's thoughts and actions.[22] In this way, Reid, like Lutes, usefully contextualizes Bradstreet's deployment of the trope of motherhood. Both critics convincingly read motherhood for its potentially subversive registers, not simply as an expected performance of, or capitulation to, motherhood as the pursuit more acceptable than writing for a Puritan woman.

Though they differ on the significance of motherhood and creativity in "The Author to Her Book," taken together, the readings offered by Sweet, Kenneth Requa, Lutes, and Reid demonstrate the extent to which the book, the very object of the poet's apostrophe, has fallen from attention. The status of the book in Bradstreet's poem is deserving of the kind of contextualizing performed by Lutes and Reid in the service of the child imagery. This has not happened even though, as I will show, a reading of the book is, in fact, consonant with the work of these two critics, who find serious questioning of social order in Bradstreet's use of metaphor. This is a particularly interesting trend in the study of a metaphor because it neglects the book—the object of comparison, the tenor of the metaphor—at the expense of the figure in its service, the child—the vehicle. Even when the important connection between rag and rag paper is made, as in Marjorie Garber's brief treatment of the poem, it attains the status of the unproblematic identification of one-to-one reference without deeper resonance, for, as she has it, "the phrase 'even feet' denotes 'regular metrics,' the 'rags' suggest rag paper, and so forth." When Bradstreet referred to her "rambling brat (in print)," however, she was not simply substituting the image of the book for the more interesting one of the child.[23]

Despite the fact that she represented her work as a *book*, there is a tendency to discuss "The Author to Her Book" as if Bradstreet easily could have titled the poem "The Author to Her Work," or "The Author to Her Writing." It is as if, in this critical tradition, all literary pursuits could be represented by the signifier *book*. To the contrary, in the mid-seventeenth century there were many other more likely forms in which Bradstreet's writing would have been expected to appear, including authors' manuscripts and manuscripts circulated in a coterie.

"The Author to Her Book" is intriguing because Bradstreet reflects on her singular status as a *published* woman, permanently set on public view in Massachusetts Bay Colony, London, and elsewhere abroad. "Anonymity and manuscript publication [in a coterie], were employed both by men and women, and writers of both genders voiced the fear of being exposed in public," writes David Hall.[24] Why, then, has so little attention been given to the status of the printed book in the poem? Attending to the way Bradstreet locates herself within the emergent technologies of the book trade focuses the reader on the poet's engagement with questions of gender and authorship. Foregrounding the materiality of the book in her address provides not merely a historical account of the circumstances under which her poems were produced and circulated but, more interesting, also demonstrates how Bradstreet constructs the book as a discursive object that challenges the gendering of authorship as masculine.

The Tenth Muse itself is framed by questions of gender and authorship, an inescapable fact foregrounded by the text's fascinating array of approving prefatory paratexts.[25] In one of the testimonials written by male relatives and friends of the family, readers are assured, for example, that Bradstreet wrote in "some few hours, curtailed from her sleep, and other refreshments."[26] The paratextual preface was designed to mediate Bradstreet's introduction to the public. Critics have speculated on the range of possible meanings and effects of the seven men whose voices, they felt, were necessary to delicately mediate Bradstreet's incursion into the world of print. The "story . . . told in the pages of prefatory material," writes Schweitzer, introduces a version of Bradstreet "into the public world where she dared not stray alone." Before a reader encounters Bradstreet's words, *The Tenth Muse*'s paratextual supports produce a pious woman whose role in the production of literature is nearly reduced to accident. Schweitzer suggests that these "adorn[ments]" at the opening of *The Tenth Muse* also "obscure it from view."[27]

If *The Tenth Muse*'s paratexts attempt to present Bradstreet's authorship as dependent on the testimony of men for its ability to circulate freely, then in "The Author to Her Book" she dislodges their claims by insisting on her book's location in a complex of material relations that escape the authority of any group of men. In "The Author to Her Book," rag paper and the animation of the scene of *The Tenth Muse*'s printing in London both call to mind the interdependence of the colony on England—and even of England on other nations. Bradstreet, who at first appears as a meek woman with a global mechanism of print at work on her, decentralizes the position of power assumed by approving men prefacing her book; they, too, are situated within widening circles of interdependence represented in the print trades.

Simply pointing to the fact that her book's existence depended on a complex transatlantic mechanism, however, is not the only way in which Bradstreet's poem challenges the notion of a hierarchical male-dominated print sphere. In the fifth line, Bradstreet's poetic production, her manuscript sheaf of poems figured as an " ill-form'd offspring," is first associated with the *book* of the poem's title when that brainchild is clothed in "raggs."[28] Bradstreet strengthens the relationship between the child and the book by pointing to common material, rags, in addition to shared parentage. "Rag" brings to mind the image of the malformed, bratty, ill-groomed child. Citing several seventeenth-century references, the *Oxford English Dictionary* tells us that "ragamuffin," noun and adjective respectively, indicates "a ragged, dirty, disreputable man or boy" or something that is "rough, beggarly, good-for-nothing, disorderly."[29] Certainly, these senses of the word have been important in common interpretations of the poem. As Winthrop and others would have it, reading and writing leads to bad mothering and so leads to children in rags. Yet, the rag is the point at which the cloth dressing the child and the cloth dressing/constituting the book are sutured together. Although a child can be "made" in rags as far as "to make" signifies "to dress," the book, the poem's object of address, is even more literally made of rags.

Though the technology for making paper was relatively unchanged from the fourteenth century through the eighteenth, the infrastructure of paper manufacture in Europe and its colonies did not develop evenly. Before the discovery and widespread use of wood pulp for paper production in the nineteenth century, the industry was volatile and subject to supply shortages, international trade negotiations, and changes in local conditions. There were no paper mills in the North American colonies during Bradstreet's life-time. The first North American mill was established in Philadelphia in 1690, but papermaking would not reach Bradstreet's Massachusetts until 1729.[30] The situation was not much better in Bradstreet's homeland. Seventeenth-century English papermaking was slowed by a lack of rags, especially for the production of print-quality white paper. According to Philip Gaskell, "Practically all the white paper used by English printers up to 1670 came from foreign mills, and much the great part of it from France, especially Normandy. There were indeed a good many mills working in England from the later sixteenth century, but they suffered from the lack both of skilled workmen and of a regular supply of linen rags (English people wore wool not linen), and with few and unimportant exceptions, they made brown paper, not white. Foreign paper continued to supply the greater part of the English market during the last quarter of the seventeenth century and the first quarter of the eighteenth, but now it came chiefly from Holland, either from Dutch mills, or from French mills trading through Dutch ports." By calling attention to the conditions of the production of her book, Bradstreet goes beyond simply reiterating the dependence of colonists on European printers for the majority of printed material they used. By citing rags, she also points to the complex trade of manufactured paper that for England meant a great deal of contingency and dependence on other nations to maintain a strong national print media. England's dependence on and vulnerability to bordering European states was a familiar one in Bradstreet's poetry. In "A Dialogue between Old England and New," which was also published in *The Tenth Muse*, Bradstreet, positioning New England as the daughter of England the mother, questions "Old England" about the potential unkind influences of "Forreign ayde." The possible reasons for Old England's ailments include treasonous barons and dukes receiving assistance from other countries, England's "allye, fair *France*" conspiring against her, and "*Holland* quit[ting]" her favor. Though Old England responds that "forraigne Foe, nor fained friend I feare," including France, there is still some question about Holland: "What *Holland* is, I am in some suspence."[31] This is not to suggest that Bradstreet's engagement with England's dependence on other nations is the same across both "A Dialogue between Old England and New" and "The Author to Her Book" but rather to point out that one of the poet's concerns was England's internal stability and the nature of its relationships with bordering states.

Bradstreet and her contemporaries knew the ingredients of paper and their significance, and her contemporaries encountered *The Tenth Muse* within this frame of the Protestant Atlantic book trade.[32] The object clothed in rags to which the poet speaks would have been made of rags owing to these very mechanisms and flows of supply. Like the child of uncertain paternity, the book itself was a physical manifestation of an unseen, indeterminate blending of liquified materials in the manufacture of an object whose "mother's" contribution was clear but whose "father" was disparate and foreign. In a single copy of that book, one held the writing of a woman from Massachusetts Bay Colony, presswork from London, paper from Holland or France, and countless mixed rag remnants from shops and households all over Europe.

Bradstreet certainly was aware of the composition of paper, as her use of the word "rags" shows, and I have offered a picture of the global issues surrounding rag production in her world so as to suggest what important connotations could reasonably be expected to have accrued to her use of the word. As a poet, Bradstreet's use of a word in a powerfully complex metaphor of book as child held together by the common factor of rags cannot be reduced to commodity history. Metaphors and paper are both devices for reading, and although metaphors are read for their rhetorical effects, paper seldom is. Bradstreet's "raggs" ground the mingling of material object and discursive text, one that often escapes contemporary scholars but was perhaps more readily perceptible by early moderns. Margreta de Grazia and Peter Stallybrass write of scholars who assume that "the clean and familiar textual surface allows reading to proceed unencumbered past matter and into the heart of the matter—into Shakespeare's 'meaning.'" The metaphysics of reading commonly dictate that meaning must reside in words on the page, not in the page itself. "The standard edition," they continue, "thereby promotes a binarism between surface and depth in which the former leads to the latter. . . . No less than depth, surface is locked into the dichotomy of outer/inner, form/content, appearance/reality. Perhaps a more helpful way of conceptualizing the text is to be found outside metaphysics, in the materials of the physical book itself: in paper." Whatever meaning might be found in the "metaphysics" of a text, de Grazia and Stallybrass, like Bradstreet before them, remind us that "any Renaissance book . . . is a provisional state in the circulation of matter."[33] These meanings are not available as long as the dichotomies of surface/depth, form/content, or body/soul are the structuring frameworks of the encounter with literature. Bradstreet's interest in the book made of rags indicates that she gave great attention to the presence of the book, to the rags contained within the page. She turns to metaphor, interpretation, and metaphysics to make an argument about paper, gender, and writing in the emergent publics of print in which she found herself. But the critical moves she makes in this moment are lost if we critics ignore the presence effects of paper in favor of our tendency to privilege the interpretation of what is written on paper.

There are suggestions in Bradstreet's work that she did not assume the Cartesian model wherein the function of paper is likened to the function of the body: the accidental carrier of the essential soul. When Bradstreet mentions the surface of writing, she speaks of inscribing herself into it. When she is writing to her children she refers to the physical book or paper on which she is writing as her worldly representation after death. In "To my dear children" she writes:

> This Book by Any yet unread,
> I leave for you when I am dead,
> That being gone, here you may find
> What was your living mothers mind.
> Make use of what I leave in Love
> And God shall blesse you from above.[34]

More than words, ideas, or text, Bradstreet explicitly chooses "This Book," the one which she had contact with, the very paper with which she interacts, as she writes to her children both in this world and from beyond the grave. Her deictics point to *this* book, *these* sheets of paper upon which her eyes fell and her hands moved. She ascribes to a specific book of writing paper the ability to contain her mind, to carry the physical trace of herself through time to her children. The physical paper is invested with the body of the mother whom it carries into the future. The transactions between the author of the these poems and their intended readers, the children, are not accomplished through the words alone but also include Bradstreet's presence carried in the objects of writing and reading. In addition, the commonsense framework that assigns the status of mere surface to paper—that surface is to depth as paper is to writing—is displaced as the ink and her tears absorb into the paper. De Grazia and Stallybrass point to this "crucial quality of paper" that "eludes . . . dichotomy. Only because of its absorbency is paper permeable by the black spots of ink."[35] In Bradstreet's poem her body is absorbed into paper, written *into* paper in such a way that demands a new way of reading. In these poems Bradstreet refers to a commonplace book in which she wrote by hand and would have expected her children to read from the same physical book. *The Tenth Muse* is different because of its manufacture and public nature, but these two poems show that she approached paper as much more than a passive surface, giving us reason to ask what about the printed page of *The Tenth Muse* led her to represent it as a child in rags.

Like "The Author to Her Book," "To my dear children" is concerned with birth, reproduction, writing, and the material forms of communication. In both, Bradstreet the mother addresses her literal and figurative children, discussing the ways in which she relates to them and cares for them via processes involving writing, books, and paper. These later, personal lyrics illustrate Bradstreet's willingness to ascribe to paper something of a material memory or the ability to carry her presence into the future. "The Author to Her Book" says something about the life of paper after Bradstreet's death too. The poem was found among others in her effects—her papers, we might say—which were arranged, collected with edited poems from *The Tenth Muse*, and issued posthumously in a new Bradstreet volume. "The Author to Her Book" was given priority of place as the first of the section of new poems in this 1678 edition.

Unlike the two poems addressed to her children, however, "The Author to Her Book" looks backward to 1650 and refers not to the paper on which her hand moves but to the paper on which *The Tenth Muse* was printed. This is an important difference, because not all acts of writing carried the same meaning in her seventeenth-century Puritan community. A women writing in manuscript to her children was one thing, but, as she writes in "The Prologue" to *The Tenth Muse*," publishing a book of poems that "sing[s] of Wars, of Captaines, and of Kings" was likely to be considered "too superior" for her; as in the case of Anne Yale Hopkins, it was an act with social consequences.[36] With a fuller sense of the meanings of books and paper in Bradstreet's world, I now want to return to the questions about gender and print publication that "The Author to Her Book" so provocatively poses.

Earlier, I took Bradstreet's reference to rag paper and placed it in its book historical context to understand the relationship she carefully develops between the rags on the child's back, the raggedness of the child's nature, and the rags constituting the paper object of *The Tenth Muse* in front of her. The rags used for paper production were, in fact, culled from old linen textiles in all their forms: clothes, undergarments, and bedsheets are just three common sources. "In the sheets of a book, bedsheets began a new life," write de Grazia and Stallybrass.[37] In "The Author to Her Book," Bradstreet relocates and retemporalizes the complex global exchange in rags and paper. The great time and distance traversed by the sheet of rag paper is suddenly localized, as the cloth used to care for the child functions at the same time as the cloth within paper. In the poem, the ways in which women work with textiles demonstrate various sources of rags for paper. She mentions washing the child's face:

> Thy blemishes amend, if so I could:
> I wash'd thy face, but more defects I saw
> And rubbing off a spot, still made a flaw.

These lines continue the dialectical turning of rags into paper and back again as Bradstreet, without warning, shifts registers between child and book. The very rags with which she washes the child's face would have gone to the rag collectors and eventually made their way into the paper mills. Linen rags, textiles, cloth, and clothing pertained to the labors of women, especially the work of caring for family and children. Having suggested the economics of rag paper, Bradstreet also explores where those pieces of cloth originate: in the hands of women. If the reference to cloth in face washing is oblique, she returns in the next few lines to an explicit exploration of the cloth-related duties of the wife and mother:

> In better dress to trim thee was my mind,
> But nought save home-spun Cloth, I' th' house I find.
> In this array 'mongst Vulgars mayst thou roam.[38]

Here the language of cloth sustains images of both the child and the book. Bradstreet the mother wishes that she were able to provide better clothes for the child. It's ill-dress contributes to the sense of the child's illegitimacy, its vulgarity, its status as ragamuffin. Bradstreet means these images to reflect on her ability as a mother, perhaps to play to expectations of those like Winthrop, who associated the woman writer with the bad wife and mother. She sends her book, such as it is, out into the world of book circulation to "roam" indiscriminately among texts high and low—the promiscuity of public life from which women were supposed to abstain.

And what would drive her to express anxiety over her capability to properly clothe the book? Perhaps Bradstreet's ability to "trim" the book is limited by the lack of presses and supplies in Massachusetts, forcing the production abroad. Such a possibility supports the idea that this poem uses connotations of the book trade to shift the structural position of feminized dependency away from her person as a woman writer and instead to the relationships at the heart of papermaking. We know that English printers, by necessity, looked outward for their supply of white paper because, as Gaskell tells us, the majority of their domestic cloth was wool not linen. The line "nought save home-spun Cloth, I' th' house I find," applies equally to English papermakers as it does to the mother addressing her child: both are limited in their ability to provide the right kinds of cloth for their purposes.

It is also worth remembering that clothing and textiles carried significant meaning in the sixteenth and seventeenth centuries. Ann Rosalind Jones and Peter Stallybrass have produced extensive documentation of the ways in which Renaissance "clothing...reminds," to borrow their stimulating phrase. Jones and Stallybrass's reading of early modern textile and clothing is analogous to how I have interpreted Bradstreet's seventeenth-century understanding of paper: textiles carry material memory, a memory that Bradstreet wants to recall in the very pages of books. Just as Bradstreet's paper could facilitate proximity and interpersonal relationships through time and distance, Jones and Stallybrass see in clothing "a world of social relations put upon the wearer's body."[39] Bradstreet's co-placement of the ragamuffin and the rag paper book should encourage us to read the world of paper as one more set of social relationships at work on the surface of the wearer's body. By pointing to the continuity of the rags used to wipe or clothe a child and the rags that constitute paper, Bradstreet suggests that the paper in her book carries the social relationships of the cloth forms that preceded it. The book is the child in an abstract metaphorical sense, but it is through that metaphor that the reader begins to see that the cloth of child-rearing literally *is* the book. We can understand this by looking at the ways in which people in the sixteenth and seventeenth centuries ascribed to objects like cloth and paper the ability to carry material memory, or we can think more practically about the stains a child leaves on the rags used to care for it. Like Bradstreet's salty tears, the bodily fluids deposited into cloth from face scrubbing, diapering, or wound dressing were carried to the paper-mills as remnants of domestic labor, where they became the matter of paper.

In the moment that Bradstreet unites the book and the child, authorship and motherhood, she draws attention to the material linkages between the two in the presence of paper. In paper are rags serving as connective tissue between biological reproduction and textual production, which is even more apparent when one holds an original copy of *The Tenth Muse* or any seventeenth-century book. One finds large pieces of rag that were not fully shredded into pulp. Figure 4, for example, shows page 172 of the Library of Congress's copy of *The Tenth Muse* held up to light. A large piece of rag can be seen and felt within the page. Since this shred was not completely reduced to pulp, it is an obvious sign of the material past of the pages onto which *The Tenth Muse* was "made . . . in raggs." Here, the presence of the rag is apparent and inserts itself into the visual and haptic world of the reader. This page fails to perform the disappearing act that is normally demanded of paper. It does not recede silently behind text. It prompts the reader to engage the text with the finger in addition to the eye, perhaps even to look at it differently by holding it to the light—to look into the page rather than at its surface alone.[40]

I. A. Richards described metaphor as the comparison of vehicle and tenor that when placed together make a deeper meaning available in the relationship between the two. This operation is at work in Bradstreet's book-child metaphor. In the moment when tenor and vehicle are coeval in the material of rags, the reader is faced with a literary object that is at the same time a domestic object, a realization that undoes the gendering of print publication as male. This amounts to nothing less than a deconstruction of the binaries of needle-pen and textile-text that structure the gendered division of creative and intellectual labors, a division that Bradstreet bristled against in "The Prologue" in *The Tenth Muse*.

Winthrop's treatment of Anne Hopkins is again useful to illustrate how these divisions permeated the perception of daily life and work in Bradstreet's

So many Princes ſtill were murthered,
The Royall blood was quite extinguiſhed
That *Tygranes* the great *Armenian* King,
To take the government was called in,
Him *Lucullus*, the *Romane* Generall
Vanquiſh'd in fight, and took thoſe kingdomes
Of *Greece*, and *Syria* thus the rule did end,
In *Egypt* now a little time we'l ſpend,
Firſt *Ptolomy* being dead, his famous ſon,
Cal'd *Philadelphus*, next ſat on the throne,
The Library at *Alexandria* built,
With ſeven hundred thouſand volumes fill'd
The ſeventy two interpreters did ſeek,
They might tranſlate the Bible into *Greek*,
His ſon was *Evergetes* the laſt Prince,
That valour ſhew'd, vertue or excellence,
Philopater was *Evergete's* ſon,
After *Epiphanes*, ſat on the Throne,
Philometer: then *Evergetes* again,
And next to him, did falſe *Lathurus* reigne,
Alexander, then *Lathurus* in's ſtead,
Next *Auletes*, who cut off *Pompey's* head

Massachusetts. If, instead of reading and writing books, "she had attended to her household affairs, and such things as belong to women, and not gone out of her way and calling to meddle in such things as are proper for men, whose minds are stronger, etc., she had kept her wits, and might have improved them usefully in the place that God had set her."[41] Winthrop's phrases delineate the domestic space of women and the intellectual space of men. In "The Prologue," Bradstreet represents "household affairs" and "such things as are proper for men" in the familiar opposition between the needle and the pen. There she expects to be chastised by her community and told that in her hand "a needle better fits" than a "Poets Pen."[42] The symbolic separate spheres of needles and pens had a long history by the time Bradstreet seized on it to preempt her critics. "Text after text throughout [early modern] Europe," write Jones and Stallybrass, "insisted on the division of these two kinds of labor: the useful industry of the private woman could save her from aspiring to the dangerous self-display of the woman in print." But, they say, even as "conservative gender politics" opposed chaste textile work to the shameful example of Sappho, the art of the needle exceeded the frameworks into which it had been conscripted. "The needle could *be* a pen" as "new technical practices opened up unpredictable possibilities for the design and display of textile work of women."[43]

Even as Bradstreet chafes against the distancing of needle from pen, women's textile work had already disrupted "any clear distinction between public and private, inner and outer spaces" in the practice of English needlewomen. Clothing, bed linens, and furniture, for example, were embellished with what are identifiably narrative forms. These textiles were also the spaces of political expression during Bradstreet's life. During the English Civil War, needlewomen stitched caterpillars, butterflies, and peacocks (Royalist symbols) into the objects surrounding them, including mirror frames and caskets, in addition to elaborate narrative panels. In "The Prologue," Bradstreet expects that her contemporaries will use the needle-pen division to insist on Bradstreet's proper place in the social structure, as a producer of proper housework, proper textile work. This is, of course, her representation of others' expectations. As a needlewoman using the same pattern books and producing needlework in the same contexts as explored by Jones and Stallybrass, the textile work she performed may have already resonated for her as one where "needlewomen clothed themselves, their intimate furnishings, and their public spaces with textiles that challenge any simple opposition between public and private, the domestic and the political, material labor and 'immaterial memory.'"[44] The textile work of the needle could already be understood as a narrative form, a literary object. Highlighting the fact that cloth lends itself as the material substrate of both stitching and printing, such a careful observer of the unequal gendering of objects and labors as Bradstreet could easily have seen the play of contradictions that inhere in the pages of *The Tenth Muse*.

Bradstreet's insistence that we be attentive to the presence of rags also raises an important question about the reception and history of women's art. The intricate textile work that women produced was categorized as lower, or decorative, art, and as such women artists were not considered producers of art worthy of inclusion in the pantheon of great artists and writers. "The Prologue" is rich with her awareness of this hierarchy of creative pursuits. But by reminding readers that the basis of paper is old textiles, she illustrates that such a hierarchy may indicate use value rather than inherent gender superiority. As art historian Ingrid Rowland writes, "If we have no Leonardos and Michelangelos from [the] embroidered world, it is partly because so many towels and handkerchiefs have worn to rags."[45] Rowland does not go on to say that those rags went on to live as paper, but Bradstreet certainly made that connection.

Bradstreet's "raggs" dissipate the discursive space between the bed linen and the book, the needle and the pen, the public and the private. Bradstreet's poetry shows that she understood paper as an object with a material memory—an object that carries past material worlds within it. If in "The Prologue" she entertains the range of possible protests against her work, chief among these the call that she remain in her domestic place, then in "The Author to Her Book" she rejects these by illustrating the undeniable constitutive link between a woman's "place" and the book. The worlds of domestic production, biological reproduction, and literary production are, contrary to the norms of her contemporaries, mutually inclusive. The textiles of women's domestic work, and in them the very traces of women's labor, she shows, are present in every act of entextualization, whether in the print production of *The Tenth Muse* or the work of her celebrated male contemporaries like Guillaume de Salluste Du Bartas.

"I've heard the veriest trifles have a voice": Lydia Sigourney's Cloth Poems

On September 7 and 8, 1859, Norwich, Connecticut, celebrated its bicentennial. Lydia Huntley Sigourney, by then near the end of her "half a century" as "America's leading poetess" and a resident of Norwich, wrote several poems for the event, one of which was printed on a broadside notice for the celebration (Fig. 5).[46] "Hymn. For the Bi-centennial Anniversary of the Settlement of Norwich, Conn.," one of the many occasional poems Sigourney wrote during her long career, praises God for the success of the town for its colonial settlement ("these cultured glades / Redeem'd from thorns and savage sway,—"); commerce and institutions ("the happy homes / The prosperous marts that thronging rise, / The peaceful academic domes,—/ The church-spires pointing to the skies"); and future ("as the past with joy is bright, / So may the unborn future prove,—").[47] The poem is set in the middle of the page, surrounded by advertisements for Manning, Perry & Co. steam book and job printers and the Chelsea Manufacturing [Paper] Company, which together published the daily *Norwich Morning Bulletin* and the weekly *Eastern Bulletin*, which are also advertised. Readers are directed to see the "*Morning Bulletin* of Thursday and Friday," which "will contain full reports of the . . . Celebration." The number of advertisements and layout of the broadside make the bicentennial seem like occasion not only for Sigourney's hymn but also to sell more newspapers, printing, and paper.

Closer inspection of the Chelsea Manufacturing Company advertisement reveals a rather strange claim about the broadside. Beneath the claim that it is "the largest paper manufactory in the world," the company informs the reader that "the material of which [this paper] is made was brought from Egypt. It was taken from the ancient tombs where it had been used in embalming mummies." The Chelsea mills were not the only firm to claim that their rags were from Egyptian mummies. Rags for papermaking were imported to the United States from Egypt for the first time in 1855, and by July 1856 the *Syracuse Daily Standard* claimed to have been printed on mummy paper: "Rags from Egypt.—Our daily is now printed on paper made from rags imported directly from the land of the Pharaohs, on the banks of the Nile. They were imported by Mr. G. W. Ryan, the veteran paper manufacturer at Marcellus Falls, in this country, and he thinks them quite as good as the general run of English and French rags."[48] In 1866, a minister told the editor of the *Bunker Hill Aurora* that he knew someone who had loaded a cargo ship headed for the

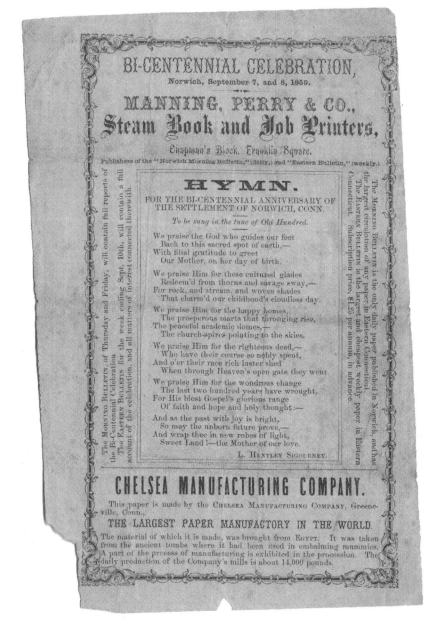

Figure 5. "Hymn. For the Bi-centennial Anniversary of the Settlement of Norwich, Conn.," broadside, 1859, Norwich, CT: Manning, Perry & Company. *Courtesy of the John Hay Library, Brown University Libraries.*

United States full of mummies. "On arriving here," we are told, "the strange cargo was sold to a paper manufacturer in Connecticut, who threw the whole mass, the linen cerement, the bitumen and the poor remains of humanity, into the hopper, and had them ground to powder. 'And,' added the speaker, 'the words I am now reading to you, are written on some of this paper.'"[49] Back in Norwich, the Chelsea mill invited locals to come see the process of turning mummies into paper and to marvel at their output: "Part of the process is exhibited in the premises. The daily production of the Company's mills is about 14,000 reams."[50] And since the paper, the mill claimed, was made of rags previously used in the "embalming of mummies," visitors who were not interested in papers mills per se might be enticed by the promise of proximity to the morbid and the exotic.

It is incredibly unlikely that paper was ever made from mummy wrappings in commercial U.S. mills, but the persistence of the myth—lasting as it does into the present—is telling. In the recent history *Mummies in Nineteenth Century America: Ancient Egyptians as Artifacts*, S. J. Wolfe takes the Sigourney bicentennial broadside and the Chelsea paper mills' assertion that its paper was made from mummies as prima facie evidence of the practice.[51] Among the skeptics, Joseph Dane notes that "references to mummy paper have much in common . . . they are vaguely documented or pure products of oral history" and often derive from secondhand accounts. The 1866 claim in the *Bunker Hill Aurora* is illustrative of the layers of hearsay behind these stories. "They have the aura of a Swiftian projection, based on real needs—the shortages of [rag] material," Dane notes. And they trade in supposed contact with the exotic, a tactic that, Dane reminds us, P. T. Barnum had perfected in the 1850s.[52] *This* newspaper that you're holding is made of mummies; *this* paper I'm reading is full of "the poor remains of humanity"; come to the Chelsea mills and see our impressive output for yourself—these deictic performances invite readers to experience the materiality of the text while reading. Or, if promising good reading doesn't sell a newspaper, perhaps the chance to touch the supposed remnants of a mummy will. At a time when the wealthy were actually purchasing mummies for "unwrapping parties" in their homes, newspapers and papermakers that claimed their product was made from mummy rags offered a more accessible promise of encountering a faraway land or transgressing social norms about disrupting graves and respecting the dead.

Frankly, whether paper was actually made from mummies matters less to me than the fact that readers everywhere were confronted with stories about the alleged mummy content of the paper they were holding. The *Syracuse Daily Standard* might fairly be accused of sensationalism in trying to sell newspapers, but its claims about mummy paper tell us something about sensation itself. Readers were receptive to enticements related to the material contents of paper. Discussions of the makeup of paper could be found almost anywhere, even on the promotional broadside for the town anniversary celebration. Readers could pick up a newspaper and be asked to think, as part of the reading experience, about where the newspaper's rags originated. The haptic experience of rag content was part of the everyday reading experience. Readers were called to think about not only what was printed or written on a page but also what was contained within it.

Bradstreet, as I have argued, sensed this too and appealed to readers' tangible sense of the page to reframe their thinking about women and print. Though the print and book trades were significantly larger and technologically different during Sigourney's life, rags were still the primary material in paper, and she, too, looked to this dimension of the page to argue against women's exclusion from the print public sphere. When she was composing and publishing three cloth paper poems (one each about linen, silk, and cotton) between 1833 and 1841, Lydia Sigourney had recently been commanded by her husband to "be less a poet and more a wife." Objecting to her increasing desire to publish and to engage in what he thought were secret dalliances with the literary men of Hartford, Connecticut, Charles Sigourney prepared an "appeal" to his wife after she requested a separation, which he, in turn, denied. In an 1837 letter he lists grievances against his wife:

> The ambition for literary distinction seems now to be occupying all your thoughts, & threatens to destroy your conjugal character . . . the apparently unconquerable passion of displaying yourself is the secret principle which of late influences your conduct. . . . It is not, my dear wife, that I have a decided objection to your writing, & improving the elegant accomplishments you possess. It is not that I object to your publishing what you write, provided it be in moderation, and . . . "like the Sun behind a cloud, *yourself unseen*." But I do object to the excess, & the abuse of this talent, the consequent *immoderate* desire of *constantly* appearing before the publick . . . which amounts, in fact, to a mental disease. . . . I do object, and it has given me great pains to see your name bandied about in the newspapers, & magazines . . . in the mouths of printers, & publishers, artists, & shop boys. . . . I do object that you sink the *woman*, & the *wife*, in *the writer*; that you appear to be more anxious, and better pleased to be known for your talents as an author, than for virtues as a wife, &

a mother. . . . Who wants, or would value, a wife, who is to be the publick property of the whole community?—She who *wishes to belong* to the *publick* never
should consent to be the private possession of any individual man.[53]

In Charles Sigourney's mind, writing was a fine talent and an adornment for
a woman, but the promiscuity of publication, combined with the increasing
professionalization of writing, disqualified a wife from her husband's full
possession.

This sense is reflected especially in his recoiling at the thought of printers
and publishers having an intimacy with her such that she is in their mouths,
an act that could be extended even to her anonymous readership voicing
her in their mouths. Charles Sigourney's appraisal of his wife's writing
is also marked by his fear of what Sandra Gilbert and Susan Gubar call the
ever-present potential "duplicity" of female authorship. Toril Moi's characterization of the masculine construction and fear of the duplicitous female
author seems relevant to Charles Sigourney's incomprehensibility of his
wife's creative mind. When her husband accuses her of having a "mental disease," it seems likely to be a product of his perception of her as a "duplicitous
woman . . . whose consciousness is opaque to man, whose mind will not let
itself be penetrated by the phallic probings of masculine thought."[54]

Despite his conventional understanding of her work, the poet and her husband did not reach a separation; nine months after he wrote the letter she bore
their first child to survive birth and two years later had another. She published
anonymously at first, and when she returned to working under her own name
(because her husband's business went into a slump and her name carried
value in the literary marketplace), she "pick[ed] up on the theme of her
husband's appeal" and published on "acceptably feminine subjects such as
education, moral reform, and female conduct."[55] It was in the feminized print
marketplace, however, that her work proved remarkably profitable while
allowing her to critique the personal and professional limits placed on her by
discourses of appropriate femininity.

One topic befitting the "virtues" of a wife and mother was cloth. Addressing silk, linen, and cotton in poetic apostrophe, however, also meant that
Sigourney's poems discussed the essential ingredients of papermaking
that good "ladies" who ran households were expected to collect. Sigourney's
cloth-to-paper poems are part of her larger project of linking the secular and
spiritual through appeals to the inner lives of both people and things.[56] More

specifically, cloth and paper link rather than separate the domestic and print public spheres. While still speaking from the "proper" terrain of the domestic, Sigourney used cloth's presence in both the home and the paper mill to explore how the public and the private were interrelated, as well as how the domestic and the literary were materially linked, challenging the partitions that circumscribed her.

The first poem in her cloth series, "To a Fragment of Silk," was published in the 1833 edition of the gift annual *The Token and Atlantic Souvenir: A Christmas and New Year's Present*. "To a Fragment of Silk" begins, as do all three cloth poems, with the speaker's notice of a piece of fabric lying out of place in an otherwise tidy household. "Well, radiant shred of silk, is it your choice, / Here on my carpet, thus at ease to lay?" The occasion of the poem is an interruption of the orderly domestic space; the speaker is one whose perception of her domestic environs ("my carpet") is so acute that the presence of a random silk strand sticks out.[57]

This interruption of the orderly domestic space immediately opens unto an expansive imaginative scene. The speaker addresses the object: "I've heard the veriest trifles have a voice / Unto the musing mind; what can you say?" It is not clear what is meant by the attribution of voice to this object. Does the silk speak; is it fully personified? Or, rather, does it present the speaker with the opportunity to engage in imaginative contemplation? In whatever manner it communicates, the silk inspires within the speaker's "musing mind" dreams of the exotic lands from which the silk has come: "You seem to wake a dream of southern bowers / Where sprang your rudiments, among Italian flowers." Like a novel or poem, the piece of cloth provides an occasion for the imaginative mind of the housewife to break from the confines of the home and its demand on her attention.[58]

The object does more than inspire romantic images of the Mediterranean— its specific material history is carried within. "Who were your ancestors?" the speaker asks. The silk replies and the speaker, surprised, repeats the answer so that the reader shares in the information: "What! those unsightly worms, with tireless maws, / And such a marvelous digestion?" The silk strand occasions a comparison between the worms that die in their "cone like urns" and "many a purblind dame" who work the "shuttle's toil." Both the worms and the women who turn silk into cloth on the looms suffer bodily harm to produce the "rainbow tinted tissue." In Sigourney's poems, cloth defies the logic of what Marx called the commodity fetish, ushering forth a narrative history of its material production.[59] We might recall that Marx's prime example in explaining the commodity fetish is "a coat and ten yards of linen" and that Sigourney's cloth poems (and the it-narratives to which they are related) predate Marx's *Capital* by thirty years. For Sigourney, this is an occasion to display both the artistry and the hardship of women's labor in an objet d'art that from a masculinist perspective appears, like women's work generally, to be the "veriest of trifles."[60]

Between the third and fourth stanzas, the poem shifts from exploring women's labor to juxtaposing the ways silk figures the public and private in the United States—or silk's "destiny in this New World." Silk is first imagined as part of the private, intimate lives of women young and old, who use it either as a "dazzling robe to make the young beauty vain" or "to hide time's ravage" of "some waning lady pranked and curled." The silk covers and uncovers women's bodies according to codes of beauty, adornment, and propriety, acting as a boundary that places the woman's body within and the public eye without. Along these lines, silk is imagined to grace "the bosom . . . with outward show doth swell," revealing as it conceals.[61] Here Sigourney's speaker interrupts the focus on women's work and women's bodies and turns radically to the world of business and finance, familiar industries to her as a resident of Hartford, Connecticut:

> Your history is not complete. Your second birth
>   is in bank-paper, to allure the eyes,
> Making the rich o'erprize the gifts of earth
> And the poor covet what his God denies:
> Man's vanity from a vile worm may grow,
> And paper puff his pride; go, gaudy fragment go![62]

Though Sigourney has used the natal image to hedge the sudden shift from the domestic and the decorative to the public and financial, the change is dramatic. What began as a noticeable mark in an otherwise clean and organized domestic space, and what seemed at first to represent women's work and women's dress, silk is, by the end of the poem, the catalyst of a critique of "Man's vanity." Certainly, the capitalization of "Man" could indicate that Sigourney means to speak of mankind in general, but it also marks a spatial and thematic shift from the domestic sphere to the public sphere that gives "Man's vanity" gendered significance.

In the choice of cloth for her subject matter, Sigourney mostly remains within properly defined feminine subject matter, but because cloth materially interpenetrates "spheres," it connects the "trifles" of women to the "vanities" of men. The link is established when the speaker sends the piece of silk to the paper mill: "go, gaudy fragment, go!" Sigourney uses this material connection as justification for a critique of the financial market's misvaluation of a piece of silk paper. Silk enwraps both the "dazzling . . . beauty" and the "allure[s] the eyes" of the investor, but she shows that at the same time it also dresses the "waning lady" and "puff[s]" the value of goods. In 1833, Sigourney's remarks about the potentially inflated value of paper money were probably occasioned by Andrew Jackson's withdrawal of all federal deposits from the Second Bank of the United States in September of that year, an act that crippled federal bank regulation and fueled speculation until the Panic of 1837 plunged the U.S. economy into a five-year depression.[63] Sigourney recognizes in silk a material connection between the private and public domains that allows her to maintain the propriety her husband wished while also momentarily venturing into the public discourse of economic critique.

Sigourney looked to linen, however, to argue for women's connection to the literary marketplace, answering her husband's objection that "you sink the *woman*, & the *wife*, in *the writer*," as if these were exclusive categories. As both a writer and keeper of what her husband called the "domestick fire," Sigourney, like Bradstreet, recognized that she was an important contributor to the processes of paper and textual production.[64] By tracing the "life" of a piece of linen, "To a Shred of Linen" highlights the irony of a situation in which women are chastised for engaging their imaginative literary faculties at the same time that they are called on to lend their labor to the production of paper. First appearing in the third edition of *Select Poems* in 1838, the poem also explores the theme of women's cloth-based public/private involvement while expanding Sigourney's reach to address women's authorship.[65]

Sigourney's "To a Shred of Linen" begins in the same manner as the silk poem. A housewife discovers an errant shred of cloth, except whereas the speaker's imagination immediately began to spin romantic images of the Mediterranean, now the occasion inspires a critical consciousness about the consequences of such readerly imagining. As Melissa Ladd Teed explains, "in 'To a Shred of Linen,' Sigourney observed that if a 'neat lady' had seen the scrap of cloth had escaped the speaker's housecleaning, that domestic critic would undoubtedly have admonished, 'this comes from reading books' or 'this comes of writing poetry.'" Teed identifies an important aspect of Sigourney's change in tone from the silk poem to the linen poem. "While the tone of the poem is playful," she says, "Sigourney raised in it an issue of central concern: that she risked public censure for writing if she failed to attend to her familiar responsibilities." Sigourney's method of dealing with this threat, however, was not simply to "walk the fine line between promoting her career" and passively "appearing not have any interest in doing so," as Teed suggests.[66] By offering an archaeology of the page in her poem, Sigourney's speaker answers the domestic critic's accusation that the intruding linen "comes from reading books" by actually demonstrating the inverse. Reading books comes from *this*, the shred of linen in a woman's home. Like "To a Fragment of Silk," "To a Shred of Linen" allegorizes the relationship between material, memory, and narration. The latter poem, however, is more focused on the category of the literary; unlike silk that was made into paper for bank notes, linen produced the finest paper for book production. Because of its well-known uses in both the domestic and the literary, linen provided Sigourney the material through which it was possible focus on the links between women and literary production, rather than the supposed necessary separation of the two.

Sigourney's characterization of the "littering shred" as "a vile reproach to all good housewifery" pertained to the gendered social expectations that constrained her own professional life, but it also alludes to the long history of female readers and poets (such as Anne Hopkins and Anne Bradstreet) having to answer to claims about their housewifery.[67] Linen refigures this commonly negative connection between housewifery and the literary, showing the domestic to be generative of the literary in *both* material and content. The "littering" is resignified as the literary.

Like Richard Frame's "Pennsilvania" papermaking poem, "To a Shred of Linen" retreats in time and space back to the flax fields. "Resolve thyself into thine elements," the speaker commands the shred. "I see the stalk and bright blue flower of flax. . . . I see thy bloom tinging . . . these New England vales." Sigourney again uses cloth production as an opportunity to discuss women's labor. The speaker imagines the flax farmer's wife, "with kerchiefed head, and eyes brimful of dust," combing the flax. Here again, working the fiber into cloth afflicts the eye, which might stand in for assumptions about women's ability to read and comprehend. Yet another woman works the flax into linen on the loom while her "rustic lover" sits by her side imagining how her labor will increase his worth: her "dextrous hand" will bear "many a keg and pot of butter to the market." He sits, she works, and Sigourney offers another reflective scene on the value women's labor relative to men's.[68] All the way back to the flax field, the loom, and the tattered garment, and, as we shall see, all the way to the paper mill and the book, women perform labor at all points along the life cycle of the flax, linen, and paper object.

What makes "To a Shred of Linen" stand out as a poem about the literary, however, is the way Sigourney describes the life of linen after it leaves the loom. The speaker's "thread of . . . discourse" turns to the scene of the domestic, and linen begins to read like a sentimental plot, set within the nineteenth-century middle-class home:

> Methinks I scan
> Some idiosyncrasy, that marks thee out
> A defunct pillow-case.—Did the trim guest,
> To best chamber usher'd, e'er admire
> The snowy whiteness of thy freshn'd youth
> Feeding thy vanity? or some sweet babe
> Pour its pure dream of innocence on thee?
> Say, hast thou listen'd to the sick one's moan,
> When there was none to comfort?—or shrunk back
> From the dire tossing of the proud man's brow?
> Or gather'd from young beauty's restless sigh
> A tale of untold love?[69]

The linen pillowcase absorbs the events that take place on and near it, from the dreams of children to the death throes of the sick. As a pillowcase, it bears witness to events that will emerge as narratives printed on the paper it will become. The cast of characters and scenes circulating around the pillow-case resemble some of the stock of sentimental narratives: finely appointed rooms, the distinguished houseguest, the innocent child, the sick and the dying, the prideful man, the sighing beauty, a hidden love. Resulting from its place in the home, the shred of linen is imagined to absorb the stories of the people who move around it. Linen becomes a container for stories, an object that can be "scanned," rather like a poem. It is threaded with discourse, plots are interwoven; Sigourney invites the reader to make as much use of these textile metaphors as possible.

In the poem's final stanza, the speaker finds the shred unsatisfactory in its current form. Unlike the fragment of silk which seemed to have the power of speech itself, the linen appears "mute." But this changes as the poem continues and the shred of linen becomes paper:

> Still, close and mute!—
> Will tell no secrets, ha?—Well then, go down,
> With all thy churl-kept hoard of curious lore,
> In majesty and mystery, go down
> Into the paper-mill, and from its jaws,
> Stainless and smooth, emerge.—Happy shall be
> The renovation, if on thy fair page
> Wisdom and truth, their hallowed lineaments
> Trace for posterity. So shall thine end
> Be better than thy birth, and worthier bard
> Thine apotheosis immortalize.[70]

Mill advertisements often described old linen as somehow deficient, thus ready to be sent to the mill and made new. The last stanza of "To a Shred of Linen" retains this structure at the point when Sigourney is most interested in shifting focus to the paper mills. For all we've heard from and about the linen, its muteness requires that it be sent away to the mills, only to return as a literary object.

As the poem closes, the linen does not, however, return as a popular novel that tells the stories pent up in the pillowcase. Sigourney, constrained by social expectations as the speaker fearing reprimand, cannot come out fully in praise of these literary forms. She modestly deflects any indication of her status as a poet, hoping that the linen emerges from the paper mill to receive the hallowed "wisdom and truth" of a "worthier bard" immortalized at his apotheosis. This imaginary representation of the literary market is the opposite of what Sigourney understood to be her market. She knew that the amount of paper being used to produce gift books, novels of sentiment and sensation, periodicals, and newspapers far outstripped the production of lofty tomes claiming to transmit immortal "wisdom and truth." In the 1830s, when linen was turned into paper for print production, it was most likely going to participate in the "carnival on the page" than in a fine volume.[71] It was, after all, in the vast world of commercial print where Sigourney's name was a valuable commodity.

If Sigourney couldn't openly celebrate the development of a literary marketplace in which women were robust producers and consumers of literary content, she could call on the familiar language of women as rag collectors and consumers of sentimental literature. The paper mill ad ensured that women were seen as essential gatherers of material for paper, and in these same ads they were promised sweet notes and interesting novels. Even if these ads pretended that "sighing beaus" would do all the writing, Sigourney shows in this poem that the subjects of popular literature are born in the home and borne to the mill by women. When the shred of linen appears at the beginning of the poem, it represents the speaker's fear of being found out as a reader and writer of poetry. By poem's end, however, that piece of linen represents the proliferation of literary material. She knew as well as we do that this desire for more paper and more reading material produced exactly the kinds of literature the home embedded in the shred of linen. Sigourney traced the production of paper from a feminist argument about the material culture of the literary public sphere. Like Bradstreet before her, Sigourney developed the public's sense of the contents of paper into an argument about the reliance of the masculine public sphere on the feminine private sphere for its very existence. By highlighting the materiality of the literary public sphere in their poetry, Bradstreet and Sigourney look to paper as a route linking domestic work and literary production.

Mediating Intimacy

In October 1970, the Dartmouth College Library recorded the accession of its one millionth volume, a copy of Bradstreet's 1650 *Tenth Muse Lately Sprung Up in America*. To celebrate this milestone, trustees of the college and friends of the library issued a copy of the Dartmouth *Tenth Muse* in ultrafiche, a type of microfiche in which the filmed images have been reduced in size by a factor of 100. Encased in a special commemorative box with a brief introduction, *The One-Millionth Volume of the Dartmouth College Library* reproduces the paper, type, and binding technologies of 1650 within the information technologies of the 1970s: compact, durable, and reproducible films. The move from paper to film alienates the rags within paper from the reader's touch and therefore removes the crossroad where Bradstreet located herself between domestic rags and public rag paper. The ultrafiche version of the book is a reminder that such textual surrogates as films or digital files replicate a version of alphabetic text while severing the reader from other contexts like touch, smell, or scale.

The Dartmouth *Tenth Muse*, however, contains annotations specific to this book copy that are remediated and transmitted in the films. In the otherwise

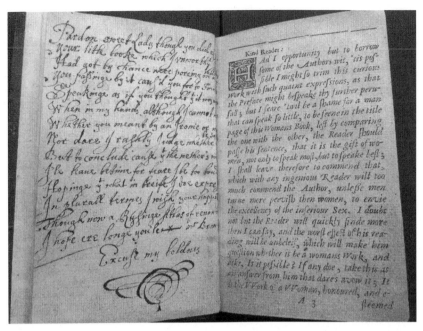

Figure 6. Verse inscription in Dartmouth College's copy of *The Tenth Muse Lately Sprung Up In America. Courtesy of Rauner Special Collections Library, Dartmouth College.*

blank endpapers before the licensing paratexts famously written by Bradstreet's male relations, a "Mr. Brown" left an amateur verse poem in his seventeenth-century hand (Fig. 6). The verse is addressed to a "sweet Lady," who has some claim to the "little booke." This woman happens upon Mr. Brown while he holds the book in hand. He reacts to the situation by writing in the endpapers. The verse reads:

> Pardon sweet Lady though you did espy
> your little booke which I unworthy
> Had got by chance were poreing on a while
> you passing by it caus'd you for to smile
> Speakinge as if you thought that it was so
> When in my hands, although I cannot know
> Whether you meant by an Ironie or no
> Nor dare I rashly Judge whether it be soe
> But to conclude cause that the wether's soul
> I'll leave betime for feare I be too foul

Hopinge that what in briefe I doe express
In plural termes I wish your happiness
Though now a Rysinge Atlas of renown
I hope ere long you'le Excuse my boldness
Mr. Brown[72]

The verse inscription is remarkable for its staging of the "boldness" that is pronounced in the space between a man, a woman, and "her book." The poem records a moment of intimacy between Mr. Brown and his interlocutor, an intimacy conducted through her book seen, unexpectedly, in his hands. It is as if he has transgressed a boundary and touched her by putting "your little booke . . . in my hands."

Provenance and other records are unhelpful in pinning down exactly who this particular Mr. Brown is. Neither do we know for sure who he addresses. Brown has, however, added his verse to the whole set of paratexts that serve as the threshold between the book's reader and its female author trying in various ways to negotiate the intimacy one gains with Bradstreet by taking her book in hand. At the very least, the verse inscription stages a personal encounter in which the intimacies of the book object occasion personal exchanges between a man and a woman. The fair lady spies her book in Mr. Brown's hand, and he is occupied by it. He "pores" over it. She smiles upon witnessing it "in [his] hands." Mr. Brown next moves literally to neuter the sexual possibilities of this encounter, saying he must move to conclusion with a "wether's soul," or the spirit of a castrated and thus less aggressive sheep. Despite figurative castration, Brown moves to end the conversation for fear of becoming "foul." The poem closes with a bold flourish of the pen under-lining his desire that she "excuse [his] boldness." What if we speculated that the poem is addressed to Bradstreet herself? She did have a "Rysinge Atlas of renown" after the publication of *The Tenth Muse*. If this is the case, then the inscription speaks to the fears about the promiscuity of print that led Bradstreet's male relatives and such others as Winthrop to be uneasy about a women's appearance in print. The book could be a conduit to possess and hold another person. That the trespass recorded within this particular book copy would be remediated through microfilming and distribution to librar-ies around the world multiplies attention to Mr. Brown's suggestive book cradling, while also divorcing readers from the paper that he touched and inscribed.

What Bradstreet and Sigourney knew is that every piece of paper occasions moments of intimacy and proximity to others. As women who worked with cloth in the home and published work that went out into the public sphere backed by rags, they understood that the private and public spheres were dissolved within the rag content of paper. Turning a page, one touched cast-off underclothes, bed linens, and cleaning rags. In a book by Bradstreet or Sigourney, one could gain intimate access to the minds of these women poets, but also intimate access to the rags hundreds of women kept in their kitchens. In holding her "little booke," Mr. Brown was not only intimate with his interlocutor, a female author or owner of a text, but also with many others whose rags and labor with them are embedded within the paper. Bradstreet and Sigourney embraced the intersection of private and public inherent within rag paper to trace a feminist genealogy of the book. Their accounts reveal that women were always already present in the print public sphere, and that without their private domestic labor, this sphere would have no material backing on which to circulate.

CHAPTER 3

THE
INEFFABLE SOCIALITIES OF RAGS IN
HENRY DAVID THOREAU AND
HERMAN MELVILLE

FOR THE CHRISTMAS season of 1966, the West Virginia Pulp and Paper Company published a special edition of Henry David Thoreau's 1854 book *A Week on the Concord and Merrimack Rivers*. The book was created for gift distribution to clients and others in the book trades. Adorned with marbling, full bleed printing, and copious engravings, this edition of *A Week* exists as much to advertise this paper company's products as it does to tell the story of Henry and John Thoreau's 1839 "fluvial excursion." The company offers it, according to its foreword, "in sharp contrast to the original edition of *A Week*, with its soporific expanses of type devoid of illustrations or visual relief of any kind." This Christmas offering was meant to "persuade the reader to savor Thoreau's words" while appreciating the West Virginia Pulp and Paper Company's products. "Selecting a natural shade of Pinnacle Book Offset in English finish for his text stock," the legendary book designer Bradbury Thompson meant to take advantage of the company's product and its "clarity and fidelity . . . [for] lithographic reproduction."[1] Since *A Week* takes its rhythms from the passing of day and night during Thoreau's trip, the designer and paper company take care to integrate the book's content and its form by including pages printed in black to signal the break in chapters at each night. "To denote the approach of night," each chapter closes with "two solid bleed pages of inky blackness, back to back, relieved only by the pin-point sparkle of stars in familiar galaxies." Before the text resumes with the next day, "the stirring of each day is . . . illustrated by three-page bleed spreads of crowing cocks and clucking hens, pensive squirrels, horses in the fields, croaking frogs, game birds, water rodents, and barking dogs."[2] Printing an entire page in crisp black bled to the very edge of its surface, leaving small bright stars to reveal the original white color of the paper, is a way of showing off what the product could do at the outer limit of paper's affordances. The book is a beautiful advertisement for high-quality paper and printing.

But given all the overt attention to its materiality, is this edition of *A Week* meant to function primarily as a marketable object? In the very pages of *A Week*, Thoreau criticizes everyone from publishers to papermakers for the devaluing of writing and thinking at the hands of market forces in bookmaking and selling. "Paper is cheap," Thoreau writes, "and authors need not now erase one book before they write another." By the mid-nineteenth century, paper had, in fact, become less expensive and easier to make given the introduction of steam mills, a global trade in rags, and advances in chemistry. Thoreau seized on these changing dynamics of the paper industry to bemoan the cheapening of thought and writing in an economic climate of fast print and high demand. "Books are for the most part willfully and hastily written, as parts of a system, to supply a want real or imagined."[3] Between the 1830s and the 1850s, the scale of papermaking had been vastly increased, and these technological and scalar shifts also changed the meaning and value of paper itself.

Traveling the waterways of New England in the mid-nineteenth century, Thoreau was navigating the terraqueous geography of industrial papermaking. New England's rivers were a source of power and water for many mill-based industries. As cities and industries grew around these rivers and mills, literary accounts of changes in labor and society proliferated between the 1850s and 1870s, including Rebecca Harding Davis's "Life in the Iron Mills," Lucy Larcom's "Weaving" and other "mill girl" poems, and Elizabeth Stuart Phelps's *The Silent Partner*. In *A Week*, Thoreau recounts paddling by mill sluices and having to navigate around artificial dams and falls erected to feed growing industry. Some writers, such as Thoreau and Herman Melville, wrote about the connection between their work as publishing writers and their embeddedness within the capital of U.S. papermaking in central and western Massachusetts. Having run out of writing paper in the process of drafting *Moby-Dick* in the winter of 1851, Melville recounts that he went directly to a nearby paper mill and "got a sleigh-load of . . . paper." "A great neighborhood for authors, you see, is Pittsfield," he wrote to his editor, Evert Duyckinck, emphasizing the relationship between prolific papermaking and prolific writing in Massachusetts.[4]

This chapter explores connections between the work of two canonical writers of the American renaissance, Henry David Thoreau and Herman Melville, and the technologies of papermaking among which they lived in Massachusetts. Both Thoreau and Melville were fascinated by what the latter called the "ineffable socialities" created by material texts and their circulation.[5] Earlier writing about rags and rag paper, like the examples studied in the preceding chapters, imagined intensely personal and localized intimacies within paper, dwelling in the possibility of knowing whose rags made up particular sheets of paper. By the 1850s, the stream-driven Fourdrinier paper machine made the scale of rag collection, papermaking, and printing many times larger. In a history of papermaking written during that same period, Joel Munsell remarked on the quickness with which the hand was replaced by the machine and how vastly the extent of papermaking increased: "In a little more than a quarter of a century, the machines have entirely superseded the diminutive hand-mills which sparsely dotted the country, and gigantic establishments have risen up in their places. Paper-mill villages, and banking institutions even, have grown out of this flourishing branch of industrial art, and we behold with satisfaction and amazement what has been brought about by the aid of a commodity so insignificant in the eyes of the world as linen and cotton rags."[6] The expansive growth of the U.S. paper industry in the 1850s was even a matter of great touristic interest for popular visiting writers from abroad. Writing for the popular English magazine, *Household Words*, Harriet Martineau reported that the U.S. paper industry was far larger than England's and that Americans throughout the country consumed unbelievable amounts of paper per person. "The great, the grand papermaker," observed Martineau, has a mill that "puffs and pants" and "covers large spaces of ground," with "machinery [that is] of the newest and best."[7]

During this period, writing about rag paper still shows fascination with the intimacies mediated by rags, but overall attention shifts toward questions about the mass mixing of rags and the mediation of raggy intimacy at very large scales. Living amongst these changes in the rag trade and papermaking industry, Thoreau and Melville address these scalar changes in their writing about paper during the 1850s. They explore how the rags within paper mediate meaning and intimacy during the rise and reign of the industrial book and society. In the midst of the mechanization of the print trades on which their livelihoods depended, Thoreau desired the direct experience of things, for rags instead of print, and Melville found within machine-made paper new forms of distributed erotic connections among people.

"That thin stratum": Of Experience and the Materiality of Print

The original publication of *A Week on the Concord and Merrimack Rivers* did not attract the interest of publishers or readers. Thoreau hired James Munroe of Boston to publish *A Week* in an edition of one thousand copies in 1849 at Thoreau's own expense. It sold so poorly that in 1853 Munroe, no longer wanting to warehouse 706 remaining copies (450 in unbound sheets and 256 bound), returned the stock to Thoreau. In his journal Thoreau wrote, with equal measure of sadness and humor, "I have now a library of nearly nine hundred volumes, over seven hundred of which I wrote myself . . . This is authorship." These books remained in Thoreau's attic until after his death. Setting pen to the paper of his journal, while also surrounded by hundreds of unsold and unread copies of *A Week*, Thoreau took stock of the ironies of "authorship" while "sitting beside the inert mass of [his] works."[8] An observer of the highest order, Thoreau seems always attuned to the relation between the human body and the material world. "All material things are in some sense man's kindred," he had written in his journal several years earlier.[9] And so, here it is significant that all those unread copies of *A Week* are figured as an "inert mass." As a college student, Thoreau both criticized the print market's interest in the price of paper over the merit of the ideas that could be printed on it and felt excitement over the audiences print could reach. He would continue to balance his professional involvement in printing and publishing with his criticism of markets and processes that could turn ideas, meanings, and expressions into "an inert mass."

Earlier that same year, in a journal entry on April 3, 1853, Thoreau figures his present moment in time as a "thin stratum," thinner even than a printed page on which news of the day will appear. The entry is exemplary of Thoreau's ongoing criticism of print culture: print mediation alienates people from firsthand experience of the world: "The last two Tribunes I have not looked at. I have no time to read newspapers. If you chance to live and move and have your being in that thin stratum in which the events which make the news transpire,—thinner than the paper on which it is printed,—then these things will fill the world for you; but if you soar above or dive below that plane, you cannot remember nor be reminded of them."[10] The sliver of time and space we call "the present," like a needle constantly moving forward from the past into the future, affords the space and time of direct experience. To read the newspaper is to mistake that competing "thin stratum" of the printed page for direct experience of the present. It was not the only time Thoreau criticized writing and print on paper for being a poor substitute for direct experience of the material world.

Thoreau frequently made this criticism of print and reading, and its clearest expression appears in the "Sounds" chapter of *Walden*. In "Sounds," Thoreau describes a train cutting across the woods near his cabin: "The Fitchburg Railroad touches the pond about a hundred rods south of where I dwell." In addition to moving consumer goods and commuters to and from the small towns and villages of central and western Massachusetts, the train carries bales of linen rags from Boston, past Concord, and to the paper mills in Fitchburg. At harbor in Boston, tattered sails were sold to papermakers who broke down the cloth and recycled ragged linen into paper. Thoreau takes note of the transport of linen rags to the mills in Western Massachusetts: "These rags in bales, of all hues and qualities, the lowest condition to which linen and cotton descend . . . gathered from all quarters both of fashion and poverty . . . [will go] to become paper . . . on which forsooth will be written tales of real life, high and low, founded on fact." Revisiting the "thin stratum" theme, he interjects that he prefers the world to paper, finding himself "more influence[d by] those books which circulate round the world, whose sentences were first written on bark, and are now merely copied from time to time on linen paper." What is printed on the page is "mere copy" compared with the direct of experience of the "book" of the world. Thoreau then asks "why should we leave it to Harper & Brothers . . . to select our reading," when the carloads of tattered sails offer a closer experience of the sea than do novels about life at sea. "This car-load of torn sails," he argues, "is more legible and interesting now than if they should be wrought into paper for books. Who can write so graphically the history of the storms they have weathered as these rents have done? They are proof sheets which need no correction."[11] Thoreau's depiction of unprocessed rags as proofs means he understands rags to be finished texts in and of themselves, before they have been processed by a mill or printed on a press. He already reads narratives embedded within them and finds the kind of unmediated intimate access to embodied experience superior to written representations of experience that could someday be printed upon them.

Peter Coviello writes of Thoreau's "prodigious and articulate fluency with the world of *things*," arguing that, unlike Ralph Waldo Emerson's turn to nature as a system or "vast unfolding metaphor," things prompt Thoreau into "meticulous scrutiny" of "an array of small, complex, and infinitely fascinating details" that "offer the possibility of nearly limitless revelation." Thoreau is absolutely serious when he says that being present with ragged tattered sails provides him a better account of the sea than does a novel published on paper made out of old ragged sails. Thoreau would rather become attuned to the presence of ragged sailcloth that might be within the pages of *Moby-Dick* than read what is printed on them. Fittingly, this argument about rags, paper, and print opens the "Sounds" chapter. Coviello would have us note that sound, as distinct from hearing or listening, has little to do with interpretation and everything to do with the firsthand experience of "flesh-vibrating modulations . . . a sensual responsiveness to the outer world that works abrupt and sweeping changes in the very organization of the corporeal self."[12] In the first paragraph of "Sounds," Thoreau warns that "we are in danger of forgetting the language which all things and events speak without metaphor, which alone is copious and standard."[13] In the midst of the massive expansion of print, and despite his own eventual successes as a professional author, Thoreau desires to "read" the world through direct experience of things rather than a representation of it on paper.

"Ineffable Socialities Are in Me": Herman Melville's Queer "Paper Allegories"

Herman Melville's life and work are full of blank paper. Marking his grave in the Bronx's Woodlawn Cemetery, Melville's headstone bears the image of what is either a blank scroll or a long unrolled sheet of machine-made paper. Provoked by his "last grave joke," as Kenneth Speirs puts it, Melville scholars have offered several readings of the blank sheet, actually a standard-model headstone left uncustomized beyond the inscription of name and dates of birth and death. "Is it the cruelest of jokes, the darkest of dead letter offices, a mum glance to posterity, or is it suggestive of something else?" asks Speirs.

He continues: "Its simplicity is finally confounding, the utterly blank scroll on Melville's grave, like the whiteness of the whale, is an invitation to further interpretation, an ending containing innumerable beginnings."[14] Others eschew interpretive possibilities in favor of biographical readings, speculating that "perhaps his family had planned to engrave titles of all his books on the scroll and then decided it 'wasn't worth the expense,' or perhaps they decided he 'hadn't written anything worth remembering.' Perhaps a daughter . . . deliberately left a blank page like a fresh pad on a writer's desk."[15] The headstone is only the last of many Melvillian scenes of blank paper. In his 1855 *Harper's* magazine story, "The Paradise of Bachelors and the Tartarus of Maids," Melville explores the industrial papermaking process and the production of long sheets of blank white paper. The paper mill, cotton and linen rags, and papermaking terms appear elsewhere in his work, including his 1852 novel *Pierre*; the whiteness of Moby Dick, which has frequently been compared to a blank sheet; and his breakdown of whale species by paper format in *Moby-Dick*.

Katie McGettigan has written that for Melville, the material text was not simply a vessel for his words but an expression of the author's ideas in its own right. In Melville's writing, she explains, "the materiality of print is more than a surface for textual transmission: it is a medium for . . . expression."[16] As I argue here, for him it was also a space of intimate and often erotic contact between people. I read Melville's fascination with paper and papermaking through his writing about it in letters to Nathaniel Hawthorne and in "The Paradise of Bachelors and the Tartarus of Maids." Melville's interest in paper, I suggest, is based in how its rag content created "ineffable socialities" and intimate communication between and among others.[17]

As perplexing as the blank headstone is, another archive of unreadable papers—the missing half of the correspondence between Nathaniel Hawthorne and Herman Melville—has raised even more questions. The surviving letters, those written by Melville to Hawthorne, are suggestive, intimate, and, in a number of registers, queer.[18] In response to a letter in which Hawthorne praises the just published *Moby-Dick*, itself dedicated to Hawthorne, Melville writes:

> Your letter was handed me last night on the road going to Mr. Morewood's, and I read it there. Had I been at home, I would have sat down at once and answered it. In me divine magnanimities are spontaneous and instantaneous—catch them while you can. The world goes round, and the other side comes up. So

now I can't write what I felt. But I felt pantheistic then—your heart beat in my ribs and mine in yours, and both in God's. A sense of unspeakable security is in me this moment, on account of your having understood the book. . . . Whence come you, Hawthorne? By what right do you drink from my flagon of life? And when I put it to my lips—lo, they are yours and not mine. I feel that the Godhead is broken up like the bread at the Supper, and that we are the pieces. . . . My dear Hawthorne, the atmospheric skepticisms steal into me now, and make me doubtful of my sanity in writing you thus. But, believe me, I am not mad, most noble Festus! But truth is ever incoherent, and when the big hearts strike together, the concussion is a little stunning.[19]

These letters, many of which sound homoerotic to a contemporary ear, are full of quite beautiful, and suggestive, passages like these. Add to them Melville's pronouncement in "Hawthorne and His Mosses" that "already I feel that this Hawthorne has dropped germanous seeds into my soul. He expands and deepens down, the more I contemplate him; and further, and further, shoots his strong New England roots into the hot soil of my southern soul," and it seems like understatement when Leland Person and Jana Argersinger write that "the question of sexuality looms like a grand hooded phantom" over these two central figures of the American Renaissance. Person and Argersinger open *Hawthorne and Melville: Writing a Relationship* with an illustration of Queequeg and Ishmael's nighttime embrace emblazoned on the book's cover and then move to the question of the missing letters. "What's in a letter? All the world. . . . But what if the letter is missing?" they ask.[20] We are invited to imagine, with a particular strain of archive fever, that more paper, a completed paper record, would pull the hood off the phantom—fill in the blank sheets that taunt us in their silence.

Jordan Stein has studied the history of scholarship on Melville's letters to Hawthorne with the aim of understanding how their suggestiveness and incompleteness was taken up by scholars with different investments over time in canonicity, influence, and sexuality. He argues that while Melville's letters to Hawthorne are frequently read as if they are love letters that provide a beautifully written trace of a consummated homosexual relationship, the erotics or the queerness in Melville's writing may be better glimpsed in a study of his style and of his practices of keeping correspondence.[21] Stein's turn to questions of style and form are important ones, for they orient us toward questions about how texts and the exchange of paper create and stage the erotics of friendship, love, and communication. When readers approach Melville's letters to Hawthorne in search of evidence of something sweet, loving, or even sexual between the two, they are apt to miss the transit of paper and what it meant to Melville to be engaged in passing rag paper between them.

The absence of Hawthorne's replies has invited rampant speculation. We know Hawthorne sent return letters, as Melville indexes the spaces left blank by his destruction of Hawthorne's paper record. "I thank you for your easy-flowing long letter," Melville writes, "which flowed through me, and refreshed all my meadows, as the Housatonic—opposite me—does in reality."[22] The desire for the papers that would alleviate some of the ambiguity is so strong that Wyn Kelley even wrote some herself, ventriloquizing Hawthorne and Melville's conversation about another enigma, the unwritten "Agatha" story. Kelley situates her fictional supplement like so: "Drawn by my admiration of Hawthorne and Melville to the Berkshires . . . I sought and gained a position as a Surveyor in . . . Lenox and Pittsfield. . . . One day, while eating a simple repast in the cornfield near Arrowhead [Farm, Pittsfield, Massachusetts,] . . . I noticed a glint—of metal?—in the grass at the margin of the field . . . I was able to dig . . . uncovering a small but heavy sea chest with the initials 'HM'. . . . Imagine my astonishment at finding within a collection of tissuey letters tied in a black ribbon with a paper marked 'Secret' pinned to the top sheet. Opening this eagerly, I read the following words: 'Being the correspondence between my self and Hawthorne from the summer and fall of 1852.' Some of the letters appear to be missing somehow?—but these remain—and remain cherished as tokens as what might have been."[23] Scholars see a blank headstone, perceive that some papers are absent, and wish immediately for some text that would fill in the supposed emptiness of these gaps in the archive. But I want to suggest that Melville saw "blank" rag paper as the mass material mediation of strangers and loved ones whose traces were mixed up together within sheets.

Kelley calls her imaginative piece about finding Hawthorne's half of the conversation "letters on foolscap." It is one part allusion to Melville's discussion of paper in "The Paradise of Bachelors and the Tartarus of Maids," one part play on the foolishness of archive fever, and one part invocation of the materiality of paper, an important fact of life in the Housatonic River Valley, where the river powered the largest concentration of paper mills in the United States during and after Melville's time in the Berkshires. Melville frequented the paper mills in Dalton, mere miles from Arrowhead, where he purchased his paper directly from its source. These trips formed the experiential base from which he wrote "The Paradise of Bachelors and the Tartarus of Maids," for example, and reminded him always of his physical location within a center of massive industrial paper production.

Living in the catchment area where rags were collected and transformed into paper also shaped Melville's thinking about what and who was present in paper. Graham Thompson has written that living in the Housatonic River valley meant that the production process that brought his writing into being was always in front of him and on his mind. "Like the Housatonic River picking up tributaries on its journey toward the ocean," Thompson writes, "other processes—transcribing, editing, printing—supplement the journey of writing toward publication that in Melville's case began with purchasing paper."[24] But Melville took seriously the fact that paper and its rags had lives before anything would be written or printed on them. He was attuned to the relationships among objects and people archived within sheets of rag paper. In this, he was not unlike the makers and users of Revolutionary-era rag paper who found structures of national feeling embedded within their shared rags, the subjects of chapter 1. But as we will see here, and as Melville explores in "The Paradise of Bachelors and the Tartarus of Maids," by the 1850s the scale of relationality within paper was neither local nor knowable. Changes in scale meant that the personal material proximities within rags could no longer be imagined as a polity or a public. Working through this issue in his writing about papermaking, Melville showed how the relationships among people that became embedded within industrial rag paper were best understood as a queer social relation. Kate Thomas's work on how paper media create queer forms of relation helps unpack what I mean by the queerness of paper. Writing about Victorian postal system, Thomas illustrates how the promiscuity of letters mixing in mailbags and other forms of stranger sociability "asked everyone to imagine themselves in relations of correspondence with each other." Queer theory approaches to media elucidate how networks, in Thomas's words, "simultaneously bind us and also show us divergent pathways, help us understand ourselves as both linked and dispersed, reveal the contrapuntal, often erotic relationships between fiction and counterfiction."[25] In Melville's imagination of his own subjectivity and his relation to others, paper signifies the ability to be in infinite correspondence with others through the touch of rags. In his writing about rags and papermaking in "The Paradise of Bachelors and the Tartarus of Maids" and letters to Hawthorne, Melville is drawn to paper because he finds a form of unlimited intimacy in its internal archive of rags and people.

ॐ

During the winter of 1850–51, Melville nearly ran out of paper for the volumi-
nous manuscript of *Moby-Dick*, necessitating a trip to Carson's Old Red Mill
in Dalton, a few miles away from Arrowhead Farm. In the heart of the Berkshires, where paper manufactories took advantage of ample running water
and immigrant labor, Melville could obtain paper directly from the source.
He and his family returned from the paper mill with "a sleigh-load of paper,"
and what Melville saw there would become the basis of novella in part about
papermaking, published four years later in "The Paradise of Bachelors and
the Tartarus of Maids."[26]

On this very same fresh supply of Berkshire paper, Melville would not only
finish writing *Moby-Dick* but also began the aforementioned correspondence
with Nathaniel Hawthorne, to whom the novel would be dedicated. Surrounded in his office and region by paper and papermaking, Melville began to
think of both his work and his relationships in terms of paper. Days after the
publication of *Moby-Dick*, he wrote to Hawthorne expressing anxiety about
the novel's reception: "Appreciation! Recognition! Is Jove appreciated? Why,
ever since Adam, who has got the meaning of his great allegory—the world?
Then we pygmies must be content to have our paper allegories but ill compre-
hended."[27] On the surface, "paper allegories" compares Hawthorne's and Melville's fictional tales to God's "great allegory—the world," and the sentence is
meant to play down readerly expectations. Further down the letter, however,
Melville writes his own "paper allegory," in which he figures his relationship
to Hawthorne through paper.

Sometimes their contact is mediated through the paper they pass between
them; bodies and minds seems to dissolve and absorb into the rags within
the page. In this passage, divisions between mind, body, and paper that seemingly fall away, leaving behind an "infinite fraternity": "Whence come you,
Hawthorne? By what right do you drink of my flagon of life? And when I put it
to my lips—lo, they are yours and not mine. I feel that the Godhead is broken
up like the bread at the Supper, and that we are the pieces. Hence this infinite
fraternity of feeling. Now sympathizing with the paper, my angel turns over
another page."[28] To sympathize with paper is to feel with it, to imagine oneself
in its place. Melville cannot but imagine the relation between himself and
Hawthorne as an intimacy conducted by the technology of paper. But the
Melvillian sense of paper is much closer to how we might imagine networked
mobile devices. Paper appears in his imagination as an always present and
always on conduit to others. Melville and Hawthorne's two bodies are figured

as the Eucharist: one body broken in two pieces, one divine spirit in two bodies. The "infinite fraternity of feeling," the oneness of the mouth or of two bodies cut from the same bread, is then transferred onto the page as Melville's spirit ("my angel") "sympathiz[es] with the paper" as he lays his finger on it to turn the page. What does it mean to sympathize with paper, to feel with paper? Other parts of this letter might help us understand his sense of what "paper allegories" are.

After initially closing his long and suggestive letter ("this is a long letter . . . gibberish," he admits), Melville adds the first of two postscripts: "P.S. I can't stop yet. If the world was entirely made up of Magians, I'll tell you what I should do. I should have a paper-mill established at one end of the house, and so have an endless riband of foolscap rolling in upon my desk; and upon that endless riband I should write a thousand—a million—billion thoughts, all under the form of a letter to you. The divine magnet is on you, and my magnet responds. Which is the biggest? A foolish question—they are *One*."[29] Here, the ideal form of intimacy is to have "infinite fraternity of feeling" in the form of a paper mill and its still-wet, never-ending sheet. Paper materializes the allegorical, the metaphorical, and the symbolic, but not by simply recording these in written or printed language on its surface; a paper allegory is not merely figurative language written on paper. For Melville, paper signifies on its own. It triggers the oscillation of presence and meaning effects. Within its rag content, it assembles archives of people, places, and affects.

The signifying dimension of the sheet of paper is sometimes obvious, as when the manufacturer's mark occupies the writing surface in Melville's correspondence. In an 1852 letter, to congratulate Hawthorne on the well-received *Blithedale Romance*, Melville looked at the embossed stamp at the top of the page, a maker's mark. He drew a feather over the embossed image of a crown, the mark of Bath papermakers. He wrote, "By the way, here's a crown. Significant this. Pray, allow me to place it on your head in victorious token of your "Blithedale" success. . . . I have embellished it with a plume."[30] In pointing to the stamped crown's meaning, Melville says that paper, before Melville has even written on it, is signifying. The raised ridges in the shape of a crown carry the congratulatory content of the letter before Melville writes it. Embossing, of course, might be understood as a kind of inscription, an imprinting without ink. But I would also argue that Melville understands this paper to have inherent signifying capacities without any kind of inscription on it, an understanding that Melville lays out in the letter and its postscript.

In the postscript to his letter, Melville imagines his desired relationship with Hawthorne, and it is to be connected to each other by a paper mill. The "endless riband of foolscap" running between himself and Hawthorne is a paper allegory about how an endless still-wet roll of paper structures subjectivity and intimacy. Rag paper represents a set of social relations through its material composition. Rag paper embodies, and the discourse surrounding it imagines, forms of relation that, as Kate Thomas has suggested, "see through or look around forms of relation that insist upon linear, discrete, and exclusive models, engaging instead structures of human relation built upon dispersed, infinitely relative, prosthetic, or virtual associations."[31] The mixing of rags within paper creates a multitude of unpredictable and unknowable relations between people and things. "The Paradise of Bachelor and the Tartarus of Maids" stages the creation of these queer paper relations, but they emerge in Melville's thinking in these letters. They are especially present in his desire for a kind of unlimited intimacy with Hawthorne through an endless riband of always wet, fresh paper.

"The Paradise of Bachelors and the Tartarus of Maids" is a set of two linked stories, one of Melville's "diptychs." The first story is about the narrator's time with bachelor legal clerks, scholars, and writers in the all-male homosocial space of London's Temple Bar. There, the bachelors enjoy the pleasures of literary discussion, leisure, and food. The apparent absence of women and children, we are told, creates conditions in which the bachelors can attend to their literary pursuits: manuscript collecting, law, architecture, travel. "It was the very perfection of quiet absorption of good living, good drinking, good feeling, and god talk," explains the narrator. "We were a band of brothers. . . . And you could plainly see that these easy-hearted men had no wives or children to give an anxious thought. Almost all of them were travelers too, for bachelors alone can travel freely."[32] Elizabeth Renker has read Melville's "Paradise of Bachelors and the Tartarus of Maids" as a record of his violence toward women and the resentment he felt toward his wife and children for both stymieing his writing and requiring him to write for a market. "Herman's metonymic chain associating writing with misery, women with misery, and women with writing is both most notable and most notably symptomatic . . . in 'The Paradise of Bachelors and the Tartarus of Maids,'" she writes.[33] It seems at first as if there are no traces of women or children in the bachelors' club, but in the second half of the diptych we learn that wherever there is paper, there are women and children.

The second part of the diptych finds the narrator in the Berkshires on his way to a paper mill. There, he goes on a tour of the mill and its Fourdrinier machine. In the rag room, where young immigrant women shred cloth for the pulping machine, he has the startling realization that the shirts the maids are cutting up might be those of the bachelors, and the reader is invited to understand the transatlantic movement of cloth as the formal link between the two parts of this diptych.

> "This is the rag-room," coughed the boy.
> "You find it rather stifling here," coughed I, in answer; "but the girls don't cough."
> "Oh, they are used to it."
> "Where do you get such hosts of rags?" picking up a handful from a basket.
> "Some from the country round about; somefrom far over sea—Leghorn and London."
> "'Tis not unlikely, then," murmured I, "that among these heaps of rags there may be some old shirts, gathered from the dormitories of the Paradise of Bachelors. But the buttons are all dropped off. Pray, my lad, do you ever find any bachelor's buttons hereabouts?"[34]

The realization that the rags being turned to paper in this mill might be "gathered from . . . the Paradise of Bachelors" provides a material link between the two parts of the diptych, prompting a reflection on the different conditions under which the male bachelor writers and the female millworkers labor. As with Bradstreet and Sigourney, we see that without women's constitutive labor in the papermaking process, there would be no paper for the bachelors to write on.

But the narrator is quickly distracted by the horrors of the paper mill, horrors that arise, mostly, from the bachelor's rags not only coming to this U.S. paper mill but also entering into the maids' bodies. The maids breathe in the shreds of linen, which become part of their bodies, which in turn start to resemble paper: "The air swam with the fine, poisonous particles, which from all sides darted, subtly, as motes in sun-beams, into the lungs" of the mill-working maids.[35] Like other industrial tour narratives, such as Rebecca Harding Davis's "Life in the Iron Mills," "Tartarus of Maids" indexes concern over the brutal working conditions that come with advancing industrialization. Here, breathing in particulate fibers is so routine that it no longer troubles the women most exposed to it. But this is also a form of intimacy amid the brutality. The airborne shreds from the bachelors' shirts enter the maids' bodies. This process makes them resemble paper:

"What makes those girls so sheet-white, my lad?"

"Why"—with a roguish twinkle, pure ignorant drollery, not knowing heartlessness—"I suppose the handling of such white bits of sheets all the time makes them so sheety."[36]

The clothes of the bachelors enter the maids' bodies—making them sick and pallid, like the sheets of paper that other shreds will make. The human relations haunting or inhering in the rags are then mixed into the maids and into a pulp, promiscuously combined in bodies as in paper.

Bachelors entering maids through their rags in the lungs is not a form of sex, but it is a kind of intimacy—one of the "intimacies" produced by the "odd companionships and dependencies" that Pastor Wright tells us rags bring to paper. The promiscuous mixing of rags takes place in the maids' bodies as they breathe in particulate pieces of shirts off the bachelors' backs. The rags are also mixed together in the vat, creating a slurry of "stuff" to run through the paper mill. Both these ways of mixing rags form peculiar assemblages of relation. The mixing of rags from different origins create "ineffable socialities": mixtures of rags that are impossible, definitively, to trace back to individual owners but that we nonetheless know trace back to someone. Or, in Kate Thomas's words, the relation of rags within paper are not "forms of relation that insist upon linear, discrete, and exclusive models." Rags in paper, rather, build queer "structures of human relation built upon dispersed, infinitely relative, prosthetic, or virtual associations."[37]

I argue that the intimate and queer forms of association within paper offer us a subtler reading of sexuality in "The Paradise of Bachelors and the Tartarus of Maids" than the story has tended to receive. And it is a reading that explains what paper and papermaking, specifically, are doing in the story. Critics have focused on symbols of sex in the story, and there are many, including the Fourdrinier machine symbolizing a womb that is inseminated by sticky white paper pulp. Sheets of wet paper emerge from the machine exactly nine minutes after the pulp enters the machine, the narrator tell us. It is a comparison that Melville invites, to be sure. After all, the title gives us "bachelors" and "maids," names that refer to marital and virginal status. The white pulp going into the paper mill is clearly coded as semen: "I crossed a large, bespattered place, with two great round vats in it, full of a white, wet, wooly-looking stuff, not unlike the albuminous part of an egg, soft-boiled." When the "stuff" enters the mill, the narrator tracks how long it takes until it emerges as paper on the other side. "Nine minutes to a second," is the answer.[38] So, there really isn't a question of whether reproductive sex happens somewhere in "The Paradise of Bachelors and the Tartarus of Maids." It just happens inside a Fourdrinier machine, and it produces paper, not children.

This is the force of Melville's critique of industrialism. It is antihuman. The bachelors remain bachelors, and the maids remain maids. There are no children, but there are commodities. "Why is it, Sir, that in most factories, female operatives, of whatever age, are indiscriminately called girls, never women?" the narrator asks. The guide replies:

> "We will not have married women; when they are apt to be off-and-on too much. We want none but steady workers twelve hours to the day, day after day, through the three hundred and sixty-five days, excepting Sundays, Thanksgiving, and Fast-days."
> "Then these are all maids," said I, while some pained homage to their pale virginity made me involuntarily bow.
> "All maids."
> Again the strange emotion filled me.[39]

Of course these girls exhibit such paleness because they have become paper-like through working in the mill, both in their pallid appearance and in their inhalation and bodily incorporation of airborne rags. Thus, by working in the mill they have supposedly become unmarriageable in this "strange" sort of "pale virginity."

In this interpretive vein, Robyn Wiegman has characterized the story as a "diptych of segregated spheres of gender relations." Leland Person expands on this thesis, describing the linked stories as Melville's exploration of his "pessimism about the possibility of mutually creative male-female relationships. The bachelors of paradise have no connection to women, the maids of Tartarus have no fruitful connection to men." Explicating the surface level imagery of the phallus and womb, Person asserts that "if the 'iron animal' that embosses the paper is phallocentrically male, the 'great machine' that makes the paper is unmistakeably female."[40] Though they correctly identify the genital and sexual imagery here, I find these readings generally unsatisfying because they have little to say about of the erotics of rag paper and papermaking with which Melville was deeply interested. In taking pulped rags and paper machines as mere symbols, typical readings of the story rush to explain the surface level correspondences of this part of the machine with the phallus, that part with the vulva and womb, and so on. They miss how the erotics of rag papermaking arrange intimate and erotic relationships beyond reproductive sex between two cisgender heterosexual people. Given all the possible anti-human reproductive effects of industrialization in his time, why write specifically about papermaking?

Adhering to a rigid male-female framework, these readings imagine that the two halves of the story are separate. But they aren't. A material connection exists between these separate spheres: the cloth that makes rags and becomes paper. Rags move from the bachelors' quarters in the first part and are worked into paper by maids in the rag room in the second. And paper cuts back from the mill in part two into the scene of reading and writing in part one. Rags become airborne and then create new assemblages of raggy bachelor matter inside sheety maiden bodies. Rather than perpetuate a "separate spheres" ideology, "The Paradise of Bachelors and the Tartarus of Maids" instead frequently invites us to consider the infinite possibilities of the dispersal and refabrication of matter and the interrelation of bodies through material traces.

Shredded rags enter bodies and make the bachelors' matter part of the maids'. Liquefied and reconstituted into paper, they unite London and the Berkshires, classes who write and classes who labor in mills; bodies of men and bodies of women enter one another across space, out of linear time, and create the infinite possibilities of the blank sheet: "It was very curious. Looking at that blank paper continually dropping, dropping, dropping, my mind ran on in wonderings of those strange uses to which those thousand sheets eventually would be put. All sorts of writings would be writ on those now vacant things—sermons, lawyers' briefs, physicians' prescriptions, love-letters, marriage certificates, bills of divorce, registers of births, death-warrants, and so on, without end." Asks the narrator when he arrives at the mill, "You make only blank paper, no printing of any sort, I suppose? All blank paper, don't you?" Replies the guide, "Certainly, what else should a paper factory make?"[41]

But even if these sheets are blank, the narrator is able, by the end of the story, to see infinite possibility in or on them. Sermons, legal documents, love letters, government papers, "and so on, without end." Renker argues that Melville was an incredibly frustrated writer who felt stymied by the women and children in his life and house. Identifying white paper with white women, Melville, Renker says, fought against the blank page and used violent metaphors for writing, such as "stabbing" at a book that indexed his abuse of the page and the women in his life.[42] I am not going to argue whether Melville was an abusive husband and father; as Renker's research suggests, he very well may have been. I do want to point out, however, that the blankness of paper was not necessarily a sign of frustration for Melville, nor is it necessarily an index of his inability to write. To the contrary, the paper rolling off the mill in "The Paradise of Bachelors and the Tartarus of Maids" signifies writing "without end." More significant, though, is what blank paper rolling off the mill figures in Melville's postscript to Hawthorne. There, the blank paper rolling off the mill allows Melville to "write a thousand—a million—billion thoughts." Why does the paper mill allow Melville to conceive of infinite writing?

The infinite mixing and blending of rags from countless sources gave Melville's writing and subjectivity a model for thinking about his expansive relations to other bodies. In her book *Dust: The Archive and Cultural History*, Carolyn Steedman discusses a kind of archive fever different from the one made familiar to us by Derrida. Steedman focuses on the inhalation of dust in the archive and how taking into one's body the particulate matter of the past affects the writing of history. "The Philosophy of Dust," she writes, "speaks of the opposite of waste and dispersal; of a grand circularity, of nothing ever going away. . . . To recognize and deal with the understanding that nothing goes away: to deal with dust. Historians writing the narrative that has no end, certainly make endings, but as we are still in it, the great slow moving Everything, in which nothing has gone away and never shall, you can produce only an Ending, which is different from an end."[43] Ultimately, I want to suggest that Melville's endless riband of still wet rag particles is his self-figuration as a writer who ingests the dust of history—the particulate matter of others—and writes the "narrative that has no end," as Steedman calls it.

Melville figures himself as a perpetually wet, always coming together, endless riband of paper, containing the multitudes of his self. In the November 17, 1851, letter, the "rapturous" reply to Hawthorne with the paper mill postscript, Melville imagines his body and his subject as constantly in flux, reconstituting itself each moment, as if new molecules had entered and rearranged him: "Ineffable socialities are in me," he writes. "This is a long letter, but you are not at all bound to answer it. Possibly, if you do answer it, and direct it to Herman Melville, you will missend it—for the very fingers that now guide this pen are not precisely the same that just took it up and put it on this paper. Lord, when shall we be done changing? Your letter was handed me last night on the road going to Mr. Morewood's, and I read it there. Had I been at home, I would have sat down at once and answered it. In me divine maganimities are spontaneous and instantaneous—catch them while you can. The world goes round, and the other side comes up. So now I can't write what I felt."[44] Melville here reiterates that he never steps into the same river twice or perhaps that he is never the same self from one moment to the next. He is constituted, reconstituted, and recirculated. He is figuring himself as a riband of still-wet paper rolling off a mill. Always becoming Herman Melville out of a set of social relations, other bodies, and other places, his subjectivity is dispersed across many Melvilles, ready for infinite becoming. Like Steedman, Julietta Singh argues for a concept of the archive as enduring material traces within the body. Singh calls the "body archive" the "assembly of history's traces deposited in me . . . an attunement, a hopeful gathering, an act of love against the foreclosures of reason . . . of scrambling time and matter . . . a way of thinking-feeling the body's unbounded relation to other bodies."[45] The endless riband of wet rags coming together as paper was Melville's object lesson in the expansive body archive. Rag paper gave Melville the image and language to conceive his "vital entanglements" to others, especially Hawthorne.[46] The mix of bodily, affective, and historical residues on each shred of rag was mixed promiscuously in the paper machine and assembled anew in relation to strangers, lovers, and things known and unknown.

What Singh identifies as the expansive intersubjectivity of the body archive, Melville calls "ineffable socialities." This is the same sense of subjectivity at which the narrator of "The Paradise of Bachelors and the Tartarus of Maids" arrives while looking upon the blank roll of paper emerging from the machine: "Then, recurring back to them as they here lay all blank, I could not but bethink me of that celebrated comparison of John Locke, who, in demonstration of his theory that man had no innate ideas, compared the human mind at birth to a sheet of blank paper; something destined to be scribbled on, but what sort of characters no soul might tell."[47] Rather than suggesting gendered separate spheres engaged in frustrated sexual nonreproduction, blank rag paper emerging from the mill signifies endless thoughts and plentiful, yet unknowable, intimate relations with others. The bachelors and maids may exist in different halves of the story, but paper moves between. Their bodies and labors are absorbed and present within shreds of rag, mixed in infinite combination within the roll. Forms of expansive personal and social relations that seem difficult to describe make sense when described in the concrete terms of rag paper production. The blank sheet contains the ineffable socialities *within* the page that creates queer impersonal intimacies between the bachelors and the millworkers and between Nathaniel Hawthorne and Herman Melville. Melville's blank headstone, then, is the riband of foolscap rolling from himself to Hawthorne. It does not represent the muteness of death but infinite possibility in the loss of self to intimate communication with another through the ever-shifting relations within a sheet of paper. Though it is constructed out of symbols for cisgender male and female heterosexual reproduction, within the wider context of Melville's writing about papermaking and material textuality, "The Paradise of Bachelor and the Tartarus of Maids" also offers a more complex account of a sort of queer relationality of bodies, texts, and archives that cannot be kept separate. We find in Melville's paper allegories a writer who sees rag paper as a technology of "infinite bodyings" where strangers and friends "lose the difference" between one another.[48]

In the opening paragraphs of "The Tartarus of Maids," we first find Herman Melville's narrator describing the Berkshires as a landscape of ink and paper, a world of black and white. It is January, so the landscape is overwhelmingly white with snow, "fairly smoked with frost; white vapors curled up from its white-wooded top, as from a chimney." He is pulled by a horse named Black through the "ebon-hue[d] . . . . Black Notch," and when we see of the paper mill we find that it "white-washed . . . like some great whited sepulchre." "The whole hollow gleamed with white," and it is "a snow white hamlet amidst the snows."[49] Once inside the mill, the narrator sees the maids and compares their white faces to the whiteness of the pulp and paper coming through the mill: "A fascination fastened on me. . . . Before my eyes—there, passing in slow procession along the wheeling cylinders, I seemed to see, glued to the pallid incipience of the pulp, the yet more pallid faces of all the pallid girls I had eyed that heavy day. . . . Their agony dimly outlined on the imperfect paper, like the print of the tormented face on the handkerchief of Saint Veronica."[50] The maids' excessively white faces could be due to the illnesses they develop from working in the mills. But the pallor of their faces also registers a particular problem about their gender: their class, ethnicity, and occupations disqualify them from proper participation in white femininity. Melville's repeated insistence on the blank whiteness of the page anchors his explorations of the maid's social positions, providing a key metaphor through which to explore how racial marking works. Unlike other writers who compare "fair maidens" to blank sheets of paper in order to extol their virginity and passivity (in chapter 4 we will encounter a poem that asks us to "Observe the maiden, innocently sweet, / She's fair white paper, an unsullied sheet"), Melville explores the pathologized reversal of this symbol.

Just as the horse "Black" and the geological formation "Black Notch" are visible against the backdrop of white snow, the whiteness of the page acts as a ground for legibility. Melville throws his narrator into a certain kind of vertigo as when he observes the paper mill and its whited sepulchre exterior against the snow. The narrator goes through the mill unable to read what is before him, always needing to be told what he is seeing. He describes the mill as the "great machine . . . a miracle of inscrutable intricacy." Seeking information about its workings, the narrator repeatedly turns to his guide, Cupid, and asks, "why?" In the whited mill, observing white paper and white maids, the narrator loses the ability to make sense of what is before him. "A strange emotion filled me," he says. Noticing the narrator's disorientation, Cupid turns and says, "Your cheeks look whitish yet, Sir. . . . You must be careful going home. Do they pain you at all now?"[51] Overcome by disorientation, the narrator himself is in danger of being absorbed into the white world of the mill. Amid all that whiteness, and while turning white himself, the narrator nearly loses himself. That threat of loss speaks to a need to maintain difference (the narrator immediately goes outside where the horse Black and the Black Notch are)—or legibility.

As a medium for intimacy, paper is a material product complexly connected to the bodies of those involved in its production and use. Given my focus on intimacy, it is perhaps unsurprising that this intimacy would extend to notions of not only gender and reproduction but also sexuality. As the bodies engaging with the material of paper are, themselves, intersectional, it is perhaps also unsurprising that paper's resonance would necessarily intersect with race. In my final chapter, I address how the relationships between paper's materiality and people's embodiment contributed to the work of racialization. Like paper itself, its whiteness was not an invisible surface but a materially constitutive and important part of its materiality, one that cannot be extracted from the larger cultural uses of whiteness as a metaphor for race. The whiteness of paper, therefore, both contributes to and is constituted by the cultural formation of race.

CHAPTER 4

THE WHITENESS
OF THE PAGE

Racial Legibility and Authenticity

WHITENESS IS A key feature of paper's function as a substrate for written and printed texts. It serves as the ground against which the figures of text and image become visible and legible to readers and viewers. Today, makers of such e-readers as Amazon's Kindle Paperwhite boast that its surface provides a reading environment in which the "whites are whiter" and "blacks are blacker" in very high contrast. In the nineteenth century, papermakers used similar language to describe the production of ream after ream of paper intended for printing. In 1833, the sales agent of a Boston papermaker wrote back to the main office that a customer was pleased with an initial shipment of fifty reams, and if the quality could be kept up, "I have a prospect of selling a considerable amount of it." "I will let you know how it ends," he continued, "I hope you will keep up the quality, make it as white as possible."[1] It took considerable work and expense to produce this valuable and marketable whiteness. Rag merchants traded in "white" and "brown" rags, terms that connoted the relative coarseness and staining of rags, and also their value on the market. Cheaper "brown rags" created "brown paper," which was less expensive stock intended to be used for wrapping paper and other utilitarian purposes, whereas more expensive "white rags" became "white paper," for printing and writing. Paper companies segregated "white mill" buildings where fine writing papers were made from "brown mills" where coarser papers were manufactured.[2] As one printer wrote to his Boston papermaker, "Please make 50 reams. . . . You will please be *particular* to make it white clean and fine, with the smoothest surface you can give. We want the best paper you can make [at the price of] 4.50 per ream."[3]

"Read against one another," writes Craig Dworkin, "blank pages tell a story not just about the development of modern art and literature, but about media themselves." Dworkin writes about modern and postmodern art's tendency to frame "blankness" and "emptiness" as themselves subjects of art and analysis—like "ready-mades"—that focus the viewer's or reader's eye on mediation itself. "Today a blank page put forward as poetry" would belong to "a minor subgenre . . . [of] avant-garde incursions and conceptual interventions," he writes. The recognizably modern and postmodern argument about media and meaning-making available in the presentation of "blank" media did not, however, suddenly become available in the mid-twentieth century. As I argue here, the whiteness of the blank page was a conceit already developed and adopted by late eighteenth- and early nineteenth-century writers. The blank sheet of white paper, real or imaginary, was called to signal various social formations, especially the gendered contours of white femininity. Contemporary media theorists find it quite provocative to ask, Was "the paper you are holding already a medium before it was brought together with ink?"[4] This question was part of the discussion about what had already been mediated within paper: rags, color, and ideas about purity and marking. The construction of white paper as blank and virginal linked ideas of race and gender to writing and inscribing.

Taking a longer view of this question in media history helps us frame the question somewhat differently. "The closer one looks at the materiality of a work—the brute fact of its physical composition," Dworkin writes, "the more sharply a social context is brought into focus." Media are never reducible to mere fact, he argues; neither are they standing reserves waiting for inscription or content from the outside. The modern and postmodern artists he looks at bring the manifest content of "blank media" to light and demonstrate the necessity of studying the contextual circumstances of their making. By reaching back to into eighteenth- and nineteenth-century conversations about paper, we find that the social context brought into focus includes discussions about how racial whiteness is formed and maintained, about gender and racial marking, and about how all these are "read" or become "legible" in the world. "Media are aptly named not only because they bear messages between writers and readers," says Dworkin, "but because they negotiate our socially mediated experience."[5]

It is no mere coincidence that during the mid-nineteenth century, the whiteness of paper was economically valued and prioritized at the very same time that norms defining and policing racial whiteness intensified. In this chapter, I argue that "whiteness" as a self-effacing, yet highly valued, backdrop against which other, usually black figures become legible was a crucially important technology of print culture and also of racialization. Put simply, whiteness, in both paper and persons, came to be understood as the common ground of representation, against which "blackness" became visible. Therefore, if learning to read words was figured as learning to "pick the black from the white," as one children's book had it, then both racial legibility and alphabetic legibility are linked by a common technique.[6] For printers and readers alike, legibility, a form of making sense, depends on the contrast between an invisible ground and a hypervisible figure. Whiteness, in both paper and persons, recedes and produces blackness, in both ink and persons, as the visible and visibly differentiated. These logics of reading and seeing have significant import in the period, as we will see, because they recruit material texts for the construction and maintenance of antiblack racism and white supremacy in the years leading up to the Civil War.

In a study of the material cultures of whiteness in antebellum domestic spaces, Bridget T. Heneghan has shown how everyday goods and spaces were literally whitened to "stanch the flow of blackness introduced by slavery, free blacks, and racial mixtures from invading the developing definition of 'America.'"[7] Home interiors, gravestones, and pottery participated in this material landscape of whitened goods, but paper was a special case, I argue, because it brought together the racial ideology of unmarked, and standardized, whiteness with the self-effacing invisibility of paper while reading or seeing what is printed or written on it. The effect is to link racial legibility and print legibility, putting what it means to read language and read bodies very close to each other by making them dependent on common visual techniques.

This chapter explores how two important discourses—print legibility and racial legibility—informed each other in the nineteenth century. By making meaning out of a field of white spaces and black marks, antebellum print carried racial significance for writers, readers, and print practitioners. First, I explore popular antebellum print culture, mainly intended for young readers, especially white girls, which constructs that young white femininity specifically as white paper. Then, I put William Wells Brown's theory of whiteness in his novel *Clotel* within the context of the everyday utterances of papermakers, printers, and engravers, arguing that the way readers perceived the whiteness of the page ultimately mirrored emergent theories of racial whiteness. Like a white page grounding black print, racial whiteness seemed to be the natural invisible background against which differently marked bodies could be read. Finally, I conclude the chapter with a look at how paper has been used to authenticate African American material texts, acting as a sort of surface or skin that can be analyzed and offered as proof.

Fair White Paper and "The Girl Who Inked Herself"

In the *American Museum* magazine of 1788, "Paper, A Poem" was first attributed to printer and paper merchant Benjamin Franklin. Though likely not written by Franklin, the poem was widely reprinted in such popular pedagogical texts as Caleb Bingham's *Columbian Orator*, where generations of students and autodidacts would have read, memorized, and recited it. "Paper, A Poem" proceeds from the assumption that people can be classified into types according to their physical appearance or the functions they perform in the world: "Men are as various: and, if right I scan, / Each sort of paper represents some man." Stanza by stanza, the poem's speaker compares "types" of people to different types of paper and their uses. For example, in the poem's typology of "man," "the fop" is equated with "gilt paper." If the fop dresses himself in "half powder and half lace," then the similarly fine and delicate gilt paper should be "lock[ed] from vulgar hands in the 'scrutoire.'" On the other hand, "Mechanics, servants, farmers, and so forth / Are copy-paper of inferior worth." Here, "mere" labor is figured as copying by the comparison with copy paper, which does not require delicate handling or to be locked away in an interior drawer of an escritoire. Laborers and copy paper alike are "free to all pens, and prompt at every need."[8] Both paper's appearance and its social functions within economies of public and private exchange factor into its mapping of social types within this poem's imaginary. In Franklin's own autobiography, he recounts deliberately wheeling a barrow of paper from his warehouse to his shop through a longer but more visible pathway through the streets to serve as a publicly visible sign of his industriousness and business. "Paper, A Poem" extends into poetry the ways Franklin habitually made visible the material technologies of print to mold public ideas about his character.[9]

"Paper, A Poem" also encodes ways of thinking visually about racial difference and social power. "The wretch, whom avarice bids to pinch and spare /
Starve, cheat, and pilfer, to enrich an heir," is, according to the poem, "course
brown paper; such as pedlers [sic] choose / To wrap up wares, which better
men will use."[10] The wretched person whose "brown" wrapper creates goods
for "better men," is "Starve[d], cheat[ed], and pilfer[ed]," so that wealth can be
extracted from it for the enrichment of heirs. Brown paper represents people
within this symbolic order of paper types. The poem associates the skin color
of the enslaved, both a visual logic and legal construction, with the brown,
rough, and unrefined surface of utilitarian brown wrapping paper. Brown
paper and brown people, in this poem's logic, are for labor, commerce, and the
enrichment of others rather than for writing, reading, or art.

Several stanzas later we find "brown paper's" social and functional opposite, "white paper." "White paper" is both a site of writing and of reproduction;
it is the only stanza in the poem that includes an explicitly female "type."

> Observe the maiden, innocently sweet;
> She's fair white paper, an unsullied sheet;
> On which the happy man, whom fate ordains,
> May write his name, and take her for his pains.[11]

Here, the whiteness of the "unsullied sheet" refers to both a blank sheet of fair
white paper and the premarital bed. Other poets used the same white paper
as a virginal woman trope, including Oliver Wendell Holmes, whose "To a
Blank Sheet of Paper" addresses its object as a

> Wan-visaged thin! thy virgin leaf
> . . . .
> looks more than deadly pale,
> Unknowing what may stain thee yet,—
> A poem or a tale."[12]

Until a "happy man" comes to "write his name" on this virginal sheet and body,
the blank sheet and the maiden lay in waiting to receive either ink or semen.
The unsullied sheet and the maiden are figured as passively receptive to the
possibilities of "inscription." By the middle of the nineteenth century, whiteness and virginity had become common metaphorical ground for description
of paper. In 1842's "The Poetry of Printing," virginal sheets are fed to "supply"
the press's appetite:

The perfect print adorns the snowy sheet,
And graces rare the reader's eye entreat.
What piles of virgin sheets the press supply!
What growing heaps of print salute the eye![13]

More recently, William Saroyan figured this possibility as a particular kind of possession and possibility, noting "what a delight it is to open a whole big ream of clean white typing paper and to behold the stack.... All that unused paper permits me to believe I can fill every sheet with writing, and not only with writing, but only the kind of writing only I can do."[14] The feminized and white body of the fair sheet of writing paper and the maiden are protected and valued for their eventual reproduction of text and the writing of "names," or the reproduction of bloodlines. Meanwhile, brown skin and brown paper both wrap commodities to be bought and sold.

The preservation of white paper's whiteness from unintended black marks was frequently taught to children, a lesson parents were instructed to offer not only to discourage wasting paper but also to encourage a certain moral cleanliness. Indeed, as both John Locke and the author of "Paper, A Poem" suggested, the infant mind was like a blank sheet of paper and could be either improved or blotted:

Some wit of old,—such wits of old there were,—
. . . .
Called clear blank paper every infant mind;
Where still, as opening sense her dictates wrote,
Fair virtue put a seal, or vice a blot.[15]

As we have seen, a wide variety of nineteenth-century children's literature and ephemera taught children how paper was made and to value it. And just as "fair virtue" could "put a seal, or vice a blot" on the paper of a child's mind, these lessons were often also about preserving the child's whiteness, and often their white femininity specifically.

In 1840, Sarah Josepha Hale edited and published an American edition of Anna Letitia Barbauld's *Things by Their Right Names*, a series of dialogues meant to instruct children through, as the long title explains, "stories, fables, and moral pieces, in prose and verse." One of the dialogues is about the manufacture of paper, as well as the care necessary to preserve its whiteness. "Father" gives "Harriet" "an account of the elegant and useful manufacture of *paper*.... this delicate and beautiful substance is made from the meanest and most disgusting materials; from old rags which have passed from one poor person to another." Following pages of technical details about rag sorting, beating, pulping, moulding, and drying—the sort of descriptions that make one wonder how strong the attention spans of nineteenth-century children could possibly have been—Harriet finally makes a short, but important, reply. She tells her father, "It is a very curious process, indeed. I shall almost scruple, for the future, to blacken a sheet of paper with a careless scrawl, now I know how much pains it costs, to make it so white and beautiful."[16] Harriet has learned that whiteness is painstakingly produced and that she should think twice before carelessly "blacken[ing]" it with a thoughtless "scrawl." She has learned to identify whiteness as a precious commodity that she must take "pains" to protect and preserve. Recall that in "Paper, A Poem," a maiden like Harriet remains an "unsullied sheet" until a "happy man" can "take her for his pains."

Just as in "Paper, A Poem," the dialogue between Harriet and her father contrasts white paper to brown paper, by way of an explanation of how the early process of bleaching worked. Here, though, brownness is depicted as in need of remediation toward whiteness. "I should mention to you," Father says, "that a discovery has been made, by which you can make paper equal to any in whiteness, of the coarsest brown rags, and even of dyed cottons; which they have till now, been obliged to throw by, for inferior purposes." Chemical processes can "discharge the colors . . . bleach[ing] the brown to a beautiful whiteness."[17] Although this lesson is ostensibly about the creation of whiteness and it preservation specifically in paper, Harriet, and the children who read along with her, are being instructed in the value of their racial whiteness and virginity.

The association of white paper and white femininity can be found throughout nineteenth-century print culture. The racial and gendered logics at work in "Paper, A Poem" and "To a Blank Sheet of Paper" turned up in many other forms. Published around 1859, for example, the brief picture book *Little Miss Consequence* included a two-page spread that tells the story, "The Girl Who Inked Herself, and Her Books, and What Happened" (Fig. 7). The girl, "Miss Mopsa," carelessly spills ink on her body and her books, which not only turns her book pages and her skin from white to black but also turns her into a thing, a black rag doll. "Seated at her writing-copy, / in the ink her hands she dips," the text begins, and soon the girl "sucks her pen, the black ink she swallows, / Smears her nose, and cheeks, and lips." Once the division between black ink and white skin, and black ink and white page has been breached, the blackness spreads, unable to be contained:

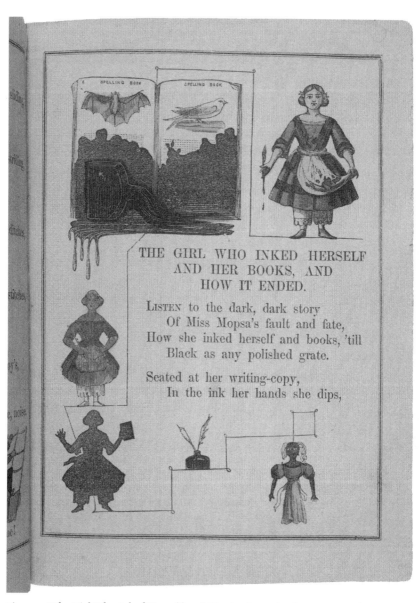

THE GIRL WHO INKED HERSELF
AND HER BOOKS, AND
HOW IT ENDED.

LISTEN to the dark, dark story
Of Miss Mopsa's fault and fate,
How she inked herself and books, 'till
Black as any polished grate.

Seated at her writing-copy,
In the ink her hands she dips,

Figure 7. "The Girl Who Inked Herself, and Her Books, and What Happened." *Courtesy of the American Antiquarian Society.*

Daily worse grow all bad habits:
> See her frock and apron soiled;
> Now the ink-stand she capsizes
> O'er her book—completely soiled.

The accompanying images show a child's book lying open with an overturned inkwell and ink spreading over more than half of the two pages. At the top of the pages we can still see the bat and bird illustrations that are soon to be overtaken by the creeping black ink, which drips into the next images. As the ink flows from the now unreadable book, we see it taking over the body of Miss Mopsa herself, whose characteristics begin to fade in the illustration. Her figure eventually becomes a flat silhouette of a girl, as if a nineteenth-century silhouette portrait and one of the contemporary artist Kara Walker's silhouetted figures were coming together on the page. The text continues,

> Next appears a thing unthought of;
> Her complexion turns to brown
> (White and red quite gone forever),
> Through the ink she has drunk down.

As Mopsa changes from white to black, "Nor alone her body changes—/ E'en the clothes upon her back" transform, until finally she transforms from a white human girl into a black rag doll on display in a rag shop:

> Blacker than a Guinea negro,
> Blacker than the sootiest sweep,
> Blacker than the shiny beetles
> O'er the chimney's back that creep.
> Dire event! Poor Mopsa's parents
> What to do with her can't tell;
> Far too hideous for a daughter,
> FOR A BLACK DOLL HER THEY SELL.
>
> At a rag-shop she's suspended,
> Swinging by an iron link.
> With one word my story's ended—
> Never stain yourself with ink.[18]

Robin Bernstein has noted that Miss Mopsa's story incorporates aspects of the Topsy/Eva topsy-turvy doll, which links the bodies of Topsy and Eva from *Uncle Tom's Cabin*, combining these two racialized figures in the body of the doll in such a way that scripts the transformation of one into the other. Bernstein also notes that "The Girl Who Inked Herself" is a forerunner to the story of "Miss Dinah Pen Wiper" in *Godey's Lady's Book* in 1861. According to Bernstein these stories imagine white girls who engage in "racial transgression" by turning themselves black, in addition to "treating [themselves] like a thing that soaks up excess."[19] Part of the material textual logic within this frame, whether in "The Girl Who Inked Herself" or "Paper, A Poem," is that white femininity cannot help but be a thing always threatened by marks from the outside. Marking can either be proper, as when a man "writes his name" in marriage, or improper, as when uncontainable and illegible blackness spills on the body or marks it intentionally, transgressively.[20] Mopsa's racial and material transformation undoes her whiteness and her status as fair white paper in two registers. She transforms from a person into a thing, following a racial logic under chattel slavery wherein "Uncle Tom" is also "the man that was a thing." This transformation is also reinforced by her move from a white-skinned girl, who, like paper, can be the ground for policing proper and improper racial marking, into a black rag doll in a rag shop. No longer a kind of paper, she has devolved back into rag.

"The Girl Who Inked Herself" quite literally draws a line of connection between the staining of white paper with black ink and the transformation of white girls into black things, encouraging white child readers to preserve the whiteness of their paper and of their bodies. Indiscriminately inking the page and "inking" their bodies threatens a loss of legibility, which is "Miss Mopsa's fault and fate."[21] This picture book instructs young white girl readers to take great care not to spread ink on their fingers and pages because their books will become illegible owing to the lack of black/white contrast, but so will their racialized bodies according to the same dualism.

Indeed, a great deal of nineteenth-century writing about race was concerned with the construction and maintenance of clearly divided white/black dualisms. But texts about the uncertain boundaries between white and black are equally familiar to us in this period. Not all racially marked women and girls have the same textual racialization as Mopsa. They do not so quickly "switch" from apparently white to apparently black. Nineteenth-century texts about mixed-race women often emphasize how the race of these characters is ambiguously denoted or connoted on the surface of the body. The white paper or brown paper / black ink or white paper dualisms we've seen so far lend themselves neatly to an antebellum U.S. juridical regime of race that demands an answer to the question of whether a body is *either* white *or* not. We know, however, as did many abolitionist and antiracist writers of the period, that the visual and juridical registers of race, of skin color and legal color, do not always so easily overlap.

If the material textual tools for representing race are black ink and white paper, or self-effacing ground and legible figure, then the mixed-race woman's body is a complex site through which to consider the representation of race. In the case of Mopsa, we were given a representational scheme in which the structures of legibility were identical for "herself" and "her books." The page and the skin were either all white or all black. The mixing of ink and paper produced a totally inked surface, and the bringing of black ink into Mopsa's body or the staining of her hand with it produced her as a "black doll." It's a "one drop"—of ink—rule for making bodies and marking pages.

Racialized negotiations between black ink and white paper were not only figural, gestured toward suggestively in poetry and story. Printers and engravers actually worked through these materials and often negotiated racial representation with these media. For example, engravers and printers of "Amalgamation Waltz and African's [*sic*] March in Turley," a circa 1850 sheet of illustrated music, used quarter and half notes, respectively, to represent the illustrated figures of black and white people. Here the blackness and whiteness of ink and paper are not only metaphors for visualizing race but also the very technology used for notating music and illustrating bodies.[22] In the next section, I explore this literal overlap of paper as skin and ink and racializing, or "coloring," content. The whiteness of paper and the blackness of ink present a technical and ideological problem in the moment when book illustrators try to represent mixed-race figures within the pages of nineteenth-century texts. Moments like these bring the literary play in "Paper, A Poem" and "The Girl Who Inked Herself" to the literal surfaces of pages in books that called for illustrations of women whose skin color often defied strict visual logics of race.

As we see in the next section, authors of mixed-race heroine narratives deliberately worked to specify different registers of racial representation. A mixed-race woman could look visibly white but be legally black; she could be an "unsullied sheet" to the eye, but be a "Mopsa" in the eyes of the law. This is certainly the case with the character of Clotel in William Wells Brown's novel *Clotel; or, The President's Daughter* (1853). But in the production of its material text, engravings were made using white paper and black ink to achieve the representation of Clotel. How these engravings work with and against the text's desire to complicate racial representation places the nineteenth-century's racialization of paper and ink in full view.

Bottles of Ink and Reams of Paper: Racializing Clotel in Print

William Wells Brown carried stereotypes with him. So we learn in an 1849 letter from William Lloyd Garrison to a British abolitionist who had inquired about the American Anti-Slavery Society's role in Brown's European lecture circuit. Brown carried letters of introduction and other credentials from influential Americans, but he went to England a free agent, relying on the generosity of friends and book sales to pay his way. "Mr. Brown does not go out officially from any anti-slavery society, simply because he prefers to stand alone responsible for what he may say and do," Garrison replied. "Nor does he go out to be a pecuniary burden or to make himself an unwelcome guest to any one; but he hopes that, by the sale of his Narrative, (the stereotype plates of which he takes with him,) he shall be able to meet such expenses as may arise beyond what the hospitality of friends may cover."[23] Existing interpretive frameworks for early African American literature tend to privilege literacy and writing in the attainment of agency and subjectivity, exploring how, William L. Andrews writes, "the *writing* of autobiography [is] in some way self-liberating."[24] As Garrison explains, however, Brown's freedom in Europe from the reaches of kidnappers and from the management of white abolitionists alike depended on his relation to the material conditions of print production as much as it did his own literacy. The stereotype plates in Brown's traveling case remind us that producing oneself as a free subject in print and in life is embedded within a set of material textual practices—practices that are (as the double meaning of stereotype suggests) also constitutive in processes of racialization.

Contrast Brown's carrying stereotype plates of his narrative as a sign and source of his independence with an event Brown recounts in the narrative itself. He describes an incident that occurred while enslaved in Saint Louis, during the period when he was hired out to Elijah Lovejoy, publisher of the *Saint Louis Times*, who would, years later, become an abolitionist printer and famous

First Amendment martyr. Brown recounts how he was often sent to the office of another newspaper to retrieve forms of standing type and on one occasion was stopped and harassed by local youth. "Once while returning to the office with type, I was attacked by several large boys, sons of slave-holders, who pelted me with snow-balls. Having the heavy form of type in my hands, I could not make my escape by running; so I laid down the type and gave them battle. They gathered around me, pelting me with stones and sticks, until they overpowered me, and would have captured me, if I had not resorted to my heels. Upon my retreat, they took possession of the type; and what to do to regain it I could not devise."[25] Just before this passage, Brown notes that his first acquaintance with literacy was made while working at Lovejoy's press, probably when sorting or setting type. "I am chiefly indebted to [Lovejoy], and to my employment in the printing office, for what little learning I obtained in slavery."[26] To perform basic tasks in the shop, Brown would have needed, at minimum, the ability to recognize basic letter shapes in order to sort pieces of type in the cases.

The beginning of literacy, commonly associated with the beginning of freedom in nineteenth-century African American narrative, does seem to stem from Brown's access to letters, but it is an alphabet in the type cases before it is an alphabet in the mind. And although Brown's literacy grows out of the material practice of print production, it is the awkward heft of these materials that encumbers him physically. As an enslaved person, Brown's movement is already restricted to the circuit between two newspaper offices, but the wooden form, furniture, quoins, and leaden type only frustrates his "escape" and exposes him to threat of "capture." Compared with frames of type, the stereotype is freeing. Of course, I am intentionally stressing the similarities and differences between stereotype printing plates and stereotypical representations to highlight the links between technologies of print and technologies of racialization. A stereotype plate is created from a mold of movable type, producing a lightweight replica in a single piece of metal; while the thousands of pieces of movable type are redistributed for new uses, the stereotype can be reprinted over and again, unchanged.[27] Thus Brown can carry his stereotypes across the Atlantic and around England without remaining tethered to a publisher or a particular print shop's type. This mobility is documented in an edition of Brown's narrative from 1849 that lists Charles Gilpin as publisher and London as place of publication on the title page, yet on the very next page we find: "Printed, chiefly from the American Stereotype Plates, by Webb and Chapman, Great Brunswick-street, Dublin."[28]

Greater attention to the significance of the material culture of print, especially in early African American print culture, shows how technologies of racialization emerge in conjunction with technologies of printed words and images. The stereotype is perhaps the most familiar case. In one sense it offers quick reproduction of legible text, and in another it offers quick reproduction of a legible social type. In the rest of this section, I examine how another technology of legibility, black/white dualism, structures both print legibility and racial legibility. The material culture of whiteness in antebellum print culture participates in nineteenth-century racial formation by modeling how whiteness is to be seen while unseen, providing the structural backdrop against which marks or types become legible.[29] As Brown himself suggests in the opening sentences of the 1867 edition of *Clotel*, blank ink and white paper transmit the author's writing about racial categorizations of blackness and whiteness while they also shape the common sense about whiteness, blackness, and structures of legibility and visibility. "The Death of Clotel," the only wood engraving providing an illustration of the namesake of Brown's novel, offers us an object of analysis wherein the materiality of the text—and the racialized meaning of whiteness in paper—forces a foreclosure of the novel's exploration of racial ambiguity by "filling in" Clotel's face with ink, signifying racial content instead of the absence implied in white paper. On display in such a moment is print's role in the construction and maintenance of dualism as a technology for making sense out of difference in both print culture and antebellum racial discourse.[30]

The minstrel riddle "What's black and white and re(a)d all over? (Answer: the newspaper)" turns on the multiple meanings of white and black and is complicated by the homophonic "red"/"read." It is a racially inflected joke, not only in its formal use of minstrelsy's comic indirection but also in the way it trades in the racialized meanings of color. The demand to think these colors together is frustrated by the assumption that a body is ultimately identified only by one color, or racial identification, "all over."[31] The joke's resolution arrives in the replacement of racial significations with a printed thing that can, without contradiction, be simultaneously black and white. This linguistic play retraces the historical process in which, through the printed page, black and white became sensible as binary opposites. Print provided a black/white structure that would later be used as a key form for the articulation of racial difference.

The emergence of the printed letter and image between the fifteenth and sixteenth centuries precipitated the partitioning of black and white from the domain of the full color spectrum, setting them in their now-familiar opposition. The visual experience of the codex shifted from the medieval manuscript culture's rich illuminations to modern print culture's black/white contrast. John Calvin, for example, saw in the stark contrast of black print against white paper the model for an aesthetic in which "the most beautiful ornament in the church must be the word of God." For the "people of the Book," the word of God appeared in black and white. Michel Pastoureau places ink, paper, and the engraved image at the center of a modern revolution in perception: "It was the circulation of the printed book and engraved images that . . . led to black and white becoming colors 'apart.' And even more than the book itself, it was undoubtedly the engraved and printed image—in black ink on white paper—that played the primary role. All or almost all medieval images were polychromatic. The great majority of images in the modern period, circulated in and outside of books, were black and white. This signified a cultural revolution of considerable scope not only in the domain of knowledge but also in the domain of sensibility."[32] The printed book, then, literally redefined "black" and "white." According to the *Oxford English Dictionary*, in 1594 "white" began to mean "blank space between certain letters or types . . . space left blank between words and lines," and four years later, "black" began to signify both "writing fluid" and "characters upon . . . paper; writing."[33] Black/white dualism is assumed in these definitions: white is sensible between black marks, and black against paper, which is white by definition.

If the black/white binary of print is an analogue of the black/white binary of race, then it seems important to ask how much cultural work this analogue performed. In other words, does the material contrast between black ink and the white page really have significant meaning with respect to the ideological contrast between black and white racially identified bodies in the period during which Brown was writing? The archives of paper mills, stationers, and publishers reveal the degree to which professionals of the material text were occupied with the production and preservation of whiteness. Professional roles in the print shop, such as the printer's devil, were part of the daily practice of maintaining the purity of paper from staining ink, and even a surprising amount of children's literature was produced to discipline children's experience of the page. The paper industry's preoccupation with and protection of whiteness as a valuable commodity cannot be seen in isolation from the production of what George Lipsitz calls the "possessive investment in whiteness."[34] Print legibility does indeed require contrast, but the adoption of whiteness as a central metaphor makes paper inextricable from the processes by which blackness becomes difference and whiteness the unmarked center. In what follows, I offer a range of contexts for the use of whiteness in the paper industry, suggest its convergences with racial discourse, and read how these convergences are at work in parts of *Clotel*.

In his 1814 *American Artist's Manual*, James Cutbush states a fact about papermaking so well known in its moment that it is axiomatic in presentation: "I will suppose that the object of the manufacturer is to obtain paper of a beautiful white."[35] Despite actual differences in the color of finished product, people in the paper industry adopted white and brown as signifiers of quality loosely related to appearance. The idea of white as pure, unmarked, and beautiful lent itself well to the purposes of an industry in search of an unobtrusive background that contrasted with black ink. "White" was adopted to signify paper with a suitably light and refined surface for printing, and "brown" to signify darker and coarser paper for wrapping and other uses.[36] By the twentieth century, the "brownness" of paper took on added racial significance through "paper bag societies" and "paper bag parties," colorist African American associations that are said to have used brown paper bags to test the tones of a potential member's skin. People with skin darker than the bag were ineligible for inclusion. But white paper wasn't necessarily visually white; "white" served as a metaphor for refinement and lightness in tone. The way whiteness functions in white paper begins to look like the function of whiteness under racial dualism: it is representative of supposed refinement and desirability and only loosely associated with the visual experience of a certain color.

Rag sales receipts show that "white" rags were worth more than others, for they were assumed to possessed a form of whiteness that made them more desirable at market. In *Clotel*, Brown depicts the sale of very fair-skinned African American women and places emphasis on the commodification of their whiteness. The "still wet from the press" advertisement that includes notice of Clotel and Althesa's sale reads: "Notice: Thirty-eight negros will be offered for sale. . . . Also several mulatto girls of rare personal qualities: two of them very superior." This marketing of "superiority" comes just before Brown's description of Clotel as having "a complexion as white as those who were waiting with a wish to become her purchasers." Here, too, the possession of whiteness has quantifiable value. When Clotel is sold to Horatio Green, the narrator offers an itemized list of her worth. Her body is worth only five hundred dollars, but the virtues of white womanhood that she is said to possess are worth one thousand more: "This was a southern auction, at which the bones, muscles, sinews, blood, and nerves of a young lady of sixteen were sold for five hundred dollars; her moral character for two hundred; her improved intellect for one hundred; her Christianity for three hundred; and her chastity and virtue for four hundred dollars more." The itemization does not explicitly include her white skin but shows Clotel's whiteness to be both physical and metaphysical, tying her physical whiteness to the trope of true white womanhood. The possession of whiteness, whether in the commodity of paper or in the body, is a promise of purity and refinement carrying with it quantifiably higher market value.[37] "Remember, Christians, Negroes black as Cain / May be refined, and join the angelic train," wrote Phillis Wheatley, noting, in a different register, how a valuable form of whiteness is produced in sugar through a refining process, one that might be applied, symbolically, to "negroes."[38]

The first order of business in the papermaking process was to distinguish between rags that could be used to make "white" paper from those that would make "brown," an action known not only to millworkers or printers but also to the general public. The separation and appraisal of rags was taught to children and linked to literacy itself. For example, in an 1837 setting of *Jack and the Beanstalk*, produced as an advertisement by a Boston printer and papermaker, an illiterate Jack does not find a giant in the clouds but rather a paper mill, a type foundry, printing press, bindery, and a schoolhouse. While visiting the paper mill in the clouds, Jack joins a group of children working in the rag pile: "[Jack] found himself in a room where there were a great many boys and girls sitting round, and picking among huge piles of cloth of every size, shape, and color, and as they picked they sang,—Pick, pick the black from the white, Assort the whole bundle before it is night. . . . The mill and the water and man with care have turned dirty rags into paper fair." Jack selects white from black through equation with dirtiness and fairness. The story's rhyming refrain, "pick, pick the black from the white," illustrates that metaphors of dualism structured the perception of rags and the paper they would become, despite whatever actual color the linens were. Upon returning to his mother, Jack says, "I should like to know what they are going to do with all this white paper," learning later that distinguishing black from white when writing is also the most basic skill required in the acquisition of literacy: "I see some strange-looking things of black on a white board . . . but I do not know what they mean."[39]

The professional practices of the print shop were shaped by the need to maintain white paper's "virginal" state, keeping ink away save for intentional marks. Shops were set up such that workers who touched ink never touched paper. The apprentice who applied ink to the type and who touched the leaden forms was called the "printer's devil," a "term [that] originated in reference to the fact that the young apprentice would inevitably become stained black from the printing ink."[40] Paper mills and print shops were ordered by metaphors of purity/deviance and cleanliness/filth constructed and circulated in the service of preserving white from black.

One papermaker, however, suggested that the orientation toward whiteness distracted from making the best quality paper, showing the preference for whiteness to be ideological, not functional. The focus on cleanliness and whiteness of rags and paper is misplaced, he claimed, and the rage for whiteness predominated other important qualities: "The degrees of fineness and whiteness, distinguished with little care, are thought to be the only objects of importance; whereas the hardness and softness, the being more or less worn, are very essential in this selection."[41] Instead of obsessing over color as a determinant of quality, papermakers are here urged to make stronger paper by selecting rags for their texture, not color. Some readers even took a contrary position on what made for the most legible paper color, arguing that the contrast of white and black was painful to the eye and that brown paper was superior. "Brown paper preserves the eye better than white," argued one reader, "and when authors and readers agree to be wise, we shall avoid printing on a glaring white paper."[42] In 1855, the *Philadelphia Public Ledger and Daily Transcript* reprinted a notice from *Scientific American* that "as a difficulty exists in getting white paper to print upon, that black paper might be substituted, with white ink." The correspondent notes that "white on a black ground is more distinct, and the eye is then relieved from the glare of rays from the white surface. We should like to see the effect of a newspaper of this kind."[43]

These experiments indicate that white color in paper was less a utilitarian need than a reflection of the importance of whiteness in the antebellum imagination. Toni Morrison suggests that Herman Melville, when writing *Moby-Dick*, "was overwhelmed by the philosophical and metaphysical inconsistencies of an extraordinary and unprecedented idea that had its fullest manifestation in his own time in his own country, and that . . . idea was the successful assertion of whiteness as ideology." In a similar deployment, the desire to have paper "as *white* as possible" made papermakers, printers, and readers into actors in the production of this pervasive ideology of whiteness in the nineteenth century.[44]

The widespread and repeated experience of ink and paper established black and white in the binary opposition that gave substance and support to the logic of racial dualism that dominated social and legal understandings of race in the nineteenth-century United States inhabited by African American writers such as William Wells Brown. The reliance of racial discourse on the binary black/white color metaphor—and the critique of this racial binary—is a key subject in much of Brown's work.

Clotel was first published in London in 1853 while Brown was on the afore-mentioned European lecture circuit. Tracing the lives of women (Clotel, Althesa, and their daughters) who are descended from Thomas Jefferson and an enslaved woman named Currer (a thinly veiled Sally Hemings), Brown devotes much of the novel to parsing the different forms of whiteness that these figures simultaneously do and do not inhabit. Clotel and Althesa are described in the novel as white women when whiteness refers to a tone of skin, but as the novel unfolds, their legal and social status as blacks under enslavement reveals itself, like the logic of hypodescent, as prevailing over all else. Though Clotel's light skin color and refined manners allow her tempo-rary inhabitance of white domesticity, she and her daughter are abandoned by the white man who, though he has promised to be a husband and father, cannot finally overcome the legal and social structures that make him their owner. After Althesa's death from fever, her daughters learn of their "true" racial status and are sold into sexual slavery to pay debts. In this way, the novel both bends binaries by indicating how unstable the chromatic metaphors for race are and explores how antebellum U.S. practices forcibly insisted that racial legibility be maintained by settling racial identification into the binary relation of black and white.[45]

As scholars in critical race studies have shown, racial binaries are unsta-ble and socially constructed yet nonetheless embedded in legal and social discourse. Addressing the rigidity of racial and symbolic dualisms com-pared with the slipperiness of the visual, Richard Dyer writes that "white as a symbol, especially when paired with black, seems more stable than white as a hue or skin tone." "White as a skin colour," he explains, "is [an] unstable, unbounded . . . category," one "that is internally variable and unclear at the edges."[46] As a symbol adopted by law, however, white is, as Cheryl Harris describes, more rigidly defined: a legal construct that "defined and affirmed critical aspects of identity (who is white); of privilege (what benefits accrue to its status); and of property (what *legal* entitlements arise from that status)."[47] Brown never misses an opportunity to complicate supposed congruities between the visual and legal syntaxes of race implied in the terms "black" and "white." Characters dwell in the spaces between apparent skin color and the legal/social privilege metaphorized through racial color. Clotel has a "complexion as white as" white men and features "as finely defined as any" white women. Clotel appears to be "Anglo-Saxon," even "Real Albino," which stresses the congruence between racial whiteness and extreme visual whiteness while also confusing that congruence by locating it in Clotel's "black" body.[48] Althesa is "as white as most white women in a southern clime," but "was born a slave."[49] Brown turns a phrase that puts white next to *white*, elegantly demonstrating the difference between visual and legal registers of race.

Despite Brown's interest in deconstructing a black/white racial binary, as a writer and printer, he traded in a material world structured by a black/white binary. And indeed, success in that world—printing—depended, one might say, on his ability to present ideas in black and white. Brown seems attuned to the contradiction that his work as a racial theorist constantly interrogated the decipherability of whiteness and blackness in opposition to each other, but that as a writer/printer his work would always depend on this very structure. Yet, in the final revision of his novel in 1867, Brown seems to capitalize on this irony. To theorize the difference between print legibility and racial legibility, Brown figures printing, the putting of black ink onto white paper, as racial intermixture, describing "Quadroon women" as products of ink and paper.

These lines open the 1867 edition: "For many years the South has been noted for its beautiful Quadroon women. Bottles of ink, and reams of paper, have been used to portray the 'finely-cut and well-moulded features,' the 'silken-curls,' the 'dark and brilliant eyes,' the 'splendid forms,' the 'fascinating smiles,' and 'accomplished manners' of these impassioned and voluptuous daughters of the two races." As Brown suggests, "mulatta" narratives were quite popular, and one in particular rewrote the limits of the possible in the book industry.[50] "One Hundred thousand volumes issued in eight weeks!" exclaimed the *New York Independent* on the publication of Harriet Beecher Stowe's *Uncle Tom's Cabin.* "The demand continues without abatement. . . . It has taken 3000 reams of medium paper, weighing 30 lbs. to the ream—90,000 lbs. of paper."[51] But *Clotel*'s 1867 opening passage (the last time Brown would edit it) does more than highlight the expanding scale of print production. In 1867, Brown begins the novel with language about print production in order to theorize the concept of legibility in both print and racial registers. Where earlier editions of *Clotel* begin with a discussion of racial intermixture under slavery, this one discusses the production of representations of racial intermixture. The first edition begins with a description of an actual population of people, described as a "fearful increase of half whites, most of whose fathers are slaveowners, and their mothers slaves."[52] In 1867, however, white fathers and black mothers are replaced with black ink and white paper, and the defining characteristics of "Quadroon women" are put under quotation: "silken-curls," "dark and brilliant eyes," and so on. Brown shifts from discussing the birth of actual mixed-race people to the production of the literary trope of "the mulatta" that over "many years" of "portray[al]" has become synonymous with these features. As Ann duCille has written, this passage seems concerned with the problem of representation, or the hypervisibility of the "mulatta" trope in antebellum popular culture, and that Brown is unlikely, for example, to have uncritically figured mixed-race women as "voluptuous." Even the replacement of "half whites" with "Quadroon women" recalls "The Quadroons," the 1842 short story by Lydia Maria Child out of which Brown built *Clotel*. Brown suggests that racial mixture is most legible, then, as a set of literary tropes just as the appearance of "silken-curls," "dark . . . eyes," and "voluptuous" bodies immediately orients readers to a set of standard characteristics and plots.[53] These figures are mixtures of black and white both because they have "fathers [who are] slaveowners, and . . . mothers [who are] slaves" and because they are formed from "bottles of ink, and reams of paper." It is only in print, however, in assembling lists of such features as "silken-curls," that these figures are legible within a structure of black/white dualism, for, as Brown emphasizes in *Clotel*, the mixture of "black" and "white" in mixed-race people does not necessarily produce the legibly "black" body demanded by the laws and logics of hypodescent.

If the portrayal of mixed-race figures like Clotel involves the mixture of black ink and white paper, then Brown's 1867 introduction also begs a practical question: how does an illustrator visually represent racial ambiguity when the tools at hand are contrasting fields of white paper and black ink? The question is particularly pertinent in the case of *Clotel* because the only

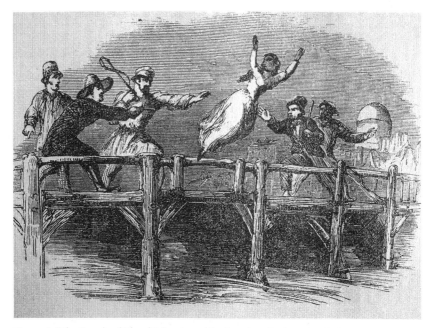

Figure 8. "The Death of Clotel." *Courtesy of the American Antiquarian Society.*

illustration of Brown's eponymous heroine, "The Death of Clotel," contradicts the author's repeated descriptions of the character's light skin and the importance of her whiteness in the narrative (Fig. 8). Clotel looks, Brown writes, "as white as . . . those who . . . wish to become her purchasers," yet in the engraving she is visibly darker than the men surrounding her. This disconnect between the verbal and visual text has not escaped scholars. Russ Castronovo, for example, notes that "even though Brown repeatedly states that Clotel . . . is so close to appearing white that she can pass as an Italian or Spanish gentleman, the illustration darkly shades her face." It is not uncommon for the visual and verbal texts within a work to create tension: "The Death of Clotel" presents what W. J. T. Mitchell calls "image/text," or "relations of the visual and verbal" that create a "problematic gap, cleavage, or rupture in representation."[54] In this instance, the rupture arises out of the link between black/white dualism in print legibility and racial legibility. Brown's deconstruction of dualism threatens to eradicate the system of black/presence and white/absence through which engravers make meaning.

Mixed-race figures break down the false logic of black/white dualism, presenting a problem for artists whose renderings are dependent on engraving as a practice of presence and absence that cannot easily mix black and white. What engravings, or "finely cut" portrayals, like 'The Death of Clotel' reveal in their attempts to depict mixed-race women is the problem of racial presence and absence, the idea of blackness as raced and whiteness as normalized, neutral, or transparent, which racial theorists ultimately expose as false. For the illustrator, though, these structures of race and legibility constitute the very form of engraving. In wood engraving, the whiteness of the page literally *is* the racial whiteness of legally white figures who go unmarked in two senses: their faces are not inked, and they are not generally understood to be "raced." The whiteness of the page makes type legible at the same time as it naturalizes the social structure of whiteness as absence, making race appear "present" on the body of its others. Working out this binary on the surface of the body was even part of an engraver's training (Fig. 9).

Michael Gaudio argues that instead of "explain[ing] away the physical substance of the engraving as the neutral agent of symbolic meaning,"

Figure 9. "Design in White" and "Design in Black," from the *Hand-book of Wood Engraving*, by William A. Emerson (East Douglas, MA: C. J. Batcheller, 1876). *Courtesy of the American Antiquarian Society.*

40   WOOD ENGRAVING.

Fig. 48.   Fig. 49.

Design in White.   *Design in Black.*

literary scholarship must grant attention "to the peculiar materiality of the engraver's art." Engravings have "a syntax," according to Gaudio, a system of meaning-making constructed through "the visible sign of a wood-engraver's concentrated efforts with his tools," the "insistently present, insistently interfering, insistently *material* lines of the engraver."[55] The material lines marking Clotel's face actualize the racial coding of the whiteness of paper and the blackness of ink, rendering Clotel's racial status legible by making it readable on the surface her skin.

"The Death of Clotel" was originally engraved for the first edition of the novel published by Partridge and Oakey, the same Protestant press that a year before had issued one of the first illustrated London editions of *Uncle Tom's Cabin*. In sharing a publisher, Brown's and Stowe's novels also had a common illustrator, Henry Anelay, and an engraver, James Johnston, a team recognizable enough to attract top billing alongside Stowe on the edition's title page.[56] Their images may even have surpassed Stowe's prose in the eyes of literary tastemakers: "All criticism on the subject of the story of Uncle Tom is superfluous; the public have settled the matter effectually by accepting the book as a sort of anti-slavery Bible not to be spoken against. The question among publishers now is, who can sell the best edition for the money? So far as real art is concerned in the illustrations, the volume before us, to our thinking, answers that question most satisfactorily. The designs of Anelay, engraved by Johnston, which adorn this edition, are alone worth the money it sells for."[57] The pair of well-known illustrators applied the same representational strategies in their depictions of both Eliza Harris and Clotel. Anelay and Johnston's Clotel and Eliza each have faces and hands similarly marked by striations designed to index a racial difference located in "blood" but not skin color. Not all engravers approached Eliza similarly. George Cruikshank, for example, does not use such lines to mark Eliza's complexion. Anelay and Johnston's lines try to register a "tint" between white and black, both visually and racially. "At one time, cross-hatching was much employed in representing flesh, which is now generally cut in tints, with white lines crossing," instructed one manual for engravers. "The lines that are [not cut away] receive ink in printing, and the lines that are cut out appear white. The quality of the plain tint depends on the evenness of the lines, which make it both black and white."[58] Anelay and Johnston's attempt to present Clotel and Eliza in "both black and white" goes beyond Brown's and Stowe's texts in order to present racial nonwhiteness as always legible on the surface of their white bodies and the surface of the white paper they inhabit. This poetics of racial representation in which "color" must be registered on the surface of the skin reflects popular thinking about the visibility of race.[59]

Despite her descriptive appearance as a "white" woman in the texts, Clotel is denied even the visual status of nineteenth-century white womanhood. That intersection of race and gender depends on ideas of racial unmarkedness and spiritual/genetic purity largely denied to mixed-race women and incompatible with the metaphorical construction of paper most clearly articulated when Franklin equates the "unsullied sheet" of "fair white paper" to "the maiden, innocently sweet." The material lines of the engraver externalize the racial blackness forbidding Clotel from entering into legal marriage with Horatio Green and indexing the sexual history of her parentage that disallows her ever having been a properly "unsullied sheet."

Given the senses of purity, beauty, refinement, and even overt white femininity sedimented on the surface page, it is no surprise that Anelay and Johnston cannot, within these racial logics, let the whiteness of the page equal the whiteness of Clotel's face described in the text. What happens on the surface of Clotel's skin here becomes inextricable from the processes of wood engraving. The wood engraver works by cutting away wood where the "white" should show, preserving the whiteness of the page from the impression of ink. Wood left raised accepts the ink and impresses it into the paper. The wood engraver, then, works by producing absences, cutting away voids that create the "invisible" whites that structure the visible blacks. Following Dyer and Lipsitz, from a visual standpoint, race, especially when articulated in color metaphors, is commonly held to be a "content" or "presence" that nonwhites carry on the surface of their bodies, a content that becomes legible as racial difference against the "background" of whiteness that claims for itself the privilege of invisibility or absence.[60] This describes the same structure through which wood engravings negotiate the figure/ground relationship: a passive, yet structuring whiteness makes visible the black marks that contrast it. But the work of the engraver actively produces these absences, just like the papermaker engages in great effort to produce a whiteness that purposefully fades out of sight. On the surface of the engraved woodblock, areas carved away (absence) "print" white, maintaining the whiteness of the page, whereas areas left raised (presence) "print" black because they accept ink from the press marking the surface of the page. Illustrating Clotel "as white as most of those . . . waiting to become her purchasers" would have required Anelay and Johnston to cut away the wood within the borders of the figure's face, creating a void, or making actual the ideology of whiteness as the absence of marking. Indeed, this is how the faces of the white men surrounding her are crafted. Leaving the wood in place to transfer ink to Clotel materially creates racial marking as presence, a "face" filled with wood on the engraving block and color on the page. Anelay and Johnston's illustrations of Clotel and Eliza demonstrate the extent to which the ideology of a racially marked blackness and a racially unmarked whiteness, reinforced in the legal institutions of "blood," guided the work of engravers for whom whiteness was literal absence and blackness literal presence.

In *Pictorial Victorians*, Julia Thomas suggests that black figures were perfect subjects for Victorian engravers seeking to demonstrate their talent:

> At a time when wood engraving was the most popular form of illustration, the reproduction of the Negro provided an opportunity for the artist and engraver to demonstrate their skills. The technique of cutting away the white parts of the image on the block and leaving the part to be inked in relief seemed designed specifically for the representation of whites. The skin could be cut away more or less in its entirety, while the inked lines served to demarcate the features. . . . Manipulating the wood engraving process and leaving all the skin in relief and therefore black, however, not only blurred the distinction between outline and content, but could obliterate the features, making the appearance of the figure too dark. The solution was to produce tonal effects by cross-hatching, cutting the wood between sets of crossed lines. . . . Such techniques . . . tested the skill and patience of the engraver, but they also showed wood engraving at its best, giving the Negro more visual impact than his white counterpart.[61]

Thomas's reading fails in its assumption that there is a discernible visual difference between "the Negro" and "whites." The image most resonant with this reading is that of Eva sitting in Uncle Tom's lap, one white and one black in visual contrast. As Brown and several other nineteenth-century writers (including Stowe) point out, however, visually identifying the legal construct of "the Negro" by complexion is not viable. Illustrating mixed-race figures that complicate the notion of racial dualism pressures both the technological limits of engraving and the tendency to equate racial status with the presence of "color." When he wrote the opening to the final revision of *Clotel*, perhaps Brown meant to emphasize that his title character challenged the duochromatic media through which she had been represented since the novel's first edition. Victorian engravers may have felt that "the Negro" figure was a showcase for the richness and possibility of the art, but once the dualisms that premise the form come under question, the figure of "the mulatta" collapses the binaries upon which wood engravings are encoded.

In "The Quadroon's Home," a chapter in *Clotel* that strategically edits Lydia Maria Child's "The Quadroons," Brown repeats Child's characterization of Clotel's daughter, Mary, as an "octoroon." "Their first-born was named Mary, and her complexion was still lighter than her mother. Indeed she was not darker than other white children. As the child grew older, it more and more resembled its mother. The iris of her large dark eye had the melting mezzotinto, which remains the last vestige of African ancestry."[62] Though Mary has the "dark and brilliant eyes" of her mother, she is imagined outside of the black/white ink/paper dualisms. Mezzotint is a different process of engraving that produces more refined shades of gray from wood or copper engraving. Rather than black lines and white lines, mezzotint creates its effects in "tones" and "halftones." In place of wood engraving's rigid separations, the mezzotint "melts" between shades. In the illustration this use of the term "mezzotint" imagines, then, that Mary's whiteness can be represented outside the black/white binary of the printed page. In place of white and black are shades of darkness and lightness. Capable of producing more mimetic representations of skin tone than the black/white dualism of wood engraving's presences and absences, the "melting mezzotinto" seems better suited to work outside the boundaries of a racial dualism never adequate to represent the people it nonetheless inscribed. William Wells Brown worked in this material world of print, a world saturated with ideological meanings related to racial difference. *Clotel* works in, through, and against these materialities and ideologies when it thematically, verbally, and visually trades in forms of legibility and illegibility—in their construction and deconstruction—and the forms of freedom and unfreedom they afford.

Authenticating Fibers

The question many mixed-race heroine narratives ask is where, exactly, race is supposedly "located" in the body, and therefore, where can it be tested? Is the skin or the blood the site or substance where race "inheres" and, finally, can be known? Antiracist and abolitionist mixed-race narratives often strike at the heart of the idea of biologically determined race by continually complicating and deferring answers to such a question. Thomas Jefferson famously asks in *Notes on the State of Virginia* where in the body race resides and can be authenticated: "Whether the black of the negro resides in the reticular membrane between the skin and scarf-skin, or in the scarf-skin itself; whether it proceeds from the colour of the blood, the colour of the bile, or from that of some other secretion, the difference is fixed in nature, and is . . . real."[63] The material surface, or its inner dimensions, we are made to believe, will reveal the material truth of racial identity.

One of the enticing features of book historical and material textual research is that they so often promise to deliver so-called hard facts about the objects of our study. Bibliography presents itself, at times, as a form of forensic analysis. Scrutiny is applied to the material textual object, it yields some hard and fast facts, and they can be known. This kind of forensic analysis is often crucially important for auction houses preparing to put manuscripts on the market. Does the paper bear a known watermark from the period? Is the organic content of its raggy contents verifiably old enough to be in a work of this purported age? What is the chemical composition of the ink used to write the manuscript? Has it oxidized at the expected rate over time? Paper, as I have been arguing here, is a site where whiteness and its others are negotiated. It is a surface and a substrate that, if kept pure, makes visible what is contrasted with it. But it, like skin, is also a site of scrutiny and of verification. In *Clotel*, we hear a list of the title character's physical features when she is subjected to the slave auction podium and watch as her white-looking skin becomes an object of scrutiny and fascination. So much of what drives the plots of mixed-race heroine narratives is whether and how a racial identification can be made, who makes such detections, and when. The body of the mixed-race woman is subjected to various tests of racial and legal identity, each of which has the highest stakes.

The methods of racial pseudoscience having to do with "where" race inheres in the skin or whether the "blush" of "black blood" on the face of the mixed-race person are certainly not the same kind of looking that we practice when we approach material texts scientifically with the expectation that they will reveal their secrets. Nonetheless, when new and fascinating archival or auction finds promise to bring new texts to our attention, we look at their surfaces and features with scrutiny so that we might authenticate them. This seems especially true when the author is purported to be an unknown or little-known nineteenth-century African American person. If a manuscript text has gone "fugitive" from the record, its materiality will give truth to its composition, age, and authenticity. While these forensic bibliographical processes are not unique to the verification of early African American writing, texts going to high-profile auction are subjected to these tests all the time; the extra rarity of early African American texts makes the process of authentication an important first step, or precursor to, any scholarship that might follow. Two high-profile examples of "recovered" African American manuscript texts do just this, and at the close of this chapter, I want to pay attention to the scrutiny they offer to paper as a site of authentication.

Caleb Smith's recent editing and publication of Austin Reed's *The Life and Adventures of a Haunted Convict* is one such text. Unknown to the wider scholarly community until it came up for auction at an estate sale, it was purchased by Yale University Library and entrusted to Smith and a team of scholars, archivists, and other experts to verify, contextualize, and eventually publish it in accessible form. When faced with a lack of positive knowledge about an authorial subject or details leading us to a story, we begin with the physical features of the text itself. Indeed, Smith recounts that it was his familiarity with Reed's distinctive hand that provided the first clues. The author listed on the manuscript is Robert Reed, so they started looking for that person. "We searched through some of New York State's prison records, but there was no sure sign" until the team found records for an "Austin Reed" in the archives of the New York City House of Refuge. "We recognized the handwriting as soon as we saw it."[64] The first connection was made toward piecing together the story of a boy and man who moved in and out of the early carceral system and crafted a remarkable pastiche of memoir, critique, and popular narrative in a singular manuscript.

Interestingly, the paper that Reed wrote on included a sheet from the Carson's paper mill, the Berkshire mill that inspired Melville's "The Paradise of Bachelors and the Tartarus of Maids." The sheet Reed used carries the same embossed stamp—a crown of flax leaves—that marks Melville's letters to Hawthorne. The embossed paper creates a distant link between the unlikely pair of Melville and Reed, while also serving to authenticate the date of Austin's writing. "Chemical testing on fibers from Reed's journal detects none of the wood pulp that would prevail in the later nineteenth century. . . . The ink from Reed's pen tests positive for iron," Smith notes, "which helps to confirm a date in the mid-nineteenth century."[65]

When Henry Louis Gates purchased a recovered manuscript version of Hannah Crafts's *The Bondswoman's Narrative*, he commissioned a full forensic analysis of the manuscript. When he published the manuscript in a modern print edition he included, in full, the authentication report prepared for Time Warner Trade Publishing by Joe Nickell. It is published as "Appendix A," included in the backmatter of the 2002 printing of *Bondswoman*. "The materiality of Hannah Crafts's novel," Russ Castronovo writes, "proves its authenticity. . . . Imprints of a thimble, stains of iron-gall ink, threads of cloth in the paper: these traces confirm the physical materials of this manuscript as products of the 1850s."[66] The physical evidence is extensive; Appendix A spans thirty pages. As Castronovo notes, happenstance impressions from a thimble and pinholes join the usual trail of evidence from paper, ink, and handwriting analysis.

Henry Louis Gates has argued that the paratexts accompanying the initial publication of Phillis Wheatley's poetry, specifically the list of prominent white men attesting to her literacy and authorship of the work, bear witness to the "trial" this enslaved woman had to endure to authenticate her work. And in publishing the list of white men's names before Wheatley's poetry, "the trial," as Gates called it, had to be carried forward to any future readers of the text.[67] This borrows from the familiar scholarly trope of the "black message" in a "white envelope," a model for thinking about racial paratexts, including these authorizing attestations that frequently attend the publication of slave narratives.[68] Gates would showcase his "Trials of Phillis Wheatley" work in the National Endowment for the Humanities Jefferson Lecture in 2002, the same year he brought out *The Bondswoman's Narrative*. Should we understand the lengthy forensic bibliography at the end of that book as a similar racial paratext, one that protects both Crafts and Gates from accusations of forgery and falsification? What sites must be submitted to scrutiny, and what evidence must be marshaled? The forensic report on *Bondswoman* contains a remarkable concatenation of detail that overwhelms the reader with evidence. Published by a trade press for a popular audience of readers unlikely to be expert judges, the appendix includes such details as whether a "potassium ferrocyanide [test] . . . yielded a prussian-blue color, thus proving the presence of iron and indicating an iron-gallotannate ink."[69] Sharing details about the manuscript's material text, rather, creates an unassailable fount of facts to back up the intellectual work of two African American writers: Crafts and Gates.

The details about paper, then, form a different kind of "white envelope" for black writing: material facts about a visually white substrate for an African American manuscript. Like Austin Reed's paper from the western Massachusetts Carson's mill, Crafts's paper bears an embossed mark reading "SOUTHWORTH / MFG. / CO.," from Southworth Manufacturing Company, in West Springfield, Massachusetts, not far from Carson's mill. Looking "inside" the paper, analysis uncovers evidence of its rag content, useful for authenticating the date of the manuscript. "I obtained some small slivers of the paper from frayed outer edges . . . moistened a sliver with distilled water and teased it apart on a microscope slide, stained it with Hezberg stain and observed the fibers microscopically," Nickell reports. "I identified rag—linen and cotton—fibers (the latter with their characteristic twist) but found no evidence of ground wood pulp," which would date the manuscript to the late 1860s.[70] Since the report is written for a general readership rather than specialists, it explains basic facts about nineteenth-century paper's construction. The report makes visible the processes of production and material dimensions of paper to twenty-first-century adult readers in ways that resemble similar instruction for nineteenth-century children. It echoes the ways nineteenth-century children learned to "see" paper as an everyday material with a remarkable production history that should not be taken for granted even if it was meant to be self-effacing.

The authenticating report's analysis also looks deep inside the manuscript's paper to reveal its whiteness. "Stereomicroscopic examination of the surface of various pages reveals the presence of bits of thread, occasionally still colored red, blue, etc., indicating the paper pulp was not bleached but was made largely of white cloth."[71] Deep within the manuscript sheets of Hannah Crafts's *The Bondswoman's Narrative* we find evidence of the whiteness of its paper. It is made from the most valuable sort of rags: white rags, never bleached. In search of authenticity for an unknown African American writer—and a well-known African American scholar—one of the significant details among others is that the paper is made up of these valuable white rags.

Whether a formal "trial" ever took place regarding the authentication of Phillis Wheatley's poetry, the authenticity and value of her authorship would be continually called into question by white figures of authority who sought to question African American literary production. These questioners would include Thomas Jefferson himself. In the same document in which he would ponder the location of blackness in the body, he dismisses African American literature and singles out Wheatley specifically, writing that "among the blacks is misery enough, God knows, but no poetry . . . Religion indeed has produced a Phyllis Whately [sic]; but it could not produce a poet."[72]

Jefferson's dismissal of African American poetry cannot be entirely separated from his desire to locate blackness in the body, as both acts stipulate notions of racial essentialism and white supremacy. In an American print landscape in which African American texts have always been—and still continue to be—called into question by white-dominated institutions of authority, the authentication documents for both Reed's and Crafts's manuscripts become necessary to their recovery and publication. What we observe in the authentication documents that Gates and Smith provide to us is yet another link that shows us how these histories of framing whiteness in U.S. print culture continue to resonate for racial production. Here, as in the other texts I discuss, the whiteness of the page allows for a particular kind of legibility for black literary production. The material culture of whiteness is hereby employed—as late as 2016—in the task of rendering racial and alphabetical legibility, showing the persistence of paper's material import for the ways in which racially marked bodies and texts are read.

"Look on every day as a blank sheet of paper," mothers are instructed to tell children as they read aloud from *The Mother's Remarks on a Set of Cuts for Children* (1803).[73] Mothers are instructed to place blank pages in front of their child and provided a text to be read aloud, instructing the children in lessons about life and everyday things. Looking upon an engraved image of a blank sheet of paper, the child is reminded, "Every object of creation may furnish hints for contemplation." "Be careful what you inscribe on it," the blank page and the day alike, "remembering that the characters are indelible and will remain forever."[74] White paper serves as the metaphorical ground for many things: white, virginal femininity; the human mind and character; a whiteness to be preserved against marks and blackness. In practice, it serves as the ground of legibility, making the figures printed on it visibly differentiated and materially manifesting ideas in the world in a given time and place. White paper's practical and figurative uses establish it as a normalized, yet often invisible, structure for making its others visible.

READING INTO SURFACES

B Y 1867, WOOD and vegetable pulp surpassed rags as the primary source material in American papermaking. Just as steam and the Fourdrinier machine dramatically changed the scale of papermaking and printing, so did a new and, at first, abundant source material. The search for a viable alternative to rags began with the earliest rag shortages. Noting that abundant paper was important for the advancement of science and the useful arts in the colonies, the American Philosophical Society frequently solicited reports about possible rag substitutes. Hector St. John de Crèvecœur, best known for his 1782 *Letters from an American Farmer*, corresponded with the Philosophical Society in 1789 to let his friends know that he had located a small French book consisting of paper samples made from many different plants. "The leaves . . . are made of the roots and barks of different trees and plants, being the first essay of this kind of manufacture," he wrote.[1] Though it is impressive that the French papermaker Pierre Alexandre Léorier-Delisle was able to make paper from reeds, nettle, hops, thistle, and many other plants, it is hard to imagine those gathered in Philosophical Hall would have been relieved by the coarse, bumpy, and dark paper surfaces they saw. Fifteen years earlier, the society sponsored a rag-collecting contest to "excite [people] to greater diligence" in rag collecting, and judging by the prospects of roots and barks to make fine white paper, their search for both rags and alternatives would continue.[2]

The production of wood pulp paper eventually solved the problem of rag shortages, but it quickly created new challenges familiar to readers and librarians who deal with print artifacts from the late nineteenth century. Ground wood pulp fibers are much shorter than shredded rag fibers and contain a much higher amount of lignin, an acidic organic compound. By the first decade of the twentieth century, paper users were already noting how quickly this highly acidic paper crumbled and darkened. Some also began to note that after forty years of mass production, wood was becoming scarce just as rags once had. In 1907, a correspondent to the *New York Times* noted that the United States' libraries and forests were both being destroyed by wood pulp paper. In a note on "the need for a new source of paper if the forests are to be saved," opinion correspondent "M. B. B." writes, "[It] is well known, wood-fibre is so perishable that newspaper files and libraries printed upon it would hardly last a generation." And while libraries of acidic paper cracked and crumbled, "the manufacture of wood paper steadily increases. . . . A mill is planted in the middle of a forest and in short time the tract is as bare as a stubble field." Once the forest has been depleted, "the portable mill is moved to another doomed forest."[3]

This change in the materiality of paper also shifted the way people wrote about paper and imagined their attachments to it. As we have seen, rag paper put readers and writers in contact with the pulped remnants of cloth, people, and the material memories and fantasies that inhered within. Wood pulp paper did not give rise to the same structures of feeling and presence. As the *Times* letter suggests, by the turn of the twentieth century, wood paper was quickly associated with environmental degradation and calls to scale back the use of paper or find a more sustainable manufacturing process. "Our beautiful poplar and spruce trees are fast disappearing. In one year, 1,500,000 cords of spruce alone were used in our paper mills," the *Times* writer complained, "woods of different kinds are devoured by the rapacious mills." This way of relating to paper continues into the present and is frequently found in the everyday ephemera of email signatures: "Save a Tree, Don't Print This Email."[4] By the early twentieth century, paper no longer signified intimacy and presence but, most famously in Walter Benjamin's description, participated in the mass production of culture that removed the "aura" from cultural artifacts.[5] The end of the rag paper period meant that paper and paperwork became an expression of alienation from others rather than a scene of intimate presence with others.

Even though wood pulp paper became dominant and over time changed the prevailing signification of paper, rag paper's sense of intimacy did not completely disappear. Just as Anne Bradstreet and Lydia Sigourney found a political claim embedded within rag paper, other artists and writers continue this tradition well into the twenty-first century. Today, we find the sense of the presences within paper held by Bradstreet, Sigourney, Thoreau, and Melville at work in the art of such paper artists as the Combat Paper and Peace Paper collectives. The way these papermakers approach rag transformation and material memory makes real in our day the structure of feeling presence effects within paper that we have seen at work throughout the long eighteenth and nineteenth century.

In 2007, Drew Cameron, a six-year veteran of the United States Army active duty and the Vermont National Guard, put on his combat-worn fatigues and began a performance. He slowly cut the United States Army uniform off his body in strips until he stood in his underwear. He then shredded the uniform, turned it into pulp, and reconstituted it as sheets of paper. Later, he printed images of the uniform cutting process on the paper along with a poem, "You are not my enemy." The end of the poem reads:

> You are not my enemy
> my child my self
> our blood
> is the same
> You are not my
> enemy
> my memories and rage
> re-making sense now
> together
> you are not my enemy
> you never were
> you are a part of me
> as I am with you
> You are not my
> enemy
> we shall stay true
> you are not my enemy
> we will change this
> with you.[6]

As Cameron cuts the uniform from his body, his speaking voice in the poem becomes increasingly able to put distance between himself and the tasks he performed in the name of the U.S. Army. As his body appears from underneath the uniform, he begins to identify with Iraqis as fellow humans ("our blood is the same"). The removal of the uniform removes the friend versus enemy frame and positions Cameron, no longer the bearer of a rifle and U.S. insignia, as a vulnerably exposed body. He takes personal responsibility for his actions but also separates himself from the military that ordered him to so act. He wants to explore solidarity between himself and his Iraqi addressee ("my memories and rage / re-making sense now"). All the while, the pile of rags on the floor grows. And from those rags Cameron produces the paper upon which all of this is printed. The uniform, which had represented the oppressive power of the U.S. military-industrial complex and the things Cameron did in its name, is transformed into the medium of reflection and reconciliation.

Cameron is one of the founding members of the Combat Paper Project, a book arts and art therapy program in which veterans cut, pulp, and transform their uniforms into paper that they then write or produce visual art upon. Participants in the Combat Paper Project (and today the related Peace Paper Project), describe the process of transforming military uniforms into paper as "cathartic." Many veteran participants in Combat Paper workshops are living with post-traumatic stress syndrome after serving in Iraq and Afghanistan. "Through papermaking workshops veterans use their uniforms worn in combat to create cathartic works of art," states the Combat Paper Project's website. That process of catharsis is dependent on understanding uniform rags as containers of material memory, objects that carry the presence of bodies, war, and experience from clothes into paper. Cameron describes how memories of combat, in addition to material traces of it, inhere in the uniforms: "The story of the fiber, the blood, sweat and tears, the months of hardship and brutal violence are held within those old uniforms. . . . Reshaping that association of subordination, of warfare and service, into something collective and beautiful is our inspiration."[7] This practice is rooted in the deep history of rag papermaking. According to their website, these papermakers say that they "[transform] military uniforms into handmade paper [using the] simple yet enduring premise that the plant fiber in rags can be transformed into paper." They have a theory of material memory carried in the presence dimension of cloth and paper: "A uniform worn through military service carries with it stories and experiences that are deeply imbued in the woven threads. Creating paper and artwork from these fibers carries these same qualities." Cameron frequently explains these capacities of rag paper during workshops and gallery installations where Combat Paper is present. In a post, an art blogger recalls seeing Cameron selling works on Combat Paper at an art fair:

> A man came up to the table and asked Cameron how much the unstenciled sheet of paper was.
> "Fifty dollars," he said.
> "But there is no image on it."
> "It's still fifty dollars."
> "It's blank. It's still fifty dollars?"
> "Yes. It's a portrait. Get it?" And then he turned to us. "Get it?"
> The short man continued, "Fifty dollars with nothing on it?"
> "It's a portrait."
> "What?"
> "It's somebody's uniform. A lot of experiences in that uniform. It's a portrait of someone."[8]

In his insistence on the presence of another within a blank sheet of paper made from their clothing, in his expression of the notion that people's life experiences are transmitted into paper through remanants of their linens, Cameron draws a direct line through American literary and book history back to Bradstreet, Sigourney, Melville, and countless others who pondered the intimacy of rag paper.

Jon Michael Turner, a veteran and Combat Paper artist who speaks of his struggles with post-traumatic stress disorder (PTSD) and substance abuse, appears in a YouTube video about how making paper from his uniforms was transformative for him. It allowed him, he says, to take the memories and experiences present within the cloth of his uniforms and to resignify the meaning of their presence once made new in paper: "I really want my voice to be heard because a bunch of my buddies have been over there, they know they've done bad things or they've seen some serious shit and they don't speak out about it, and that's what's causing them to drink as much as they are and doing the drugs and all that shit. I've been to hell and back a couple of times, between Iraq twice and all the pills that were given to me and all the booze . . . that shit ain't worth it. Making the whole paper out of my camis has been such a fucking big experience. Dealing with my shit has been great. So much better in just the last couple of days just from doing that." Turner notes that the process is more meaningful when he uses his own uniforms because they carry his memories: "It's one thing when you're pulling someone else's camis, but I've done the whole process with mine. It's been such a let go. So much weight has been lifted off my shoulders since I started the whole thing." Turner continues by saying that Combat Papermaking blurs the line between wearing a uniform and writing a book: "I put . . . there's so much history going into that paper, and that's what I'm going to write my book with." What exactly does Turner mean when he says "I put . . . there's so much history going into that paper"? The "I put . . ." refers to the parts of himself that went into the uniform during and beyond combat. Blood, sweat, dirt, and dust are in the fibers of the camis from his time in Iraq, as are his memories of what he has seen and done, the "history going into that paper" when he shreds the camis into rags. When he says, "that's what I'm going to write my book with" does he mean, literally, "this is the paper I will use to write my book"? Or, following the sense of release he feels when making the paper itself, will the narratives, histories, and relationships emerge out of the paper, releasing stories of blood, sweat, dirt, and trauma from within each sheet's rags? Drew Cameron describes the process as "reclaiming . . . taking something that . . . holds a lot of negative history for people . . . blood, sweat, and tears, horrible experiences, positive experiences. Taking that old uniform and turning it into something of our own, turning it into art . . . not some old dirty rag sitting in the closet." The process is a "reclamation . . . and reconciliation" of "old dirty rags that are full of bad memories."[9] Combat Paper and Peace Paper artists keep early and nineteenth-century American sensibilities of reading the intimacies of rag paper alive in their artwork and their communal practices.

Combat Paper and Peace Paper do not only work through individual notions of personal experience and personal memory. They also use rag paper to create paper publics, or communal affiliations rooted in shared material text creation. In his introduction to Greg Delanty's *The New Citizen Army*, a book of poetry bound in Combat Paper covers, Cameron draws on the material history of uniforms and rags to remind readers that the rag paper they now hold materially implicates them in the U.S. nation-state that pursued decades of war in Iraq:

> For us at the Combat Paper Project, [collaboration] is our defining characteristic. We utilize the uniforms and remnants of those who have survived conflict and military service to create paper with the traditional hand papermaking techniques. By working with veterans, survivors, citizens and artists, we turn

complex and often violent experiences into a collective memory and cultural response to the things we have had to bear witness to. . . . It strengthens our voice and resolve to allow our honest assessment to never again be disallowed. With this collection of poetry bound in the paper we have made from our combined uniforms, we perpetuate our belief in collective expression. This poetry lives in its various ways. It may be our uniforms that you now hold, but in a way they are yours as well.[10]

Cameron shares, or shifts, the burden of bearing witness from his group of friends and other veterans to the community of readers holding the Combat Paper–bound book in their hands. It is as if to say, "We have had to bear witness to war for you." But the rag paper made of U.S. Army uniforms provides a material trace that refuses the separation of GI and citizen. As the book's colophon says: "The Combat Paper covers were produced by John La Falce, Drew Matott, Pam DeLuco, Drew Cameron, Jon Turner and Jerry Kovis using military uniforms. These uniforms carry a lineage of over one hundred military service members, serving from WWII to the current and ongoing conflicts."[11] When Cameron points out that "it may be our uniforms that you now hold, but in a way they are yours as well," he reminds his audience that readers touch all that these cloth remnants carry and leave oils from their fingers too. The reader is drawn into the "collaborative" process of coming to terms with war—a war that can no longer be distant or abstract for the audience because the reader holds its material remnants in hand. Thus a community of material relations is drawn together and manifested in the material text.

Drew Matott, one of the founders of the Combat Paper Project and originator of the Peace Paper Project, also imagines a different kind of community growing out of the movement, what he calls the "People's Republic of Paper." Documentary videos of the early days of the Combat Paper movement show groups of veterans getting together to work on the Combat Paper Project and in the process talking, joking, laughing, and socializing with one another. In one clip, Drew Cameron toasts a gathering of maybe ten veterans and says, "We've determined this is the largest IVAW [Iraq Veterans against War] group that we've had together in a long ass time." He continues, "I have this dream now. We have this pretty small group of veterans here that are actively engaged in art making. The People's Republic of Paper and its approach will be a production paper mill of radical anti-war veterans, and that just makes me so excited!" In another clip, Phil Ailiff says "having the opportunity to hang around and work on a project with my fellow vets, no matter what we're doing . . . is always positive and beneficial to me." Matott adds: "The People's Republic of Paper is going to be a papermaking hub of activity of veterans. There's going to be veterans making paper all over the country. The goal would be to have enough people who know how to make paper, and their objective will be to teach other people how to make paper, so that they'll just continue to teach. And the veterans will be able to share their experiences, pass the torch that way."[12]

Combat Paper provides a productive outlet for these veterans to gather in community. In each of their statements, they speak to the project's ability to bring them together, to bind them into one. Its members' ragged camis comingle in new sheets of paper, and these veterans arrange themselves into new and sustaining social assemblages. These art and community projects show that the presence and meaning dimensions of rag paper continue working together, asking us to sense with both our bodies and our minds what and who inheres within and on the page.

Today, Combat Paper and Peace Paper artists travel around the United States, stopping at colleges, community centers, and artist workshops, holding papermaking sessions for veterans and others. More recently, Margaret Mahan Sheppard started a related program for survivors of intimate partner violence: the Panty Pulping Project. As with Combat and Peace Paper projects, trauma survivors create paper out of clothing, in this case panties or other intimate apparel, to create something new out the material memories embedded within. As these groups travel and make paper, they pull more and more pulped remnants of war or sexual violence into their network of remade paper. A 2015 Peace Paper broadside print by Matott and Mahan Sheppard beautifully sums up the transformative emotional and material processes at the heart of these papermaking projects (Fig. 10). It reads: "Cut the cloth to free the fibers. Pull through pulp to rinse your hands. Press the post to release rivers. Make paper to heal."

To close, I'd like to turn from today's Combat and Peace Papermakers back to the nineteenth century, and in particular to another scene of military uniforms, national and communal affiliations, and paper. In July 1863, fifty-one thousand people died fighting on the battlefields of Gettysburg. Almost all of them had linen and cotton on their bodies when they fell. Before President Lincoln rode to Pennsylvania to deliver his famous address consecrating the battlefield, the fields were scavenged by ragpickers. Ragpickers from the nearby town of Spring Grove descended on Gettysburg in the days after

Figure 10. "Make Paper to Heal," Drew Matott and Margaret Mahan Sheppard relief printing on handmade rag paper, 14 inches by 20 inches (2015). *Courtesy of the artists.*

the battle and began to pick rags from the bodies of the dead, intending to sell them to the Hauer paper mill on nearby Codorus Creek. They scavenged clothing, bandages, slings, and handkerchiefs from bodies that had already begun to decay, some of which they dug up out of shallow graves. These rags never made it back to the paper mill because the ragpickers were arrested by surviving Union troops. As punishment, the scavengers were made to bury dead horses.[13]

Those blood-soaked rags from Gettysburg were not made into paper, but many products, probably including paper, were made from materials scavenged from the remains of war.[14] In light of the ways all the writers discussed here felt rags carried people, stories, and historical circumstances into paper, I cannot help but think about how such paper would have signified to them. Picked from the bodies of Union and Confederate dead, the rags would have been broken down and brought together in the mingling of the sheet. Just as the Combat Paper and Peace Paper artists see their experiences of war archived within the fabric of paper they make from their uniforms, the Gettysburg rag paper would have contained traces of blood as material memory of the battle and remnants of the dead. Some may have seen the sheet of Gettysburg rag paper as a model of a reconstructed union, whereas others may have viewed its internal tensions as evidence of the difficult and incomplete reconstruction efforts that followed. To touch and to read such a sheet of paper would have been to encounter the contradictions of the Civil War and the bleakness of the aftermath of Gettysburg. It would have archived in material form what was done at Gettysburg beyond what words could say about it. Like Combat Paper today, rag paper made from the rags of the dead at Gettysburg would have made the dead and the bodies politics they fought for present within our archives of paper.

One of *The Intimacy of Paper's* primary goals has been to bring our contemporary encounters with rag paper more in line with how it was experienced by readers and writers of the seventeenth through nineteenth centuries. I think doing so is important for book historical and literary historical research because it helps restore to our senses ways of being with or being in paper that was often familiar to our research subjects. We are also able, I have argued, to raise different questions about what is *in* a book and in our archives of paper. We find there not simply writing but remnants of rags that are freighted with material memory and with traces of the lives they touched—literally and figuratively. Sometimes writers left accounts of how they understood these material memories and traces to matter and signify. Other times we are left to make our own strings of association and speculation about what is present to us in any given sheet of rag paper. At this book's close, I reiterate contemporary papermaker Drew Cameron's call to arrange our senses so that we understand how blank rag paper is already a portrait.

NOTES

Preface and Acknowledgments

1. Jerome McGann, *The Textual Condition* (Princeton, NJ: Princeton University Press, 1991), 3; G. Thomas Tanselle, *A Bibliographer's Creed* (Cambridge, MA: Houghton Library of Harvard University, 2014), 2.
2. Alexandra Alter, "Hot Off the Presses, for the Lucky," *New York Times*, December 24, 2018, B1; Mike Connelly, "What Happens When a Newspaper Runs Out of Paper?," *Buffalo News*, May 6, 2018; Catie Edmondson and Jaclyn Peiser, "Stopping the Presses," *New York Times*, August 9, 2018, B1; Alex Lichtenstein, "From the Editor's Desk," *American Historical Review* 132, no. 4 (October 2018): xvi.

Introduction

1. John Bidwell, "The Study of Paper as Evidence, Artefact and Commodity," in *The Book Encompassed: Studies in Twentieth-Century Bibliography*, ed. Peter Davison (Cambridge: Cambridge University Press, 1992), 69; Georges Poulet, "Phenomenology of Reading" *New Literary History* 1, no. 1 (1969): 54; Ronald McKerrow, *An Introduction to Bibliography for Literary Students* (New York: Oxford University Press, 1927), 97.
2. Jerome McGann suggested the entwining of these layers of meaning, calling them a "double helix of perceptual codes . . . linguistic codes on one hand, and bibliographical codes on the other." To these, Michael F. Suarez S.J. adds the extratextual social and political contexts of social codes (quoted in Emma Rathbone, "What's the Future of Books in a Digital World?," *University of Virginia Magazine*, https://uvamagazine.org/articles/whats_the_future_of_books_in_a_digital_world. Jerome McGann, *The Textual Condition* (Princeton, NJ: Princeton University Press, 1991), 77, 4 (emphasis in original).
3. Hans Ulrich Gumbrecht, *The Production of Presence: What Meaning Cannot Convey* (Stanford, CA: Stanford University Press, 2003), xiv–xv, xii.
4. The musicologist Carolyn Abbate has written about the split in attention between

"the material acoustic phenomenon" of "music that exists in time" and space versus the "metaphysical mania" that pulls scholars to "retreat" to the "to the abstraction of the work." Carolyn Abbate, "Music: Drastic or Gnostic?," *Critical Inquiry* 30, no. 3 (Spring 2004): 505.

5. M. Emory Wright, *The Parsons Paper Mill at Holyoke, Mass. Embracing a Minute Description of the Paper Manufacture in Its Various Departments* (Springfield, MA: Samuel Bowles & Company, Printers, 1857), 5–6.

6. John C. Holbrook, *Recollections of a Nonagenarian* (Boston: Pilgrim Press, 1897), 30. For the most part, discussions of paper money, though relevant to thinking about paper in the nineteenth century, have been omitted from this book because the historical and literary writing about paper money is vast and would require its own book. See Kevin McLaughlin's *Paperwork: Fiction and Mass Mediacy in the Paper Age* (Philadelphia: University of Pennsylvania Press, 2005), for literary scholarship that begins to do this work. On the subject of ragpicking and paper money, see my essay "Rags Make Paper, Paper Makes Money: Material Texts and the Creation of Capital," *Technology and Culture* 58, no. 2 (April 2017): 545–55.

7. Wright, *Parsons Paper Mill*, 6. Herman Melville to Nathaniel Hawthorne, November 17, 1851, in *The Writings of Herman Melville*, vol. 14, *Correspondence*, ed. Lynn Horth (Chicago: Northwestern University Press, 1993), 212.

8. Major centers, fellowships, and university press series have adopted the "material text" as their organizing object. See, for example, the Centre for the Material Text at Cambridge University, fellowships in material textual studies at the University of California at Los Angeles (UCLA) and the University of Pennsylvania (UPenn), UPenn's "Material Texts" seminar, and the Material Texts book series at Penn Press. For further information about these resources, see Centre for the Material Text at Cambridge University (http://www.english.cam.ac.uk/cmt/); fellowships in material textual studies at UCLA and UPenn (http://www.c1718cs.ucla.edu/content/postdoc-sup.htm and http://www.mceas.org/dissertationfellowships.shtml, respectively); and the Material Texts book series at the University of Pennsylvania Press (http://www.upenn.edu/penn press/series/MT.html).

9. Michelle Moylan and Lane Stiles, *Reading Books: Essays on Literature and the Material Text in America* (Amherst: University of Massachusetts Press, 1997), 13; Meredith McGill, "Literary History, Book History, and Media Studies," in *Turns of Event: Nineteenth-Century American Literary Studies in Motion*, ed. Hester Blum (Philadelphia: University of Pennsylvania Press, 2016), 33.

10. Roger Chartier, "Laborers and Voyagers: From the Text to the Reader," *Diacritics* 22 (1992): 50; Bill Brown, "Introduction: Textual Materialism," *PMLA* 125, no. 1 (January 2010): 25–26

11. Karen J. Winkler, "In an Electronic Age, Scholars Are Drawn to Study of Print," *Chronicle of Higher Education*, July 14, 1993; David Scott Kastan, *Shakespeare after Theory* (New York: Routledge, 1999), 18; Matthew P. Brown, "Book History, Sexy Knowledge, and the Challenge of the New Boredom," *American Literary History* 16, no. 4 (2004): 688–706.

12. See, for example, McGill's argument about format (pamphlets versus books) in "Frances Ellen Watkins Harper and the Circuits of Abolitionist Poetry," in *Early African American Print Culture*, ed. Lara Langer Cohen and Jordan Alexander Stein (Philadelphia: University of Pennsylvania Press, 2012), 53–74.

13. The Friends of Dard Hunter is the scholarly and craft community most responsible for shepherding this field today. See www.friendsofdardhunter.org.

14. See Dard Hunter, *Papermaking: The History and Technique of an Ancient Craft* (New York: Knopf, 1943), Cathleen A. Baker, *From the Hand to the Machine: Nineteenth-Century American Paper and Mediums: Technologies, Materials, and Conservation* (Ann Arbor, MI: Legacy Press, 2010), and Nicholas A. Basbanes, *On Paper: The Everything of Its Two-Thousand-Year History* (New York: Knopf, 2013).

15. Keith Arbour, "Papermaking in New England before 1675? A Document and a Challenge," *Papers of the Bibliographical Society of America* 96, no. 3 (September 2002): 351–79; John Bidwell, *American Paper Mills, 1690–1832: A Directory of the Paper Trade with Notes on Products, Watermarks, Distribution Methods, and Manufacturing Techniques* (Hanover, NH: Dartmouth College Press, 2013), 82n26.

16. For a concise history of the Rittenhouse Mill, see James Green, *The Rittenhouse Mill and the Beginnings of Papermaking in America* (Philadelphia, PA: Library Company of Philadelphia and Friends of Historic Rittenhouse Town, 1990).

17. Horatio Gates Jones, "Historical Sketch of the Rittenhouse Papermill; The First Erected in America, A.D. 1690," *Pennsylvania Magazine of History and Biography* 20, no. 3 (1896): 318.

18. Michael Winship's study of the Ticknor and Fields cost books is indispensable for understanding the processes and decisions behind the mid-nineteenth-century industrial book trade. See Michael Winship, *American Literary Publishing in the Mid-Nineteenth Century: The Business of Ticknor and Fields* (New York: Cambridge University Press, 1995), 95.

19. For "cloth parchment," see Steven Roger Fischer, *History of Writing* (London: Reaktion Books, 2001), e-book. For a comprehensive global history of papermaking, see Dard Hunter, *Papermaking: The History and Technique of an Ancient Craft* (Mineola, NY: Dover Publications, 1978). Hunter's several books on the art and craft of papermaking are informed by his own mastery of the art of papermaking.

20. Descriptions and technical details of the hand papermaking process come from Baker, *From the Hand to the Machine*, 20–49 and Timothy Barrett, Mark Ormsby, Robert Shannon, Irene Brückle, Joseph Lang, Michael Schilling, Joy Jazurek, Jennifer Wade, and Jessica White, *Paper through Time: Nondestructive Analysis of 14th- through 19th-Century Papers*, University of Iowa, last modified May 04, 2016, http://paper.lib.uiowa.edu/index.php, and Barrett, *European Hand Papermaking: Traditions, Tools, and Techniques* (Ann Arbor, MI: Legacy Press, 2018). Barrett and his team at the University of Iowa Center for the Book endeavored to re-create the process of making 2,000 sheets of handmade "Chancery" format paper in one day with a team of three. They documented the process on video. Short of doing the work oneself, the video is the best resource for appreciating the work of mass-producing hand paper. See Timothy Barrett, *Chancery Paper*, YouTube, last modified May 28, 2013, https://www.youtube.com/watch?v=e-PmfdV_cZU.

21. *Ithaca (NY) Journal*, March 17, 1830 (emphasis in original).

22. "Trench's Paper Mill," *Burtons' Gentleman's Magazine and American Monthly Review*, May 1, 1840, 246.

23. Baker, *From the Hand to the Machine*, 28, 50–65.

24. February 1818 article in *The Federal Gazette and Baltimore Advertiser*. Quoted in Baker, 53–54.

25. Lyman Horace Weeks, *A History of Paper-Manufacturing in the United States, 1690–1916* (New York: Lockwood Trade Journal Company, 1916), 235.

26. Wright, *Parsons Paper Mill*, 5.

27. Luca Beltrami, *Per la facciata del Duomo di Milano* (Milan, 1657). The call number for this copy at the University of Illinois Urbana-Champaign is Cavagna 17604.

28. "The Adventures of a Quire of Paper," *London Magazine, or Gentleman's Monthly Intelligencer* 48 (October 1779): 355–98, 448–52. The best recent scholarship on paper it-narratives and "The Adventures of a Quire of Paper" in particular is Leah Price, *How to Do Things with Books in Victorian Britain* (Princeton, NY: Princeton University Press, 2012).

29. *Odds and Ends*, Rochester, NY, March 1, 1850. Amateur newspapers and periodicals collection [manuscript], 1737; 1795–1892, American Antiquarian Society, Worcester, MA.

30. G. W. Henry, *The Tell-Tale Rag and Popular Sins of the Day* (Oneida, NY: G. W. Henry, 1861), title page.

31. Carolyn Steedman, *Dust: The Archive and Cultural History* (New Brunswick, NJ: Rutgers University Press, 2002), 128 (emphasis in original).

32. N. Katherine Hayles, *Writing Machines* (Cambridge, MA: MIT Press, 2002), 22.

33. David S. Barnes, "Cargo, 'Infection,' and the Logic of Quarantine in the Nineteenth Century," *Bulletin of the History of Medicine* 88, no. 1 (Spring 2014): 88.

34. Bill Brown, *Other Things* (Chicago: University of Chicago Press, 2015), 9.

35. Stéphane Mallarmé, "L'Action réstreinte," quoted in Maurizio Ferraris, *Documentality: Why It Is Necessary to Leave Traces* (New York: Fordham University Press, 2013), iv.

36. Walter Benjamin, "Unpacking My Library," in *Illuminations: Essays and Reflections*, ed. Hannah Arendt (New York: Schocken Books, 1968), 59, 67.

37. Christina Lupton, "The Theory of Paper: Skepticism, Common Sense, Post Structuralism," *Modern Language Quarterly* 71, no. 4 (2010): 426; Jennifer Schuessler, "The Paper Trail through History," *New York Times*, December 16, 2012, C1.

38. Lisa Gitelman, *Paper Knowledge: Toward a Media History of Documents* (Durham, NC: Duke University Press, 2014), 7; Ben Kafka, *The Demon of Writing: Powers and Failures of Paperwork* (New York: Zone Books, 2012). Before Kafka and Gitelman, Kevin McLaughlin was working at the intersection of paper, mediation, and literature/history. McLaughlin's take on "paperwork" in the nineteenth century is that it represents a decline of what Walter Benjamin would later call "aura." McLaughlin links the "mass mediacy" enabled by "the paper age" to the "withdrawal of the here and now" through readings of paper money, the novel, and the historical essay. See McLaughlin, *Paperwork*. McLaughlin's focus on paper and the withdrawal of aura conflicts with the readings I offer in this book about rag paper's intimacy, enchantment, and presence.

39. See Augusta Rohrbach, *Thinking outside the Book* (Amherst: University of Massachusetts Press, 2014).

40. Alexandra Socarides, *Dickinson Unbound: Paper, Process, Poetics* (New York, Oxford University Press, 2012), 4.

41. Emily Dickinson, *The Letters of the Emily Dickinson*, ed. Thomas H. Johnson and Theodora Ward (Cambridge, MA: Belknap Press of Harvard University Press, 1958) 77 (emphasis in original); Socarides, *Dickinson Unbound*, 168.

42. Bonnie Mak, *How the Page Matters* (Toronto, ON: University of Toronto Press, 2011), 6, 3.

43. Sarah Kay, *Animal Skins and the Reading Self in Medieval Latin and French Bestiaries* (Chicago: University of Chicago Press, 2017), 3.

44. For a review and critique of the recent robust interest in new materialisms, see Andrew Cole, "The Call of Things: A Critique of Object-Oriented Ontologies," *Minnesota Review* 80 (2013): 106–18.

45. Sonia Hazard, "The Material Turn in the Study of Religion," *Religion and Society* 4, no. 1 (2013): 65. More recently, Hazard challenged those who study early American material texts to think more speculatively about the thingly vitality of books through new materialism's modes. See Sonia Hazard, "Thing," *Early American Studies: An Interdisciplinary Journal* 16, no. 4 (2018): 792–800.

46. Bill Brown, "Thing Theory," *Critical Inquiry* 28, no. 1 (October 2001): 4–5; Roland Barthes, *Camera Lucida: Reflections on Photography*, trans. Richard Howard (New York: Hill and Wang, 1981), 26–27; *Oxford English Dictionary Online*, s.v. "accident."

47. Bill Brown, *Other Things*, 11.

48. Gumbrecht, *Production of Presence*, xiv.

49. Margreta De Grazia and Peter Stallybrass, "The Materiality of the Shakespearean Text," *Shakespeare Quarterly* 44, no. 3 (1993): 255–83, 257 (emphasis in original).

50. Gumbrecht, *Production of Presence*, 9, 11.

51. See Friedrich A. Kittler, *Discourse Networks, 1800/1900*, trans. Michael Metteer and Chris Cullens (Stanford, CA: Stanford University Press, 1990). The original German title of *Discourse Networks* was *Aufschreibesysteme*, which David Wellerby tells us in the preface translates literally to "systems of writing down," or "notation systems," xii.

52. On the relationship between book history and media studies see McGill, "Literary History, Book History, and Media Studies." Kittler's influence on Gitelman is most readily seen in her book *Scripts, Grooves, and Writing Machines: Representing Technology in the Edison Era* (Stanford, CA: Stanford University Press, 2000).

53. Gumbrecht, *Production of Presence*, 18, 11–12.

54. Hans Ulrich Gumbrecht, *The Powers of Philology: Dynamics of Textual Scholarship* (Champaign: University of Illinois Press, 2003), 6; Friedrich A. Kittler, *Gramophone, Film, Typewriter*, trans. Geoffrey Winthrop-Young (Stanford, CA: Stanford University Press, 1999).

55. Gumbrecht, *Production of Presence*, 54.

56. Isaiah Thomas, printer, papermaker, and founder of the AAS, the first historical society to focus on the entirety of the United States, published *History of Printing in America, with a Biography of Printers, and an Account of Newspapers* in two volumes in 1810, providing some of the earliest bibliographical and book historical knowledge we have. The gathering of blank paper from his mill is collected in Isaiah Thomas, Papers, 1748–1874, box 1, folder 4, American Antiquarian Society, Worcester, MA.

57. See Bidwell, *American Paper Mills, 1690–1832* for a definitive history of handmade paper mills in colonial North America and the early national United States. Notes on the Thomas mill and its watermarks are on pp. 109–10.

58. Paul J. Erickson has written about the account book of Thomas's paper mill, noting that he often paid millworkers and mould makers in paper and books. Paul J. Erickson, "The

Business of Building Books," *Common-place: The Journal of Early American Life* 17, no. 4 (Summer 2017), http://common-place.org/book/business-building-books/.

59. *Boston News-Letter*, March 6, 1769.

60. Isaiah Thomas, *The History of Printing in America*, ed. Marcus McCorison (New York: Weathervane Books, 1970) 3, 21–28.

61. Eric Gill, *An Essay on Typography* (Boston: David Godine, 1988), 82; *The Massachusetts Spy*, February 7, 1776.

Chapter 1: Paper Publics and Material Textual Affiliations in American Print Culture

1. M. Emory Wright, *The Parsons Paper Mill at Holyoke, Mass. Embracing a Minute Description of the Paper Manufacture in Its Various Departments* (Springfield, MA: Samuel Bowles, 1857), 19–20.

2. "Beautiful Machinery," *Scientific Tracts: Designed for Instruction and Entertainment and Adapted to Schools, Lyceums and Families*, April 15, 1835, 258. It was reprinted a week later in the *New England Farmer and Gardner's Journal*, April 29, 1835, 332, and by June had been reprinted in the *Cincinnati (Ohio) Mirror and Western Gazette of Literature and Science*, June 20, 1835, 276.

3. Laura Rigal, *The American Manufactory: Art, Labor, and the World of Things in the Early Republic* (Princeton, NJ: Princeton University Press, 2001), 9; "Beautiful Machinery."

4. In the colonies that would become the United States, paper was made from the recycled rags of linen, and eventually cotton, from at least 1690. Rags would continue to be the primary ingredient until 1867, when wood pulp–based production surpassed rag-based. For an up-to-date history of papermaking during this period, see the introductory chapters of John Bidwell's *American Paper Mills, 1690–1832: A Directory of the Paper Trade with Notes on Products, Watermarks, Distribution Methods, and Manufacturing Techniques* (Hanover, NH: Dartmouth College Press, 2013).

5. Wright, *Parsons Paper Mill*, 7–8.

6. Sandra M. Gustafson, "American Literature and the Public Sphere," *American Literary History* 20, no. 3 (2008): 465; Michael Warner, *The Letters of the Republic: Publication and the Public Sphere in Eighteenth-Century America* (Cambridge, MA: Harvard University Press, 1990), xiii; Benedict Anderson, *Imagined Communities: Reflections on the Origin and Spread of Nationalism*, rev. ed. (New York: Verso, 2006).

7. Trish Loughran's *The Republic in Print: Print Culture in the Age of U.S. Nation-Building, 1770–1870* (New York: Columbia University Press, 2007) is a notable exception.

8. Quoted in Dard Hunter, *Papermaking: The History and Technique of an Ancient Craft* (Mineola, NY: Dover Publications, 1978), 310.

9. Gillian Silverman, *Bodies and Books: Reading and the Fantasy of Communion in Nineteenth-Century America* (Philadelphia: University of Pennsylvania Press, 2012), 7.

10. Joseph Addison, *Spectator*, no. 367, May 1, 1712, 193.

11. Addison, *Spectator*, 193.

12. Printer and stationer Richard Tottel petitioned Elizabeth I for a monopoly on papermaking and a ban on exporting rags out of England, chiefly because French papermakers imported English rags and then sold paper back to English stationers at prices cheaper than could be found for English-made paper. Ronald B.

McKerrow, *An Introduction to Bibliography for Literary Students* (New York: Oxford University Press, 1965), 99.

13. Addison, *Spectator*, 193.

14. Addison, 194.

15. *The Providence Gazette; and Country Journal*, March 22, 1777, 4.

16. Frank O. Butler, *The Story of Paper-Making, an Account of Paper-Making from Its Earliest Known Record Down to the Present Time* (Chicago: J. W. Paper Company, 1901), 37–38. This story may be apocryphal; Tennent's "Defensive War" was printed by Franklin in 1748, and thirty years seems a long time to keep twenty-five hundred sermon pamphlets pending payment. As with most stories about Franklin, however, the persistence of its circulation and the value of the story for those who retell it seem more significant than its veracity. Another version of this story is told about the pacifist *Martyrs' Mirror* being used at wadding. See David Luthy, "The Ephrata *Martyrs' Mirror*: Shot from Patriots' Muskets," *Pennsylvania Mennonite Heritage* 9, no. 1 (1986): 2–5.

17. Jacques Derrida, "Paper or Me, You Know . . . (New Speculations on a Luxury of the Poor)," in *Paper Machine*, trans. Rachel Bowlby (Stanford, CA: Stanford University Press, 2005), 58.

18. Matthew S. Hull, *Government of Paper: The Materiality of Bureaucracy in Urban Pakistan* (Berkeley: University of California Press, 2012), and Ben Kafka, *The Demon of Writing: Powers and Failures of Paperwork* (New York: Zone Books, 2012).

19. Derrida, "Paper or Me," 57.

20. Kate Vieira, *American by Paper: How Documents Matter in Immigrant Literacy* (Minneapolis: University of Minnesota Press, 2016), 3–4.

21. *A Poetical Dream Concerning Stamped Papers*, in *A New Collection of Verses Applied to the First of November, A.D. 1765, &c. Including a Prediction that the S—p-A-t shall not take Place in North-America, Together with A poetical Dream Concerning Stamped Papers* (New Haven, CT: B. Mecom, 1765), 19.

22. *A Poetical Dream Concerning Stamped Papers*, 20–22.

23. Benedict Anderson, *Imagined Communities*, 35–36.

24. *A Poetical Dream Concerning Stamped Papers*, 23.

25. *A Poetical Dream Concerning Stamped Papers*, 23.

26. Robert Darnton, "What Is the History of Books?," *Daedalus* 111, no. 3 (1982): 68.

27. For a study of how colonial American discussions and political debates were often projected into London, the scene of their publication, see Jonathan Beecher Field, *Errands into the Metropolis: New England Dissidents in Revolutionary London* (Hanover, NH: Dartmouth College Press, 2009). Joe Rezek has shown that these routes between London and the "provinces" did not end in the eighteenth century. See his *London and the Making of Provincial Literature: Aesthetics and the Transatlantic Book Trade, 1800–1850* (Philadelphia: University of Pennsylvania Press, 2015).

28. Dard Hunter, *Papermaking in Pioneer America* (Philadelphia: University of Pennsylvania Press, 1952), 18, 24.

29. Henk Voorn, *Old Ream Wrappers: An Essay on Early Ream Wrappers of Antiquarian Interest* (North Hills, PA: Bird & Bull Press, 1969), 96.

30. Eugenie Andruss Leonard, "Paper as a Critical Commodity during the American

Revolution," *Pennsylvania Magazine of History and Biography* 74, no. 4 (October 1950): 488–99.

31. "New-Haven Paper-Mill," *Connecticut Journal*, February 19, 1777.

32. "To the Ladies," *Connecticut Courant and Hartford Weekly Intelligencer*, September 29, 1777.

33. Richard Frame, "A Short Description of Pennsilvania, Or, a Relation What things are known, enjoyed, and like to be discovered in the said Province Presented as a Token of Good Will to the People of England" (Philadelphia, PA: William Bradford, 1692), 7–8.

34. "New-Haven Paper-Mill."

35. John Locke, *An Essay concerning Human Understanding*, ed. Peter Nidditch (Oxford: Clarendon Press, 1975).

36. Linda Kerber, *Women of the Republic: Intellect and Ideology in Revolutionary America* (Chapel Hill: University of North Carolina Press, 1980), 11, 10. The Fort Edward newspaper was quoted in the "The Rag Supply a Hundred Years Ago," *World's Trade Paper Review*, January 20, 1893.

37. *Eastern Herald* (Portland, ME), August 17, 1795, 4; Linda K. Kerber, *Toward an Intellectual History of Women: Essays* (Chapel Hill: University of North Carolina Press, 1997), 16.

38. Quoted in the *World's Paper Trade Review*, January 20, 1893, 30.

39. Quoted in Joel Munsell, *A Chronology of Paper and Paper Making* (Albany, NY: J. Munsell, 1857), 41.

40. Henry Charles Carey, "The Paper Question," in *Miscellaneous Works* (Philadelphia: Collins, 1865), 10.

41. Oliver Wendell Holmes, "Bread and the Newspaper," *Atlantic Monthly*, September 1861, 347, 348.

42. Holmes, "Bread and the Newspaper," 347.

43. "Want of Paper," *Southern Literary Companion*, April 15, 1863.

44. "Paper Is King," *New York Times*, June 22, 1861.

45. "Suspension of the Marietta Paper Mills," *Savannah Republican*, September 14, 1863; Mary Deborah Petite, *"The Women Will Howl": The Union Army Capture of Roswell and New Manchester, Georgia, and the Forced Relocation of Mill Workers* (Jefferson, NC: McFarland, 2008), 8.

46. *Pictorial Democrat*, April 8, April 15, 1863.

47. *Daily Citizen Vicksburg, Miss.*, July 2, July 4, 1863.

48. The AAS call number for this particular book copy is G526 D751 N866.

49. Anita Singh, "Jonathan Franzen: E-Books Are Damaging Society," *Telegraph*, January 29, 2012, http://www.telegraph.co.uk/culture/hay-festival/9047981/Jonathan-Franzen-e-books-are-damaging-society.html.

50. Electronic books are no less material than paper books, despite popular imaginaries of the digital as immaterial. For a study of how book historical methods inform digital forensics of electronic texts, see Matthew Kirschenbaum, *Mechanisms: New Media and the Forensic Imagination* (Cambridge: Massachusetts Institute of Technology Press, 2007).

51. R. R. Bowker, "A Sheet of Paper," *Harper's New Monthly Magazine*, June 1887, 113.

52. Joseph Dumbleton, "The Paper-Mill," in *Colonial American Poetry*, ed. Kenneth Silverman (New York: Hafner, 1968), 326–27.

53. "To the Ladies," *Connecticut Courant and Hartford Weekly Intelligencer*, September 29, 1777.

54. "The *Courant's* Centennial Anniversary: From the *Hartford Courant*, Oct. 29, 1864," broadside circular.

55. Hans Ulrich Gumbrecht, *The Production of Presence: What Meaning Cannot Convey* (Stanford, CA: Stanford University Press: 2004), 8. See also Hans Ulrich Gumbrecht and K. Ludwig Pfieffer, *Materialities of Communication*, trans. William Whobrey (Stanford, CA: Stanford University Press, 1994).

56. Gumbrecht, *Production of Presence*, xiii.

57. Henk Voorn, *Old Ream Wrappers: An Essay on Early Ream Wrappers of Antiquarian Interest* (North Hills, PA: Bird & Bull Press, 1969).

Chapter 2: The Gender of Rag Paper in Anne Bradstreet and Lydia Sigourney

1. On Franklin's financial interests in the colonial paper industry and trade, see James N. Green and Peter Stallybrass, *Benjamin Franklin: Writer and Printer* (New Castle, DE: Oak Knoll Press, 2006), 40; J. A. Leo Lemay, *The Life of Benjamin Franklin*, vol. 1, *Journalist, 1706–1730* (Philadelphia: University of Pennsylvania Press, 2005), 327; and Jill Lepore, *Book of Ages: The Life and Opinions of Jane Franklin* (New York: Knopf, 2013), 67.

2. Benjamin Franklin, *Benjamin Franklin's Autobiography*, ed. J. A. Leo Lemay and P. M. Zall (New York: W. W. Norton, 1986), 54.

3. Franklin, *Benjamin Franklin's Autobiography*, 64–65.

4. Lepore, *Book of Ages*, 67.

5. M. Emory Wright, *The Parsons Paper Mill at Holyoke, Mass. Embracing a Minute Description of the Paper Manufacture in Its Various Departments* (Springfield, MA: Samuel Bowles, 1857), 19.

6. Lydia Maria Child, *The American Frugal Housewife: Dedicated to Those Who Are Not Ashamed of Economy* (London: T. T. and J. Tegg, 1832), 14–15.

7. Lyman Horace Weeks, *A History of Paper Manufacture in the United States, 1690–1916* (New York: Lockwood Trade Journal Company, 1916), 64.

8. Benjamin January, "Ready Money or Good Writing Paper Is Given in Exchange for Clean Linen," *Pennsylvania Gazette*, February 7, 1781.

9. "Save Your Old Papers and Rags," *Delaware County Republican*, December 5, 1862.

10. This poem is often quoted without attribution in histories of the paper trade, including in Benjamin S. Van Wyck's "The Story of Paper," *Publisher's Weekly*, April 9, 1921, 1118, and in Weeks, *A History of Paper Manufacture*, 115. Weeks notes that the verse originated with an unnamed New York State paper mill in 1807.

11. Elizabeth Wade White, *Anne Bradstreet: The Tenth Muse* (New York: Oxford University Press, 1971), 267.

12. Ivy Schweitzer, *The Work of Self-Representation: Lyric Poetry in Colonial New England* (Chapel Hill: University of North Carolina Press, 1991), 151.

13. Anne Bradstreet, "The Author to Her Book," in *American Poetry: The Seventeenth and Eighteenth Centuries*, ed. David S. Shields (New York: Library of America, 2007), 55–56.

14. Bradstreet, "The Author to her Book," 56.

15. Quoted in Schweitzer, *The Work of Self-Representation*, 128.

16. John Bidwell, "The Study of Paper as Evidence, Artefact and Commodity," in *The*

Book Encompassed: Studies in Twentieth-Century Bibliography, ed. Peter Davison (Cambridge: Cambridge University Press, 1992), 69; Bradstreet, "The Author to Her Book," 46.

17. Schweitzer, *The Work of Self-Representation*, 173.

18. Timothy Sweet, "Gender, Genre, and Subjectivity in Anne Bradstreet's Early Elegies," *Early American Literature* 23 (1988): 168, 169.

19. Kenneth Requa, "Anne Bradstreet's Poetic Voices," *Early American Literature* 9 (1974): 4, 3.

20. Jean Marie Lutes, "Negotiating Theology and Gynecology: Anne Bradstreet's Representations of the Female Body," *Signs* 22 (1997): 310.

21. Lutes, "Negotiating Theology and Gynecology," 312, 310.

22. Bradstreet, "The Author to Her Book," 45; Bethany Reid, "'Unfit for Light': Anne Bradstreet's Monstrous Birth," *New England Quarterly* 71 (1998): 519, 542.

23. Marjorie Garber, *Quotation Marks* (New York: Routledge, 2003), 187; Bradstreet, "The Author to Her Book," 46.

24. David D. Hall, "Readers and Writers in Early New England," in *A History of the Book in America*, vol. 1, *The Colonial Book in the Atlantic World*, ed. Hugh Amory and David D. Hall (New York: Cambridge University Press with the American Antiquarian Society, 2000), 150.

25. The prefatory material to *The Tenth Muse* is clearly a threshold negotiating the uncommonness and even the unseemliness of the promiscuous relationship between the world of readers and the woman author, though as Schweitzer argues, such paratexts can obscure as easily as they can better reading. Schweitzer, *The Work of Self-Representation*, 163–66.

26. John Woodbridge, "Kind Reader," in Anne Bradstreet, *The Tenth Muse (1650), and, from the Manuscripts, Meditations, Divine and Morall, together with Letters and Occasional Pieces by, Anne Bradstreet: Facsimile Reproductions with an Introduction*, ed. Josephine K. Peircy (Gainesville, FL: Scholars' Facsimiles & Reprints, 1965), iv.

27. Schweitzer, *The Work of Self-Representation*, 145, 146.

28. Bradstreet, "The Author to Her Book," 45.

29. *Oxford English Dictionary*, 2nd ed. (1989), OED Online, Oxford University Press, s.v. "Ragamuffin," nn. 2 and a.2b.

30. We can say for certain only that papermaking did not begin in the North American colonies until 1690. New evidence, however, suggests that "paper may have been made in Massachusetts in the early 1670s"; see Keith Arbour, foreword to Thomas L. Gravell and George Miller, *American Watermarks: 1690–1835* (New Castle, DE: Oak Knoll Press, 2002), xii. This possibility is incredibly enticing for my reading of "The Author to Her Book" because it means that Bradstreet could have seen or heard of the process taking place near her. As Arbour says, the evidence of this "tentative assertion . . . is slender, but it is interesting to think of a counter-narrative to the one that begins in Philadelphia in 1690 (Arbour, foreword, xii). The evidence, as Arbour presents it, is that "on 4 February 1674/5, the English polymath Sir William Petty sat down in London with two New Englanders, surnamed Frost and Bartholomew [sic], and recorded what they told him about their part of the world." Petty's informants were knowledgeable and trustworthy. Among the 300 or so data they communicated was one Sir William recorded thus: "*Paper hath been made in New England*" (Arbour, xii–xiii). Also pertinent to my argument about the global

implications of the rag and paper trade is that, according to Arbour, Petty was concerned about papermaking in his economic writings because "he thought paper largely a French product, the importation of which depleted England's coffers while filling her historic enemy's" (Arbour, xiiin7).

31. Philip Gaskell, *A New Introduction to Bibliography* (New Castle, DE: Oak Knoll Press, 1995), 60; Anne Bradstreet, "A Dialogue between Old England and New," in Shields, *American Poetry*, 40, 41.

32. On the Protestant Atlantic public sphere, see Jonathan Beecher Field, *Errands into the Metropolis: New England Dissidents in Revolutionary London* (Hanover, NH: Dartmouth College Press, 2009).

33. Margreta de Grazia and Peter Stallybrass, "The Materiality of the Shakespearian Text," *Shakespeare Quarterly* 44, no. 3 (1993): 280.

34. Anne Bradstreet, "To my dear children," in Shields, *American Poetry*, 58.

35. de Grazia and Stallybrass, "The Materiality of the Shakespearian Text," 280.

36. Anne Bradstreet, "The Prologue," in Shields, *American Poetry*, 36.

37. de Grazia and Stallybrass, "The Materiality of the Shakespearian Text," 280.

38. Bradstreet, "The Author to Her Book," 46.

39. Ann Rosalind Jones and Peter Stallybrass, *Renaissance Clothing and the Materials of Memory* (New York: Cambridge University Press, 2000), 3.

40. For more on flax and other vegetable inclusions visible within rag paper, see Joshua Calhoun, "The Word Made Flax: Cheap Bibles, Textual Corruption, and the Poetics of Paper," *PMLA* 126, no. 2 (2011): 327–44, particularly the section titled "Flax and the Materials of Memory."

41. Quoted in Schweitzer, *The Work of Self-Representation*, 128.

42. Bradstreet, "The Prologue," 37.

43. Jones and Stallybrass, *Renaissance Clothing and the Materials of Memory*, 141, 144.

44. Jones and Stallybrass, 148, 165–66, 171.

45. Ingrid D. Rowland, "Women Artists Win!," *New York Review of Books*, May 29, 2008, 27.

46. Gordon S. Haight, *Mrs. Sigourney: The Sweet Singer of Hartford* (New Haven, CT: Yale University Press, 1930), ix, 168.

47. Lydia H. Sigourney, "Hymn. For the Bi-centennial Anniversary of the Settlement of Norwich, Conn.," broadside, [1859], Norwich, CT: Manning, Perry & Company.

48. Joel Munsell, *Chronology of the Origin and Progress of Paper and Paper-Making* (Albany, NY: J. Munsell, 1876), 142; the *Syracuse Daily Standard* quoted in Joseph A. Dane, *The Myth of Print Culture: Essays on Evidence, Textuality, and Bibliographical Method* (Toronto, ON: University of Toronto Press, 2003), 174.

49. Munsell, *Chronology*, 198.

50. Sigourney, "Hymn. For the Bi-centennial Anniversary."

51. S. J. Wolfe, with Robert Singerman, *Mummies in Nineteenth Century America: Ancient Egyptians as Artifacts* (Jefferson, NC: McFarland, 2009), 178–79.

52. Dane, *Myth of Print Culture*, 180. S. J. Wolfe, author of *Mummies in Nineteenth Century America*, on the other hand, believes that this very broadside, with Lydia Sigourney's poem on it, is proof that the books printed by Manning, Perry and Company are, in fact, made from mummies.

53. Charles Sigourney, "A Husband's 'Appeal'—Be Less a Poet and More a Wife" [October

1837], in *Lydia Sigourney: Selected Poetry and Prose*, ed. Gary Kelly (Toronto: Broadview Press, 2008), 311–15 (emphasis in original).

54. Sandra Gilbert and Susan Gubar, *The Madwoman in the Attic: The Woman Writer and the Nineteenth-Century Literary Imagination* (New Haven, CT: Yale University Press, 1979), 34; Toril Moi, *Sexual/Textual Politics: Feminist Literary Theory* (New York: Methuen, 1985), 58.

55. Gary Kelly, introduction to Kelly, *Lydia Sigourney*, 23.

56. On Sigourney's use of the apostrophe to invest secular objects with interiority and spirit, see Joan R. Wry, "A Sense of the Material Object: Sigourney's Fabric Poems," in *Lydia Sigourney: Critical Essays and Cultural Views*, ed. Mary Louise Kete and Elizabeth Petrino (Amherst: University of Massachusetts Press, 2018), 48–66.

57. Lydia Sigourney, "To a Fragment of Silk," in Kelly, *Lydia Sigourney*, 107.

58. Sigourney, "To a Fragment of Silk," 107.

59. For a discussion of the relationship between narrative and commodity fetishism and the ways in which commodities "speak" in Marxian terms, see Bill Brown, *A Sense of Things: The Object Matter of American Literature* (Chicago: University of Chicago Press, 2003), 25–30. Brown characterizes Marx's construction of the commodity as the container of "the whole truth of Capital understood as a system—lurking at the bottom of a mystery.... This mystery story [is] predicated on the difference between the commodity's apparent and actual source of value." See Brown, *A Sense of Things*, 29.

60. Karl Marx, *Selected Writings*, ed. Lawrence H. Simon (Indianapolis, IN: Hackett Publishing, 1994), 226; Lydia Sigourney, "To a Fragment of Silk," 107.

61. Lydia Sigourney, "To a Fragment of Silk," 107. There is a connection here to the work of Elizabeth Maddock Dillon in *The Gender of Freedom: Fictions of Liberalism and the Literary Public Sphere*. Dillon explores notions of publicity and the establishment of the literary public sphere, familiarized by Jürgen Habermas, while tracing the ways in which these set themselves against notions of privacy and femininity as necessary backdrop. She identifies a tendency for the literary public sphere to construct itself on the revelation or exposure of the feminized private sphere, which leads me to think of how these women were constantly asked to send their underclothes into the public for the technological realization of the print public sphere. To use Dillon's provocative phrase, "we might say that women have been indecently exposed in print." See Elizabeth Maddock Dillon, *The Gender of Freedom: Fictions of Liberalism and the Literary Public Sphere* (Stanford, CA: Stanford University Press, 2007), 25.

62. Lydia Sigourney, "To a Fragment of Silk," 108.

63. Elsewhere I have written about the significance of rag paper in nineteenth-century discussions of paper money. See Jonathan Senchyne, "Rags Make Paper, Paper Makes Money: Material Texts and Metaphors of Capital," *Technology and Culture* 58, no. 2 (April 2017): 545–55.

64. Charles Sigourney, "A Husband's 'Appeal,'" 314, 316 (emphasis in original).

65. Lydia Sigourney, "To a Shred of Linen," in Kelly, *Lydia Sigourney*, 168n1.

66. Melissa Ladd Teed, "A Passion for Distinction: Lydia Huntley Sigourney and the Creation of a Literary Reputation," *New England Quarterly* 77, no. 1 (March 2004): 56.

67. Lydia Sigourney, "To a Shred of Linen," 169.

68. Sigourney, 169.

69. Sigourney, 169.

70. Sigourney, 170–71.

71. Isabelle Lehuu, *Carnival on the Page: Popular Print Media in Antebellum America* (Chapel Hill: University of North Carolina Press, 2000), 14.

72. Inscription found in Dartmouth College's copy of Bradstreet's 1650 *The Tenth Muse Lately Sprung Up in America* held in the Rauner Rare Books Library, Hanover, NH. Thank you to Meredith Neuman, Cristobal Silva, and Yvonne Seale for their expert assistance with transcription.

Chapter 3: The Ineffable Socialities of Rags in Henry David Thoreau and Herman Melville

1. West Virginia Pulp and Paper Company, foreword to *A Week on the Concord and Merrimack Rivers*, by Henry David Thoreau (New York: West Virginia Paper Company, 1966), 5.

2. West Virginia Pulp and Paper Company, foreword, 8.

3. Henry David Thoreau, *A Week on the Concord and Merrimack Rivers* (Boston: James R. Osgood, 1873), 104.

4. Herman Melville to Evert Duyckinck, February 11, 1851, in *The Writings of Herman Melville*, vol. 14, *Correspondence*, ed. Lynn Horth (Chicago: Northwestern University Press, 1993), 180.

5. Herman Melville to Nathaniel Hawthorne, November 17, 1851, in Horth, *Writings*, 14:212.

6. Joel Munsell, *A Chronology of Paper and Paper-Making* (Albany, NY: J. Munsell, 1857), vi.

7. Harriet Martineau, "How to Get Paper," *Household Words*, 10 (October 28, 1854), 243.

8. Henry David Thoreau, October 28, 1853, in Thoreau, *Selections from the Journals*, ed. Walter Harding (New York: Dover Thrift Editions, 2005), 17.

9. Henry David Thoreau, *The Writings of Henry David Thoreau: Journal*, vol. 2, *1842–1848*, ed. Robert Sattelmeyer (Princeton: Princeton University Press, 1984), 354.

10. Henry David Thoreau, *The Journal of Henry David Thoreau*, vol. 5, *March 1853–November 1853*, ed. Bradford Torrey (Boston: Houghton Mifflin, 1906), 87.

11. Henry David Thoreau, *Walden and Resistance to Civil Government*, 2nd ed., ed. William Rossi (New York: W. W. Norton, 1992), 78, 81, 75.

12. Peter Coviello, *Tomorrow's Parties: Sex and the Untimely in Nineteenth-Century America* (New York: New York University Press, 2013), 30, 44.

13. Thoreau, *Walden*, 75.

14. Kenneth Speirs, "Scriptural Stones and Barn Mending: At the Grave of Herman Melville," *Markers XV: Annual Journal for Gravestone Studies* (1998): 36.

15. Judy Logan, "Melville's Last, Grave Joke?," *Melville Society Extracts*, no. 122 (February 2002): 9.

16. Katie McGettigan, *Herman Melville: Modernity and the Material Text* (Durham, NH: University of New Hampshire Press, 2017), 1.

17. Herman Melville to Nathaniel Hawthorne, November 17, 1851.

18. On the queer registers of the Hawthorne-Melville relationship, see Jordan A. Stein, "The *Blithedale Romance*'s Queer Style," *ESQ* 55, no. 3–4 (2009): 211, and "Herman Melville's Love Letters," *ELH* 85, no. 1 (Spring 2018): 119–40.

19. Melville to Hawthorne, November 17, 1851.

20. Herman Melville, "Hawthorne and His Mosses," in *Nathaniel Hawthorne, the Contemporary Reviews*, ed. John L. Idol Jr. and Buford Jones (Cambridge: Cambridge

University Press, 1994), 112; Leland S. Person and Jana L. Argersinger, "Hawthorne and Melville: Writing, Relationship, and Missing Letters," in *Hawthorne and Melville: Writing a Relationship*, ed. Jana L. Argersinger and Leland S. Person (Athens: University of Georgia Press, 2008), 2.

21. See Jordan Alexander Stein, "Herman Melville's Love Letters," *English Literary History* 85, no. 1 (Spring 2018): 119–40, and Stein, "The Blithedale Romance's Queer Style," *ESQ: A Journal of the American Renaissance* 55, no. 3–4 (2009): 211–36.

22. Melville to Hawthorne, July 22, 1851, in Horth, *Writings*, 14:199.

23. Wyn Kelley, "Letters on Foolscap," in Argersinger and Person, *Hawthorne and Melville*, 156.

24. Graham Thompson, *Melville among the Magazines* (Amherst: University of Massachusetts Press, 2018), 11.

25. Kate Thomas, "Post Sex: On Being Too Slow, Too Stupid, Too Soon," *South Atlantic Quarterly* 106, no. 3 (Summer 2007): 618.

26. Augusta Melville to Helen Maria Melville, January 14, 1851, in *Herman Melville: A Biography, 1819–1851*, by Hershel Parker (Baltimore, MD: Johns Hopkins University Press, 1996), 810.

27. Melville to Hawthorne, November 17, 1851.

28. Melville to Hawthorne, November 17, 1851.

29. Melville to Hawthorne, November 17, 1851.

30. Herman Melville to Nathaniel Hawthorne, July 17, 1852, in Horth, *Writings*, 14:230.

31. Thomas, "Post Sex," 619.

32. Herman Melville, "The Paradise of Bachelors and the Tartarus of Maids," in *Herman Melville: Tales, Poems, and Other Writings*, ed. John Bryant (New York: Modern Library, 2002), 153.

33. Elizabeth Renker, "Herman Melville, Wife Beating, and the Written Page," in *No More Separate Spheres: A Next Wave American Studies Reader*, ed. Cathy N. Davidson and Jessamyn Hatcher (Durham, NC: Duke University Press, 2002), 106.

34. Melville, "The Paradise of Bachelors and the Tartarus of Maids," 161.

35. Melville, 161.

36. Melville, 162.

37. Thomas, "Post Sex," 619.

38. Melville, "The Paradise of Bachelors and the Tartarus of Maids," 162, 164.

39. Melville, 166.

40. Robyn Wiegman, "Melville's Geography of Gender," *American Literary History* 1 (1989): 736; Leland S. Person, "Gender and Sexuality," in *A Companion to Herman Melville*, ed. Wyn Kelley (Malden, MA: Blackwell Publishing, 2006), 233, 234.

41. Melville, "The Paradise of Bachelors and the Tartarus of Maids," 164–65, 161.

42. Renker, "Herman Melville, Wife Beating, and the Written Page," 106–11.

43. Carolyn Steedman, *Dust: The Archive and Cultural History* (New Brunswick, NJ: Rutgers University Press, 2002), 167.

44. Melville to Hawthorne, November 17, 1851, 213.

45. Julietta Singh, *No Archive Will Restore You* (New York: Punctum Books, 2018), 29.

46. Singh, *No Archive Will Restore You*, 31.

47. Melville, "The Paradise of Bachelors and the Tartarus of Maids," 165.

48. Singh, *No Archive Will Restore You*, 31.

49. Melville, 155–57.

50. Melville, 165.
51. Melville, 166.

Chapter 4: The Whiteness of the Page

1. The figure/ground relation in perception tests is often represented in the white/black optical illusion that presents the viewer with either two faces or a vase—or really both. Marshall McLuhan extended the figure/ground concept into media studies by arguing that no content, or figure, can be properly considered outside its larger, though often "invisible" media or social context, the ground. The work of the critic, to McLuhan, is thus to consider the "total situation as obvious figures against hidden ground." Matie Molinaro, Corinne McLuhan, and William Toye, eds., *Letters of Marshall McLuhan* (Toronto: Oxford University Press, 1987), 478; see marketing campaign materials for the Amazon Kindle Paperwhite at http://www.anandtech.com/show/6244/live-from-amazons-press-conference; D. Elliot to Tileson Hollingsworth Sons, March 9, 1833, Tileson and Hollingsworth Papers, American Antiquarian Society, Worcester, MA.
2. W. T. Hewitt, *Landmarks of Tompkins County, New York including a History of Cornell University* (Syracuse, NY: D. Mason, 1894), 172.
3. Norton and Yale to Tileson Hollingsworth Sons, July 13, 1850, Tileson and Hollingsworth Papers (emphasis in original).
4. Craig Dworkin, *No Medium* (Cambridge, MA: MIT Press, 2013), 27, 29.
5. Dworkin, *No Medium*, 30, 31.
6. *Jack and the Beanstalk: A New Version* (Boston: T. H. Carter, 1837), 15.
7. Bridget T. Heneghan, *Whitewashing America: Material Culture and Race in the Antebellum Imagination* (Jackson: University Press of Mississippi, 2003), 4.
8. Jared Sparks, ed., *The Works of Benjamin Franklin* (Chicago, 1882), 161–62.
9. The most prominent example that comes to mind is when Franklin recounts accidentally dumping a galley of type at the end of the regular workday but stays late resetting it. Because he is visible in the shop window working into the night, he imagines being credited as hardworking rather than bungling. "One night, when, having impos'd my forms, I thought my day's work over, one of them by accident was broken, and two pages reduced to pi, I immediately distributed and compos'd it over again before I went to bed; and this industry, visible to our neighbors, began to give us character and credit." In another instance, Franklin carries paper through the streets in a wheelbarrow, again associating himself with the materials of the print trades in a way designed to build his credibility. "I sometimes brought home the paper I purchas'd at the stores thro' the streets on a wheelbarrow. Thus being esteem'd an industrious, thriving young man, and paying duly for what I bought, the merchants who imported stationery solicited my custom; others proposed supplying me with books, and I went on swimmingly." Benjamin Franklin, *The Autobiography of Benjamin Franklin* (New York: American Book Company, 1896), 79, 85.
10. Sparks, *The Works of Benjamin Franklin*, 162.
11. Sparks, 162.
12. Oliver Wendell Holmes, *The Early Poems of Oliver Wendell Holmes*, ed. Henry Ketcham (New York: A. L. Burt Publishers, 1900), 70–71.

13. A. Votary, "The Poetry of Printing," Boston, 1842.

14. William Saroyan, *Where the Bones Go*, ed. Robert Setrakian (Fresno: Press at California State University, Fresno, 2002).

15. Sparks, *The Works of Benjamin Franklin*, 161.

16. Sarah Josepha Hale, *Things by Their Right Names, and Other Stories, Fables, and Moral Pieces, in Prose and Verse, Selected and Arranged from the Writings of Mrs. Barbauld with a Sketch of Her Life by Mrs. S. J. Hale* (New York: Harper and Brothers, 1840), 71, 74; ibid 74.

17. Hale, *Things by Their Right Names*, 75.

18. "The Girl Who Inked Herself and Her Books and How It Ended," *Little Miss Consequence* (New York: McLoughlin Bros. Publishers, 1859).

19. Robin Bernstein, *Racial Innocence: Performing American Childhood from Slavery to Civil Rights* (New York: New York University Press, 2011) 224.

20. One trope of Indian captivity narratives includes the threat of tattooing the body of the white woman or girl, leaving a mark on its whiteness. Melissa Gniadek discusses one such story where a young girl's facial tattoo serves as a record of her New Zealand captivity. See Melissa Gniadek, "Mary Howard's Mark: Children's Literature and the Scales of Reading the Pacific," *Early American Literature* 50, no. 3 (2015): 797–826.

21. "Girl Who Inked Herself."

22. Brigitte Fielder has discussed how this unusual piece compares with other depictions of racialized bodies in movement, as the musical notation itself conveys narratives of race and racial mixture. See Brigitte Fielder, "Visualizing Racial Mixture and Movement: Music, Notation, Illustration," *J19: The Journal of Nineteenth-Century Americanists* 3, no. 1 (Spring 2015): 146–55.

23. Garrison to Elizabeth Pease, July 17, 1849, in *William Wells Brown: Author and Reformer*, by William Edward Farrison (Chicago: University of Chicago Press, 1969), 143.

24. William L. Andrews, *To Tell a Free Story: The First Century of Afro-American Autobiography, 1760–1865* (Champaign: University of Illinois Press, 1986), xi (emphasis in original).

25. William Wells Brown, *Narrative of William W. Brown, a Fugitive Slave, Written by Himself* (Boston: Anti-Slavery Office, 1847), 29. Lovejoy's story was a national sensation in the late 1830s, and in this passage Brown may be casting himself in Lovejoy's role. Brown is attacked while ferrying type, and readers would remember Lovejoy's murder by an antiabolitionist mob while defending his printing press.

26. Brown, *Narrative of William W. Brown*, 27.

27. *Oxford English Dictionary*, 2nd ed., s.v. "stereotype" (n., def. 2, 3a, 3b).

28. William Wells Brown, *Narrative of William Wells Brown, an American Slave, Written by Himself* (London: Charles Gilpin, 1849), http://books.google.com/books?id=JWE6AAAAcAAJ.

29. Michael Omi and Howard Winant theorize racial formation as a "process of historically situated *projects* in which human bodies and social structures are represented and organized." See their *Racial Formation in the United States: From the 1960s to the 1990s*, 2nd ed. (New York: Routledge, 1994), 55–56. For other, more recent work on material textuality and early African American literature, see Marcy J. Dinius, "'Look!! Look!!! at This!!!!': The Radical Typography of David Walker's *Appeal*,"

PMLA 126 (January 2011): 55–72, and Beth A. McCoy, "Race and the (Para)Textual Condition," *PMLA* 121 (January 2006): 156–69.

30. I refer to *Clotel*, or "the novel," across its title changes and revisions, as an ongoing project called *Clotel*. Samantha Marie Sommers develops the idea of *Clotel* as an unfolding project in "A Tangled Text: William Wells Brown's *Clotel* (1853, 1860, 1864, 1867)" (undergraduate thesis, Wesleyan University, 2009), http://wesscholar.wesleyan .edu/cgi/viewcontent.cgi?article=1264&context=etd_hon_theses. Except as noted, references to *Clotel* will be to Robert S. Levine's reprint of the 1853 edition: William Wells Brown, *Clotel; or, The President's Daughter: A Narrative of Slave Life in the United States*, ed. Robert S. Levine (1853; repr., Boston: Bedford/St. Martin's, 2000).

31. For further discussion of this joke's history and a reading of its racial significance in terms of print, publicity, and visual culture, see Marjorie Garber, *Shakespeare and Modern Culture* (New York: Pantheon Books, 2008), 154–77.

32. Michel Pastoureau, *Black: The History of a Color* (Princeton, NJ: Princeton University Press, 2009), 114–18; Calvin quoted on 127, 114. For more on the meaning of black and white in the development of the modern science of sight, mind, and thought, see Gary Taylor, "White Science," in *Buying Whiteness: Race, Culture, and Identity from Columbus to Hip Hop* (New York: Palgrave Macmillan, 2005), esp. 294–302.

33. *Oxford English Dictionary*, 2nd ed., s.vv. "black" (n., def. 2a; adj., def. 15b) and "white" (n., def. 7a).

34. George Lipsitz, *The Possessive Investment in Whiteness: How White People Profit from Identity Politics* (Philadelphia, PA: Temple University Press, 2006), 1.

35. James Cutbush, *The American Artist's Manual; or, Dictionary of Practical Knowledge in the Application of Philosophy to the Arts and Manufactures*, vol. 2 (Philadelphia: Johnson and Warner, and R. Fisher, 1814), reprinted in *Early American Papermaking: Two Treatises on Manufacturing Techniques*, ed. John Bidwell (New Castle, DE: Oak Knoll Books, 1990), 59. In his introduction to *Early American Papermaking* Bidwell notes that Cutbush cribbed entire passages from the *Encyclopedia Britannica*, including the one from which this quote was taken.

36. See Audrey Elisa Kerr, *The Paper Bag Principle: Class, Colorism, and Rumor and the Case of Black Washington, D.C.* (Knoxville: University of Tennessee Press, 2006).

37. Brown, *Clotel*, 84, 85, 88.

38. Phillis Wheatley, *Poems on Various Subjects Religious and Moral* (London: A. Bell, 1773), 18.

39. *Jack and the Beanstalk*, 15, 30.

40. *Ink: Webster's Quotations, Facts, and Phrases* (San Diego: ICON Group International, 2008), 305.

41. Cutbush, *American Artist's Manual*, 59.

42. Quoted in John Power, *A Handy-Book about Books, for Book-Lovers, Book-Buyers, and Book-Sellers* (London: John Wilson, 1870), 135.

43. "Black Paper and White Ink," *Philadelphia Public Ledger and Daily Transcript*, April 13, 1855.

44. Toni Morrison, "Unspeakable Things Unspoken: The Afro-American Presence in American Literature," *Michigan Quarterly Review* 28, no. 1 (Winter 1989): 16; D. Elliot to Tileson Hollingsworth Sons, March 9, 1833, Tileson and Hollingsworth Papers.

45. I am aware that the question of racial identification in the nineteenth century can

be cut different ways depending on local contexts, laws, customs, and so on and that these do not always result in categorization as either black or white. I remain interested here, however, in Brown's exploration of black and white as racial signifiers which are flexible or ambiguous in certain registers like the visual yet which are, in *Clotel*, answerable in the end to the legal constraints of hypodescent or "one drop" logic.

46. Richard Dyer, *White* (New York: Routledge, 1997), 60, 57, 48.

47. See Cheryl Harris, "Whiteness as Property," *Harvard Law Review* 106, no. 8 (1993): 1707–91. While stating that legal whiteness is more defined than visual whiteness, I do not mean to suggest that it is homogeneous. Indeed, as Ian Haney López has shown, local differences in population and power structures have mediated which populations are invited to participate in the property rights of whiteness. See his *White by Law: The Legal Construction of Race* (New York: New York University Press, 2006).

48. Brown, *Clotel*, 87.

49. Brown, 196.

50. Brown, *Clotelle; or, The Colored Heroine* (Boston: Lee and Shephard, 1867), 5. Since the term "mulatto/a" is historically pejorative, I use it only to quote or paraphrase another text or when addressing the figure of "the mulatta," which I take to be a cultural trope, not a descriptive term.

51. Announcement in the *New York Independent*, May 13, 1852, quoted in Trish Loughran, *The Republic in Print: Print Culture in the Age of U.S. Nation Building, 1770–1870* (New York: Columbia University Press, 2007), 364.

52. Brown, *Clotel*, 81.

53. Ann duCille writes of this passage that Brown's reference to ink and paper and his "use of quotation marks around the defining phrases he cites, indicate that he himself is addressing the problem of representation" and notes how fiction "position[s] . . . black women as objects of the white male gaze." Ann duCille, *The Coupling Convention: Sex, Text, and Tradition in Black Women's Fiction* (New York: Oxford University Press, 1993), 22–23. In his annotations to the 1867 *Clotelle* in the Electronic Scholarly Edition, Christopher Mulvey notes, "The passage . . . is possibly taken from a printed source, but, if so, it has not been identified. [Brown] uses quotation marks for six of its phrases. These express stereotypes of exotic, particularly of mixed race, beauty. The quotation marks may indicate that they are quotations, or they may indicate that they are simply stock expressions." I would argue that Brown does not need a specific source for these lines because he is quoting print culture's habitual representation of mixed-race women. See Mulvey, ed., *Clotel: An Electronic Scholarly Edition* (Charlottesville: University of Virginia Press, 2006), https://www.upress.virginia.edu/content /clotel-william-wells-brown-electronic-scholarly-edition.

54. Russ Castronovo, *Necro Citizenship: Death, Eroticism, and the Public Sphere in the Nineteenth-Century United States* (Durham, NC: Duke University Press, 2001), 41; W. J. T. Mitchell, *Picture Theory: Essays on Verbal and Visual Culture* (Chicago: University of Chicago Press, 1994), 89.

55. Michael Gaudio, *Engraving the Savage: The New World and Techniques of Civilization* (Minneapolis: University of Minnesota Press, 2008), xii, 132.

56. See the title page of Harriet Beecher Stowe, *Uncle Tom's Cabin; or, The History of a*

Christian Slave, by Harriet Beecher Stowe; with an Introduction by Elihu Burritt; Illustrated by Sixteen Engravings by Johnston, from Original Designs by Anelay (London: Partridge and Oakey: Saunders & Otley, 1852).

57. William Tait and Christian Isobel Johnstone, eds., review of *Uncle Tom's Cabin; or, The History of a Christian Slave*, by Harriet Beecher Stowe, *Tait's Edinburgh Magazine* 19 (December 1852): 761.

58. S[arah] E. Fuller, *A Manual of Instruction in the Art of Wood Engraving* (Boston: J. Watson, 1867), 46, 21.

59. For more on the nineteenth-century idea that race would always be manifest on the surface of the body, see Walter Johnson, "The Slave Trader, the White Slave, and the Politics of Racial Determination in the 1850s," *Journal of American History* 87 (June 2000): 27, 34. Johnson describes the case of *Morrison v. White*, in which the defendant sued for her freedom using her white-looking body as evidence and arguing that "colored blood will stick out."

60. Jean Genet also makes this connection between critical race theory and print legibility explicit: "In white America the Blacks are the characters in which history is written. They are the ink that gives the white page a meaning." See Genet, *Prisoner of Love* (New York: New York Review of Books, 2003), 245.

61. Julia Thomas, *Pictorial Victorians: The Inscription of Values in Word and Image* (Athens: Ohio University Press, 2004), 35–36.

62. Brown, *Clotel*, 101.

63. Thomas Jefferson, *Notes on the State of Virginia*, ed. David Waldstreicher (Boston: Bedford/St. Martin's, 2002), 176.

64. Caleb Smith, editor's introduction to *The Life and the Adventures of a Haunted Convict*, by Austin Reed (New York: Random House, 2016), xvi.

65. Caleb Smith, "Editor's Note on the Text," *The Life and the Adventures of a Haunted Convict*, lxiii.

66. Russ Castronovo, "The Art of Ghost-Writing: Memory, Materiality, and Slave Aesthetics," in *In Search of Hannah Crafts: Critical Essays on* The Bondswoman's Narrative, eds. Henry Louis Gates, Jr. and Hollis Robbins, (New York: Basic Civitas Books, 2004), 195.

67. See Henry Louis Gates, *The Trials of Phillis Wheatley: America's First Black Poet and Her Encounters with the Founding Fathers* (New York: Basic Civitas Books, 2010). Joanna Brooks has argued, convincingly, that such a "trial" never took place and that the paratext is, rather, evidence of Wheatley's manipulation of elite networks of patronage, especially her ability to trade in white women's sympathy. See Brooks, "Our Phillis, Ourselves," *American Literature* 82, no. 1 (2010).

68. John Secora, "Black Message/White Envelope: Genre, Authenticity, and Authority in the Antebellum Slave Narrative," *Callaloo* 32 (Summer 1982): 482–515.

69. Joe Nickell, "Authentication Report," in Hannah Crafts, *The Bondswoman's Narrative*, ed. Henry Louis Gates (New York: Warner Books, 2002), 314.

70. Nickell, "Authentication Report," 311.

71. Nickell, 311.

72. Jefferson, *Notes on the State of Virginia*, 150.

73. *The Mother's Remarks on a Set of Cuts for Children* (Philadelphia: Jacob Johnson, 1803), 44.

74. *Mother's Remarks*, vii, 44.

Conclusion: Reading into Surfaces

1. Early Proceedings of the American Philosophical Society, *Proceedings of the American Philosophical Society*, vol. 22 (1885), 173. The book, *Oeuvres du Marquis de Villette*, was published in London in 1786. Its main text is printed on lime tree bark and at the end includes the "essay" of 20 samples of other vegetable paper mentioned by Crèvecœur. For more on Léorier-Delisle's paper samples and late eighteenth-century scientific societies' interest in technologies of paper, see the article by Reed Gochberg, "Circulating Objects: Crèvecoeur's 'Curious Book' and the American Philosophical Society Cabinet," *Early American Literature* 54, no. 2 (2019) 445–76.

2. "The American Philosophical Society," *Pennsylvania Gazette*, March 31, 1773.

3. M. B. B., "Need of a New Source for Paper If the Forests Are to Be Saved" *New York Times*, June 13, 1907.

4. M. B. B. "Need of a New Source for Paper." The "Think before Printing" movement aims to reduce waste by using "gentle reminders" about the environmental impact of printing in everyday electronic communications; see www.thinkbeforeprinting.org.

5. Walter Benjamin, "The Work of Art in the Age of Mechanical Reproduction," in *Illuminations: Essays and Reflections*, ed. Hannah Arendt (New York: Schocken Books, 1968), 217–51.

6. Drew Cameron, "You Are Not My Enemy, Vol IV," *Combat Paper Project*, https://www.combatpaper.org/portfolios.html.

7. "The Combat Paper Project," *Iowa Review* vol. 43, no. 1 (Spring 2013), 29.

8. See https://www.combatpaper.org/about/. The art fair conversation is reported at "From uniform to pulp/ Battlefield to workshop/ Warrior to artist" *Nexus* (blog), February 1, 2016, https://connectere.wordpress.com/2016/02/01/from-uniform-to-pulp-battlefield-to-workshop-warrior-to-artist/.

9. "Combat Paper Making," *YouTube*, http://youtube/cM4creJI1OI (site discontinued).

10. Drew Cameron, foreword to *The New Citizen Army*, by Greg Delanty (Burlington, VT: Combat Paper Press, 2010), 5.

11. Colophon to Delanty, *The New Citizen Army*, 68.

12. "Combat Paper—Paper over Iraq," *YouTube*, https://www.youtube.com/watch?v=wUtXYCihavw.

13. Mark Kurlansky, *Paper: Paging through History* (New York: W. W. Norton, 2017), 245–46.

14. Martin Medina, *The World's Scavengers: Salvaging for Sustainable Consumption and Production* (New York: AltaMira Press, 2007), 45.

INDEX